COMPARATIVE RELIGION

COMPARATIVE RELIGION

KEDAR NATH TIWARI

MOTILAL BANARSIDASS PUBLISHERS
PRIVATE LIMITED • DELHI

2nd Reprint: Delhi, 2014
Second Revised Edition: Delhi, 2009
First Edition: Delhi, 1983

ISBN: 978-81-208-0293-3 (Cloth)
ISBN: 978-81-208-0294-0 (Paper)

MOTILAL BANARSIDASS
41 U.A. Bungalow Road, Jawahar Nagar, Delhi 110 007
8 Mahalaxmi Chamber, 22 Bhulabhai Desai Road, Mumbai 400 026
203 Royapettah High Road, Mylapore, Chennai 600 004
236, 9th Main III Block, Jayanagar, Bengaluru 560 011
Sanas Plaza, 1302 Baji Rao Road, Pune 411 002
8 Camac Street, Kolkata 700 017
Ashok Rajpath, Patna 800 004
Chowk, Varanasi 221 001

Printed in India

by RP Jain at NAB Printing Unit,
A-44, Naraina Industrial Area, Phase I, New Delhi–110028
and published by JP Jain for Motilal Banarsidass Publishers (P) Ltd,
41 U.A. Bungalow Road, Jawahar Nagar, Delhi-110007

CONTENTS

FOREWORD

Comparative Religion is a very interesting and important area of philosophical research and study. That is why universities of India are steadily including it as a part of their teaching courses.

Dr. Kedar Nath Tiwari has done a great service to the cause of promoting the study of Comparative Religion by writing a book on the subject. His book is written in a very lucid style and contains enough material for initiating students and scholars for further research and study in the field. The aim of a study like this is partly to acquaint readers with the main aspects and features of the living religions of the world and partly to suggest the points of agreement and difference among the different religions. The book very well succeeds in serving both these ends. I am confident that the book will be well received both by students and teachers of Philosophy and also by general readers.

Basant Kumar Lal,
University Professor & Head,
Department of Philosophy,
Magadh University,
Bodh Gaya.

PREFACE

Second Edition

When the book was first published in 1983, I never thought that it would be as popular as it has actually proved to be. I am proud of saying that the book has been well received not only by the students and teachers of almost all the Indian Universities, but also by readers abroad. I am sorry that although at least four times the book had to be reprinted since 1983, I could not be able to present before my readers a revised edition of it. I am extremely happy to find myself at least now in a position to bring about a fresh edition of the book with several additions, enlargements and elaborations at appropriate places. At certain places where I have felt that some material could be more appropriately presented in somewhat a changed way, I have made the necessary changes. The essential framework of this book, however, remains the same.

An idea of the changes made, including the additions and elaborations, may be had from the following. There was no 'Introduction' to the book in the first edition, but the present edition contains a brief 'Introduction'. The chapter on Zoroastrianism has been, more or less, rewritten. There has been a totally new addition in terms of the religions of China and Japan in the Appendix. Of course, there may be a genuine doubt in the minds of the readers whether any of these religions (except Buddhism) may be regarded as a living religion, still I thought it worthwhile to present at least an introductory idea of these religions before my readers so that they could know at least something about them, which were once taken to be very important faiths of the world and which, in some direct or indirect manner, do not fail even now to influence and shape the life-pattern of the people of the countries to which they belonged. However, I have not thought it proper that they should intrude into the general framework of this book, partly because of the fact that they seem hardly amenable to this framework and partly due to the fact that they are not living. I hope the readers will appreciate my stand. Besides these, many suitable changes at appropriate places, such as, in chapters 1, 2, 3, 4, 8, 9 and 11 have been made. For the convenience of the readers an index of names and subjects has also been added towards the end of the book.

I have every hope that the readers will be highly benifitted by the above noted changes and they will receive this new edition of the book with a still greater interest and zeal. Even now there may be spots where changes in various terms might be necessary or desirable. I shall be grateful if such spots are pointed to me by learned readers. That will enable me to do the necessary work of editing in respect of them at any time in future when I find an opportunity to present yet another edition of the book.

KEDAR NATH TIWARI

Shantisadan,
Burhanath,
Bhagalpur-812001

PREFACE

First Edition

Although Comparative Religion as a subject of serious study has found a relatively late start, it has been realised for quite some time now that it is a very useful and important study. Many universities, both in India and abroad, have therefore included the subject in their academic curricula. Books on the subject are also not rare now. But still I have always felt the need of having a book on the subject which could effectively meet the requirements of the Honours and Post-Graduate students of Philosophy and Religion of the Indian Universities. This feeling of mine has found ample support from the difficulties which they have been reporting to me from time to time. Most of the books that are available on the subject dwell more upon the history of the origin and growth of the different religions rather than upon the basic principles, beliefs and practices that these religions inculcate and emphasise. I have, therefore, instead of going into the history of the religions, tried in the present book to deal with them with reference to certain specific topics relating to the important beliefs and practices of the followers of these religions. My study has, therefore, in brief, been more topical and less historical. Then again, to make the study really comparative, I have added a separate chapter of comparing religions on the specific topics with which I have been concerned here in this book. On the basis of these comparisons, I have also made an attempt towards the end of the book to assess the possibility of a Universal Religion, which is being much talked of for some time now by the religionists and philosophers of the world alike.

The book is specially meant for the use of the students and therefore moderate critical appraisals also have been made here and there. But general readers interested in the subject will also, I hope, not be frustrated and will find the book much to their interest, use and purpose. I cannot claim that the book will be really useful for those whom it is meant for, but I must hope so. Readers themselves will be the best judges of the merits and demerits of the book and I will be very much obliged to them if they write to me the shortcomings of the book in frank and definite terms.

I am really very much thankful to those of my students who have inspired me to write this book for the solution of their difficulties. I am also thankful to Shri Jainendra Prakash Jain, the Partner of Motilal Banarsidass, who very much liked the idea of publishing a book on the subject and asked me to prepare the manuscript. I cannot forget Sri Kamala Shankar Singh, a very sincere and enthusiastic executive of the Patna Branch of Motilal Banarsidass, who played a significant role in initiating the idea of writing a book on the subject and thereafter pursuing relentlessly the task of getting the manuscript prepared by me. Last, but not the least, I must extend my heartfelt gratitude to my elder, Dr. Basant Kumar Lal, who took the trouble of going through the manuscript, making valuable suggestions here and there, and finally writing the Foreword.

KEDAR NATH TIWARI

INTRODUCTION

Religion is perhaps the oldest human pursuit, but still no precise definition of it has been finally given till today. We also on our part are not going to give here any definition of religion in some precise terms. We will simply point to the two broad forms of religion, one of which may be called 'individual' and the other 'social'. By individual form of religion, we mean that form in which an individual in his solitariness makes silent efforts to establish communion with whatever he takes as divine. It is perhaps by keeping this form in mind that Whitehead takes religion 'as something which an individual does with his solitariness' or Dr. Radhakrishnan takes it as 'the culture of the soul'. By the social form of religion we mean that form under which several people form one religious group by virtue of entertaining, more or less, the same set of spiritual convictions and observing, more or less, the same kind of religious practices, either individually or congregationally. Hinduism, Buddhism, Christianity, Islam etc. are the examples of this form of religion, because each one of them binds several people together in matter of spiritual beliefs and religious practices. We will be obviously concerned here with the latter form of religion, because we are going to make here a comparative study of the prevailing religions of the world, some examples of which have been given above. What exactly will be the nature, aim and objective of the kind of study that we are going to make here under the title 'Comparative Religion' will be given in chapter one ahead. But here in our introductory remark we will like to mention that it will be a purely academic and scientific study having no extra-academic aims such as promoting the social value of religions in a fresh perspective or bringing about an environment of mutual understanding between them.

We have avoided giving any precise definition of religion, but we will not avoid giving a general idea of the very essential character (or characters) of the prevailing religions which makes them all called 'religion' in spite of some very important differences between them. We may mark, for example, that there are religions like Buddhism and Jainism which do not believe in any God, while religions like Judaism, Christianity and Islam obviously believe in God. But still all of them are called religions alike. What, after all, makes them all called by the same name 'Religion' in spite of the above important difference as well as some other important differences too? It is perhaps due to the following two general features possessed by each one of them alike – (1) Each one possesses certain specific convictions or beliefs with regard to the world-and-life situation as a whole and (2) In the light of these convictions, each one prescribes a specific way of life for its followers. It is possible that there are certain similarities between two religions in respect of both the convictions and the way of life, but there may be (and actually are) certain important differences too. It is really due to the specific convictions as well as the specific way of life that a particular religion has in contrast to others that it assumes its specific identity as a particular religion. Having specific convictions and then having a way of life in the light of those convictions seem to be, then, the essential character of every religion. Keeping in view the above two features of every prevailing religion of the world, 'religion' may be most generally defined as 'a specific way of life based on certain specific convictions with regard to the world-and-life situation as a whole'. On this definition, however, even an ideology like communism may be regarded as religion, provided it possesses specific convictions with regard to world-and-life situation as a whole and depicts a way of life for its followers in the light of those convictions. Communism perhaps fulfills both these conditions, and therefore a communist is as much a religious man, as a Buddhist, if the former also like the latter lives up to the convictions incorporated in his ideology. But communism is hardly regarded as a religion. Why? Perhaps because its convictions are all materialistic in nature and it very conspicuously lacks in spirituality which is traditionally regarded as the core of religion. Thus in the light of this essential characteristic of religion, we will have to make the following modification in our definition – 'Religion is a way of life based on certain specific *extra-mundane* or *spiritualistic* convictions with regard to world-and-life situation as a whole.' We may very well see that all our traditionally recognised world-religions fulfil this condition. Buddhism does not believe in God, but it believes in a spiritual sphere and a spiritual goal and in the light of its spiritualistic outlook, it depicts a specific way of life. Christianity believes in God, a spiritual reality, as well as in a spiritual goal, known generally as the 'Kingdom of God'. In the light of this spiritualistic outlook, it also depicts a specific way of life. Similar is the case with all other prevailing religions, and hence all of them are called religions.

This definition needs a lot more analysis and explanation, but that we are not going to do here for more than one reason. Interested readers may see the author's book *The Logic Of Religious Belief* (published by the Classical Publishers, New Delhi) in this connection. But whatever is said above gives sufficient hint for the sense in which the prevailing religions of the world are called religions. Here under the title 'Comparative Religion', we are going to make a study of the main beliefs (convictions) and practices (way of life) of these religions in a comparative perspective.

The subject of Comparative Religion as a scientific study of the various features of the different religions of the world in a comparative perspective is relatively a late development. It is hardly for a hundred years or so that the name 'Comparative Religion' has gained currency and studies in this direction have been taken up in right earnest. One important reason of this late beginning of the study of the subject may be attributed to the fact that most of the scientific studies of modern times have originated from the west and western people until recently entertained such a sense of supremacy in their head and heart regarding their own religion that they hardly thought it worthwhile to compare it with the religions of the east. Consequently, they did not see the necessity of undertaking any study of religions other than their own. Even when they sometimes did so, they did it only with a view to exposing the weak points of those religions so as to belittle their importance and, in contrast, to exalt their own. But this is not the right spirit in which a comparative study of the different religions can be made. Such a study requires an impartial, neutral and tolerant outlook and if at all there is any leaning or sympathy for any religion, it must be for religions other than one's own. The attitude of India has always been one of tolerance and respect for other religions and the Indian people have never regarded themselves as the "chosen people of God." Attempts at comparative study of religions have been made in India since very old days, but due to political subjugation that she had to suffer for long, her voice was not recognised and cared for in the family of nations. It is not only on a theoretical level that India has recognised the value and worth of other religions, but also on the practical level she has set exemplary evidence of her tolerant attitude by accommodating many foreign religions of the world on her soil from time to time. She has always taken the various religions of the world as nothing but the different ways, suited to the cultural environments of different people, leading to the same goal. As Parriender has very nobly and honestly recognised, "India is used to many religions and regards them as different ways to the one goal with a rare tolerance."[1] It is only when a few saner western thinkers have begun looking to eastern faith as certain valuable heritages of mankind that the western people have realized the need and importance of a comparative study of religions and a science of comparative religion has consequently come about. Moreover, when the modern scientific developments have made world in a sense very small such that mutual contacts among various cultures have become inevitable, the westerners have to recognise the existence and value of religions other than their own also. And thus comparative religion has now become an important subject of study and research amongst students, teachers and scholars of the world.

What 'Comparative Religion' precisely is will be seen, as we have said earlier also, later on, but here we will have to recount certain practical difficulties in making the kind of study we are going to make, possible. We will particularly like to discuss here the difficulties connected with the collection of materials which will make the comparison between the various features of the world-religions possible. What method or methods have we to adopt for the purpose?

Here the whole question regarding the methodology of a comparative study of religions may come up. And as a matter of fact, this is a very important and lively subject of discussion and debate for quite some time now. But apart from any such detailed discussion on the problem of methodology, we may see that at least two things seem necessary (though not sufficient) for collecting relevant materials which will make our study faithful and authentic – (1) A thorough study of the basic text or texts, along with

1. G. Parriender, *Comparative Religion* (George Allen & Unwin, 1962), p. 22.

the related works, belonging to a particular religion, and (2) An extensive dialogue with the followers of a particular religion along with a personal survey, both intensive and extensive, of the various religious practices carried on by them. The first one is easy to carry out. Perhaps most of the writers on Comparative Religion adopt this way. But adopting the second one in a serious and sincere spirit is not an easy task and therefore very few or hardly any adopt this method for studying religions.

But we can very easily note the hazard that is involved in ignoring the second one. A study of the texts and related works of a particular religion, howsoever extensive it may be, will give us only an idea of the basic principles, beliefs and practices of the religion which were either propounded and propagated by the original prophet or propounder or which came about by way of the authentic interpretations of a few great followers of the original propounder. In other words, a mere study of the texts will give us an idea of the beliefs etc. of a religion which are associated with it at the time of its origin or till a few years after. But as time passes on, a host of such beliefs and practices go on finding place in a particular religion that it is sometimes difficult to recognise that it is the same religion as the original one. There is a tremendous gap between the original principles and the actual practices carried on by the followers of a particular religion. The gap sometimes is so big that there hardly seems to be any worthwhile comparison between the original form of a religion and its later phase. We may cite here for example the early phase of Buddhism, *i.e.*, that phase which is the direct outcome of the teachings of Lord Buddha and its later phases of Mahāyāna Buddhism, specially those which have taken root in countries like China and Japan. We will see for ourselves in this very book towards the end that the latter hardly seem to be an extension or a form of the former. A.C. Graham has put the above kind of situation in his own way in the following words: "Buddhism is a 'Nay saying' religion, rejecting all life as suffering and promising release from it; yet whenever one is actually in a Buddhist country it is hard to resist the impression that one is amongst the liveliest, the most invincibly cheerful, the most 'Yea-saying' people on earth."[2] A similar situation may be seen in relation to Christianity also. To quote Graham again, "The ordinary Christian does not simply fail to live up to the moral teachings of Jesus, on many points he has always implicitly rejected it; he believes that it is improvident not to take thought for the morrow, swears in a court-of-law with a good conscience and regards any one who turns the other cheek as a coward."[3] In fact, it is the case with any and every religion that the view of life or the various principles of belief and conduct reflected in its basic form is hardly typical of the people who claim to belong to that particular religion. A very glaring example of this big gap may be seen in case of Taoism. When we go through the basic principles of Taoism as enunciated by the great Chinese thinker Lao Tzu, we are really filled with wonder how there could be a thinker in so ancient China who could propound such lofty philosophical and religious ideas. But again when we later on come across the heinous magical practices performed by those who claimed themselves to be Taoists, we are filled up with a second wonder to find the lofty philosophy of Taoism fallen to such a low level. There is sometimes an unimaginable chasm between the basic theoretical principles of a religion and the various ritualistic and magical practices that later on grow under its umbrella.

On the basis of the above we may see that a picture of some religion drawn merely on the strength of the sacred texts associated with it may not tally with the ground

---

2. R.C. Zeahner (ed.), The Concise Encyclopeadia of Living Faiths (Hutchinson London, 1959), p. 357.

3. *Ibid.*

realities regarding the observance of that religion. To avoid this and to present a picture which strikes an appropriate balance between the two (that is, between the basic principles involved in the texts and the actual ways in which the religion is being observed in practice), an extensive dialogue with the actual followers of the religion or a serious watching of their various practices seems necessary. But apart from the fact that for a majority of the writers on Comparative Religion the above kind of endeavour is not at all possible, there are difficulties in carrying out the endeavour itself. These difficulties may be enumerated as follows:

1. Very few followers of a particular religion actually know and are able to say something about the principles, beliefs and practices of their own religion. They belong to their religions mostly as a matter of heredity. Their beliefs and practices are something transmitted to them by their forefathers and they observe them more or less blindly. They have hardly ever thought anything about them, so that when someone enters into a dialogue with them in relation to these, they can hardly narrate something in clear and convincing terms.

2. The second difficulty arises due to the variety of this beliefs and practices. Unless the dialogue is of a very extensive nature, it is possible to miss many of the beliefs and practices of the followers. The difficulty aggravates in the light of the fact that more often than not followers of a religion cross the boundaries of nations and there are bound to be differences in beliefs and practices due to the local or cultural factors of a particular country. Even if someone is very courageous and meticulous in his approach to face and manage all these difficulties, it is very difficult to pick out certain essential points from the vast variety of beliefs and practices.

3. The most difficult task, however, seems to be that of striking a proper balance between the original principles of

a religion as depicted in the sacred texts and the variety of actual beliefs and practices adopted and observed by the followers. The example of Buddhism as cited above may illustrate this difficulty very vividly.

It is due to the kind of difficulties noted above that what is presented in the various studies on Comparative Religion about the nature, characteristics etc. of different religions is, perhaps, for the most part, based on the sacred texts and some other related works connected with these religions. The present work also, on the whole, may be taken as suffering from this limitation. However, like the work of any other Indian writer on the subject, the present work has the advantage of utilising, at least to some extent, the second source also. India is a secular country in which people of almost all the living religions of the world reside and have the freedom to observe their respective religions with perfect openness. Thus an Indian writer has the advantage to mix with the followers of different religions and watch their religious practices. He has the opportunity to have an idea of the ground realities regarding the beliefs and practices of a particular religion by entering into a dialogue with its followers . Nevertheless, if a surveyor of the various features of different religions marks a discrepancy between what is written in the present work about the principles, beliefs and practices of a particular religion and the ground realities regarding it, that is due to the fact that the bulk account given here is chiefly based on the sacred literature connected with that religion.

One point of caution must be added here. Howsoever distant sometimes the connection between the basic principles and actual practices of a religion may seem to be, still on closer examination the link will be visible. For example, howsoever different (from the original) a religious trait a Japanese Buddhist might exhibit today, on examination it may be seen that his chief beliefs and practices have some connection with the original teachings of Lord

Buddha. Similar is the case with a Jew or a Christian, or for that matter, with a follower of any religion. It is by virtue of such a connection that a Christian is recognised as a Christian, and a Buddhist as a Buddhist. In other words, distinctions between the followers of different religions are well maintained on account of their beliefs and practices having at least some connection with the original principles of their respective religions. This book itself will give a brief account of the various offshoots in which a religion divides itself in course of time, but again we will see therein that howsoever far drawn a particular offshoot or sect seems to be from the original, it has some distinctive connection with the latter.

We have said above several times that we are going to make here a study of the prevailing religions of the world. By 'prevailing', however, we mean 'living' and by 'living religions', we mean such religions which are still observed and followed by a considerable number of people. Such religions include Hinduism, Buddhism, Jainism, Zoroastrianism, Judaism, Christianity, Islam, and Sikhism. So these form the subject-matter of our study here. Some may have doubts in accepting Zoroastrianism as a living religion and their doubts may not be taken as totally unfounded. For, hardly a few people, and those also mostly in a corner of India, observe this religion at present. But still we feel that there is justification for taking this religion as living, at least, on the following two grounds – (1) It is still being observed as a religion by some people, howsoever small their number may be, and (2) As a religion it exhibits certain such important features which are worth considering and which have exerted considerable influence upon some of the great living religions like Judaism, Christianity and Islam. Towards the end (in the Appendix), we have also included for our brief study some of the ancient Asian religions like Taoism, Confucianism etc. These religions cannot, of course, be regarded as living religions, but still, in our opinion, they merit at least some of our attention due to the respect and regard they once commanded and the indelible impression they have left upon the minds of the people of the countries in which they once flourished.

1

Comparative Religion
Nature, Aims and Objectives

The title 'Comparative Religion' is generally used to cover a historical and comparative study of the different religions of the world. Sometimes the expression 'History of Religions' has also been used for the kind of study that one is deemed to make under the title 'Comparative Religion'. But if by means of some study someone aims to make a comparative study of the various features of the different religions of the world, the name 'Comparative Religion' seems to be more suggestive. Of course, in any such study, the history of religions also forms an important part, because a knowledge of the origin and growth of religions in a historical perspective gives us a better insight into their overall nature and characteristics. But again for that matter Comparative Religion must not be made simply a study of the history of religions. In the main, it must be a topical study, *i.e.*, a study based on the analysis of the various beliefs and practices associated with different religions. That will facilitate an honest and loyal comparison between religions on specific points.

A.C. Bouquet, while making his aim behind writing a book on Comparative Religion clear, asserts that it is a "survey and comparison of the great religions of the world.'[1] The survey, no doubt, includes history, but for making the survey a meaningful and transparent basis for comparison between the religions, a description and analysis of some of the key beliefs, practices, principles etc. of a particular religion must also be brought out. This description or analysis must, however, be objective and impartial. Moreover, if a comparative study of religions is to be an academic study, the survey must also be critical. Comparative Religion, therefore, precisely speaking, must be a comparative study of the important features of the different religions of the world in a perfectly scientific spirit. What this 'comparative study of religions in a scientific spirit' actually means, we shall try to make clearer and more precise in what follows, but for the time being we can say that Comparative Religion is comparative study of the important features of the different religions of the world in a perfectly objective, impartial and critical spirit. This is why we sometimes speak of the Science of Comparative Religion. No other aim but having a real and objective picture of the nature and characteristics of the different religions of the world in a comparative and critical perspective is the guiding principle of such a study. It is , so to say, a comparative study of religions for their own sake, and all this for a better understanding of their specific features and characteristics.

In this sense, 'Comparative Religion' must be distinguished from what is known as 'Interreligious Dialogue' or 'Interfaith Dialogue'. The former is a purely academic pursuit with the sole aim of having an understanding about the religions of the world in as objective and impartial a manner as possible. In other words,

---

1. A.C. Bouquet, *Comparative Religion* (Cassel and Company Ltd., London, 1961).

we may say that the aim of such a study is to have a better understanding about religions without having any bias or favour for any one of them. The latter, on the other hand, may be regarded as a social or pragmatic pursuit, whose aim is to promote mutual understanding amongst religions with a view to remove any possible or actual sense of animosity amongst them. It is, of course, a fact that a better understanding of the nature and characteristics of different religions with a perfectly unprejudiced or unbiased attitude will help a lot in promoting mutual understanding amongst them, but that does not mean that the two are one and the same. Similarly, as we have already noted in our Introduction, a comparative study of religions may involve dialogue, debate or discussion with or amongst members of different faiths (interfaith dialogue), but that is meant here only for achieving a better understanding about those faiths, and for no other purpose. Thus the two pursuits may co-operate with each other for achieving better results in both the fields, but they are not one and the same. The two may have certain cross points in their paths, but in their aims they are completely different. The aim of the former is *better* understanding, the aim of the latter is *mutual* understanding.

Similarly, 'Comparative Religion' as an academic discipline must be distinguished from 'Theology' or 'Philosophy of Religion.' The aim of Theology is to rationalise and systematise the claims of a particular religious faith. It is in this sense that there is Judaic or Christian theology or, for that matter, a theology related with any particular religion. Comparative Religion has obviously no such aim. It is not concerned with any one specific religion, and much less with the problem of rationalising or systematising it. Similarly, Comparative Religion has no such aim as that of Philosophy of Religion. The aim of the latter is to have a rational or critical assessment of the transcendental or spiritual claims of religion as such, but the former has no such aim. That is, it is not to be involved at all in questions about the truth or validity of the transcendental claims of religions; it studies religious phenomena as empirical facts, *i.e.*, as objective facts of human experience. In other words, its aim is simply to study the facts presented by world-religions in an objective, critical and comparative manner.

On the basis of whatever we have said and discussed so far, we may see that the title 'Comparative Religion' does not carry the full sense of the kind of study that is made under it, although it carries some sense. It is rather synoptic in nature. More properly, perhaps, it is to be called 'Comparative Study of Religions' although this caption also does not give the full idea of the nature of the subject. But that is perhaps quite natural, because it is the case with nearly every subject that the mere title does not provide the full idea about the nature of its subject- matter. In any case, however, 'Comparative Religion' in precise terms, is a comparative and critical study of the important features of the religions of the world in a scientific spirit. Although in whatever we have said above, we have thrown hints regarding the specific points involved in this characterisation, we feel that they require further clarification in which we will enter below. First we shall take up what a 'comparative study of religions in a scientific spirit' actually is and then we shall try to see what kind of criticism or evaluation is actually suitable for a field of study like Comparative Religion. All these will add further towards the clarification of the precise nature, aims and objectives of the subject.

We may very well see that in clarifying what a comparative study of religions in a scientific spirit is, we have to be clear about two points: (1) what a comparative study of religions is, and (2) what it means to make such a study in a scientific spirit. As regards the first point, it may be seen that whenever we embark on a study of various religions on different specific points related to the important principles, beliefs and practices involved in them, we have first to collect relevant materials. But here apart from other difficulties regarding the method of the collection of materials, we have to face the problem of the selection of materials also. We are in difficulty as to what to include and what to leave aside out of the vast mass of materials that we come across. But then this should not be a very serious point of difficulty. After due consideration of materials, points of relevance and importance may be marked out and comparisons of those points may be made. But again there is a difficulty regarding the comparison itself. No comparison seems possible at first sight, because each religion in its wholeness appears to have its own distinctive character with specific features of its own. How to make comparisons then? Moreover, in making comparison, there are always chances of overemphasis, both in respect of the similarities and differences found amongst different religions. As a matter of fact, religions of the world both agree and differ together in many important points. But over-enthusiastic persons exhibit maniac tendencies in either bringing useless and farfetched points of similarity or in exposing unnecessary, unimportant and artificial points of differences amongst religions. In making honest and objective comparisons, both these extremist tendencies are to be avoided. Factual comparisons with points of real similarities and differences must be brought about in making a real comparative study of the religions of the world. And this is a not an easy task. The task becomes all the more difficult due to natural and unavoidable leaning that one has towards one's own religion. In making comparisons, one is generally inclined towards taking one's own religion as the standard of comparison and judging other religions in the light of that. This tendency vitiates the real academic spirit of making a comparative study of religions, because the person instead of making honest comparisons begins to pass judgments which are prejudiced and unwarranted.

As a precaution against such tendencies, Parriender very honestly and amply remarks," Comparison, however to be justified seriously, must not imply judgement, and still less description of any faith."[2] The comparative study of the main points of various religions must be made in a neutral and detached manner characteristic of a scientist. In making comparisons, as we have said, there is always a danger of swaying towards the strong points of one's own religion and weak points of others. But in a scientific study, this tendency must be avoided. And these points inevitably lead us to the consideration of the scientific nature of the study of comparative religion, *i.e.*, to the consideration of the second point made out above.

Comparative Religion is a scientific study. In the foregoing paragraph we have indicated in an implied manner what a scientific study of religions would be like. It must not be unrealistic and biased, rather it should be factual and realistic. No point concerning any religion, either one's own or of any other is either to be overemphasised or underestimated. It is an objective study, a study of religions for their own sake. The sole aim of such a study is better understanding, and for that an attitude of objective knowledge – seeking will have to be adopted so that all sorts of preferences and prejudices for or against any religion are completely shunned. A study of the main points of various religions will have to be made in a neutral and detached manner which is characteristic of any scientific study. No value judgements on any religion by going outside the range of that particular religion are, therefore, to be passed. The study must be such that the members of a particular religion are able to recognise themselves in the description of their own religion. For this a kind of emphathetic understanding of any religion may be highly desirable. In other words, for presenting a really objective

2. G. Parriender, *Comparative Religion* (George Allen & Unwin).

picture of any religion, it will be highly desirable on the part of the comparative religionist to have the capacity of empathetically entering into the world of that particular religion. Such an empathetic entering will automatically eradicate all sorts of preferences or prejudices for any particular religion and a real and objective picture of the religion being studied will emerge. This will also promote a sense of sympathy or tolerance in regard to that religion, which is also sometimes regarded as something necessary in course of a scientific study of any religion. To be able to carry on a really scientific study in the sphere of religion, it is perhaps desirable that one is a bit more sympathetic towards religions other than his own. Religion is a very touchy and sensitive affair and therefore even in being neutral, there is always a danger of leaning towards one's own faith. It is for avoiding this danger that in matters of making a comparative study of religions, one is advised to adopt somewhat a special kind of scientific attitude. And that consists in being a bit sympathetic towards other religions (other than one's own) instead of being completely neutral in respect of all of them. Charity towards other religions, therefore, is a necessary ingredient of the scientific study of religions.

A second precaution must also be taken in making the study of religions scientific. A scientific study as we have said above, is a detached study. But too much of detachment in the study of religions is in a sense harmful and undesirable. Being detached sometimes means adopting a cut-and-dry attitude, confining oneself only to the externals of a thing without entering into its real depth. Religions are all living faiths and their essence does not consist in their bare externals such as rituals, methods of prayer, ceremonies etc. It rather consists in the inner beliefs and convictions which they carry along with them and which give their followers a distinctive character and way of life. To understand these internals of a religion, a little of involvement, not into any particular religion, but into religion in general, is necessary. In other words, some kind of religious sensitivity is essential on the part of a man who wants to make a study of religions in a comparative perspective. A purely cut-and-dry attitude cannot be regarded as a really scientific attitude in this sphere of study. That may be helpful in studying the dead and unconscious materials of the external world, but that can hardly help in a faithful study of the living faiths which concern the inner convictions of people. In a way, the study of religions is not only a study of their objective features as found in them externally, but also of the inner faiths and commitments associated with them in reference to their followers. Therefore, any scientific study in this sphere will have to be scientific in somewhat a specific sense.

Moreover, as we have hinted above, Comparative Religion to be a real academic study (and not only a study of general interest), must not only be a comparative description of the various points in a scientific spirit, but also be to some extent evaluative and critical. Really this aspect of comparative religion is the most delicate and it is here that tolerance and sympathy towards other religions are most required. Evaluation always requires a standard and one is always naturally tempted towards making one's own faith the standard of evaluation. And here the entire aim of comparative study of religions is destroyed. In making evaluations or critical estimates, therefore, one has to take utmost care of not being unfair to any faith. To make a critical appraisal of a religion other than one's own is an exceedingly difficult and delicate task. But then it has to be done. In fact, many scholars have taken up this task and have accomplished it wisely and successfully. Thus evaluations are to be made, but the important thing to see is that they are rightly made.

But the question is, how are such right evaluations to be made? In fact there is no straight and well-knit answer to this question? In other words, no straight and well-defined path can be shown to accomplish the job. It much depends upon the personal will and worth of the appraiser. One has to combine here his genuine critical acumen with his real sense of sympathy and large-heartedness for other religions. And this is not an easy task. However, some valuable hints have been thrown by certain thinkers on this point and in our humble way of thinking, we will suggest that they are to be followed in utmost sincerity and seriousness, if Comparative Religion is to become a useful study. One such hint is that, when evaluative statements are made about other religions, it must be kept in mind that they are recognised as fair in the context of the particular religion regarding which they are made. This clearly means that external criticisms of religions must be avoided as far as possible. Criticisms of a religion must be made within the framework of its own beliefs, ideas and practices. There is no limit to external criticisms. They all depend upon the personal convictions, likes and dislikes of the appraiser. But such criticisms based on personal likes and dislikes, or based on criteria drawn out of one's own faith and religion are hardly justified and desirable. A very prudent and at the same time valuable hint has been thrown in this regard by Cantwell when he says, "It is the business of comparative religion to construct statements about religion that are intelligible within at least two traditions simultaneously."[3] The two traditions meant here are: (1) The tradition to which the appraiser belongs and (2) The tradition of the religion he is appraising. In a similar vein Prof. Bahm observes, "My own view is that 'Comparative religions' does not exit in its fullest and fairest sense until judgements are based upon standards common to all of them and until each religion that proposes a standard of its own by which to measure other religions is

---

3. Comparative Religion: Whither and why?, p. 52.

also measured by standards proposed by other religions. 'Comparative religions' as a study cannot approach being an 'objective science' until those who study it become willing to commit themselves to comparisons based on objective standards."[4] It is clear that the general spirit lying behind all those hints is that, in making critical appraisals of other religions, one must give up preference for the beliefs and ideas of one's own religion or of any particular religion. Evaluations must be made with an open mind such that standards derived from one's own religion are not imposed upon others.

The above may give us an idea of the nature, aims and objectives of Comparative Religion. It also gives us an ample hint of the difficult and delicate task that a writer on Comparative Religion may have to perform. He has to be realistic in approach and has to adopt objective standards. He has to be neutral and scientific in his essential spirit, but that also in a special sense, *i.e.*, in the sense of being somewhat sympathetic towards other religions. He has to carry on a detached study, but still he is not to be completely uninvolved and devoid of religious sensitivity. He has to make evaluations but very sympathetically and carefully. Thus a very balanced mind – unbiased, unprejudiced, trained in scientific neutrality and yet sensitive to the deeper convictional aspects of religion – is required to undertake and accomplish these various aspects of the task. Yet the task is not impossible. In fact, valuable comparisons and evaluations have been made and they can very well serve as our guides in the stupendous task that we have embarked on undertaking. Let us hope and believe that in the following pages we shall be able to do justice to the claims of various living religions of the world in so far as we will be engaged in the delicate task of comparing, contrasting and evaluating them.

---

4. A.J. Bahm, *The World's Living Religions* (Arnold Heinemenn, 1964), p. 13.

2

Hinduism

1. Introductory

Hinduism is perhaps the oldest of all the living religions. It has neither any definite date of its origin nor has it any definite founder associated with it. It is called *Sanātana dharma,* a religion coming down to people through eternity. It is thus a unique religion in one very important sense. Nearly every religion of the world is associated with a definite personality claimed to be its first originator or founder and has a definite text which is regarded as its basic religious text. But Hinduism has none. It can more be regarded as a spontaneous growth assisted at various stages of civilisation from various sides rather than a creation or construction of somebody. As Sir Charles Eliot remarks in this connection, "Hinduism has not been made, but has grown. It is jungle, not a building." Similarly, K.M. Sen makes the following observations in his book *Hinduism,* "Hinduism is more like a tree that has grown gradually than like a building that has been erected by some great architect at some definite point in time. It contains within itself the influences of many cultures and the body of Hindu thought thus offers as much variety as the Indian nation itself."[1] The names of a host of sages and saints are of course associated with Hinduism, but none can claim to be its founder; they have all simply contributed to its growth in their own specific ways. Similarly, an enormous corpus of sacred literature is also associated with Hinduism to which one is to refer for having an idea of its chief beliefs and practices, but none can claim exclusive authority. Some of the important religious texts of Hinduism are – the Vedas, the Upaniṣads, the Purāṇas, the Dharma Sūtras and Dharma Śāstras, the Rāmāyaṇa, the Mahābhārata and the Bhagavadgītā. But this list also is not exhaustive. Of these, Vedas are the oldest, rather they are regarded by the Hindu tradition as beginningless (*Anādi*) and in a way exert the highest authority. Nevertheless other texts also are regarded as no less sacred.

Not only it is that Hinduism has no one as its definite founder and no book as its one exclusive text, but also that it has got no well-defined, rigid and dogmatic principles of faith or practice. Varying beliefs and practices can be found amongst those who call themselves Hindus. A polytheist is as much a Hindu, as a monotheist or a monist or even an atheist. Hinduism is really a vast and apparently incoherent religious complex. It is rightly characterised as a vast jungle in which it is very difficult to mark out how many kinds of trees and plants flourish. In fact, to summarise the main principles, beliefs and practices of any religion is very difficult, but in case of Hinduism it seems impossible. The variety and complexity of Hindu beliefs and practices can be seen implied into the very basic philosophy (of religion) that Hinduism entertains and professes. There is only one

1. K.M. Sen, *Hinduism* (Penguin Books), pp. 14-15.

basic reality underlying everything which is differently named in different religions. All the different religions are really like different paths leading to the same goal. So there is no question of prescribing any rigid set of principles or practices. Everyone has got the right to follow his own path and approach God in his own way. Hinduism never claims that a particular prophet is *the* prophet and a particular faith is *the* faith. It does not believe in inflicting rigid rules of prayer, worship etc. As a matter of fact, the way of worship or prayer or any other such way is not the only way of realising God or attaining salvation. There are various ways, of which Hinduism more often speaks of three – the way of knowledge (*Jñāna mārga*), the way of action (*Karma mārga*) and the way of worship and prayer (*Bhakti mārga*). Anyone according to his temperament may adopt any of these ways and attain to salvation. Thus Hinduism is in its very temperament against any rigid rules of religion. It is very liberal and broad hearted in its approach and outlook.

Hindu religion, as we have said above, is an amalgam of various kinds of beliefs and practices. Although this religion has generally been recognised as a religion of the Aryans, in fact, various ethnic and cultural groups have exerted their influence from time to time in shaping and reshaping the various beliefs and practices that are prevalent in Hindu religious complex. At least the two ethnic groups present in India from before the advent of the Aryans had their definite marks on Hindu religious beliefs. Aryans made no effort to convert everyone to their own faith. Instead Aryan beliefs and practices themselves assimilated a great deal with the beliefs and practices of both the Dravidians and the aboriginals. So the overall culture or religion which is now known as Hinduism is a gradual growth out of the amalgam and synthesis of beliefs and practices of various strands. Hinduism has very appreciably retained within itself all these kinds of beliefs and practices ranging from most profound religious thoughts and ideas to gross superstitions and magic which may very well be seen amongst the people who go to compose the Hindu pantheon. Thus Hindu religion, in general, may be said to be something that is lived by Hindu people. No other characterisation can do full justice to it.

Hinduism is not only a religion, but a social system and a tradition too. The most obvious and important mark of this social system has been its *varna dharma*. As a matter of fact, traditionally only he has been able to be a Hindu who has belonged to any of the four varnas present in Hindu social system. This has been rather the distinguishing mark of being a Hindu. One may have any kind of belief regarding God etc. and one may follow any kind of religious practice of his choice. That will not check anyone from being called a Hindu. But he cannot be a Hindu unless he belongs to one or other class or *Varna*. Formerly, the classification seemed more based upon the aptitude and worth that one had, but in course of time birth became the only criterion of distinction. It may be said here that in spite of all the varieties of beliefs and practices that a Hindu has, belongingness to one or other of the four varnas has been an essential mark of someone being a Hindu. Any other thing which has bound Hindus together as one religious group in spite of their differences in beliefs and practices can be said to be their faith in the supremacy of the Vedas as well as their regard and respect for some other religious texts such as the Rāmāyaṇa, the Mahābhārata and the Bhagavadgītā. Some other features which have been able to bind Hindus together as one religious group have been their common beliefs in the immortality of soul, the law of *karma* and rebirth, the possibility of *Moksha* etc. Thus in spite of varieties and differences in beliefs and practices, there are certain common grounds which Hindus generally share.

2. Basic features of Hinduism as a religion

As there are hardly any well-defined criteria of Hindu religion and one can be a Hindu by simply coming under the fold of one of the classes specified by the Varna Dharma notwithstanding his other beliefs and practices, it is very difficult to enumerate any such feature or features of Hinduism which may be characterised as basic in the sense that they are commonly and essentially shared by all Hindus. However, we have seen above that in spite of the differences of beliefs and practices, there are certain such features of Hinduism which bind its followers together, howsoever loose that bond may be. There are certain beliefs which a good majority of Hindus seems to hold and also there are certain practices which are more or less common amongst the Hindus. Such beliefs and practices may form the basic features of Hinduism as a religion and they can be summarised as follows:

1. Hinduism is a complex religion admitting of vast differences of beliefs and practices amongst its followers. That is, there is neither any definite set of beliefs nor any definite set of practices which are observed and followed by each and every Hindu alike.

One obvious point which demonstrates the complex nature of Hinduism as a religion is that it is polytheistic, monotheistic, monistic and atheistic all at the same time. In other words, a believer in many gods and goddesses is as much a Hindu, as a believer in only one God. Similarly, a believer in a personal God is as much a Hindu, as a believer in an impersonal Absolute or Brahman. Even a believer in no God can be, and is very much, a Hindu. Again, as there are different kinds of believers, so there are different kinds of practices also, and this further adds to the complex nature of Hindu faith.

2. As a natural corollary to the above, Hinduism has neither any one definite religious text nor any definite creed,

as several or almost all other religions of the world have. The Vedas, however, are regarded as the most ancient and authentic religious texts. Besides the Vedas, there are many other texts, such as, the upaniṣads, the Rāmāyana, the Mahābhārata, the various Purāṇas, the Bhagavadgītā etc., which are regarded as sacred texts of Hinduism and Hindus so often repeat lines from them as a mark of their sacred practice.

3. The above points may give us a sufficient hint of the fact that there can be hardly any definite mark of someone being called a Hindu, but with certain reservations it may be said that belief in the overall authority of the Vedas and belongingness to one of the four Varnas are, more or less, the essential marks of being a Hindu. Of these two also, the latter is perhaps more important than the former, because one may continue to be a Hindu even if he refuses to believe in the authority of the Vedas, but he will not be a Hindu unless he belongs to one of the four classes. It is perhaps this condition which has deterred Hinduism from being a missionary religion. If anyone is converted from other religion to the Hindu fold, the problem of the settlement of his Varna will at once arise: to what Varna, after all, will he be taken to belong? Of course, belongingness to one of the four Varnas seems more to be a social mark than a religious one, nevertheless, it is essentially associated with Hindu religion.

4. Hinduism, whether it be theistic or atheistic, believes in an overall supremacy of the spiritual over the profane and the material. It is generally believed in it that behind and beneath the mundane world-order, there is a spiritual order or realm, which is the basic, the essential and the eternal. Man, therefore, even while living in this material world should always bear in mind that he essentially belongs to the spiritual order, and therefore he is never to be overinvolved in or unduly attached to the attractions of this material world-order.

5. Quite in consonance with the above belief, Hinduism firmly believes that the essential nature of man is spiritual. The bodily aspect of man is only external and superficial. In his inner and essential being man is a soul. This soul in man is immortal. Nothing can destroy it. The Bhagavadgītā describes this indestructibility of the soul in the following manner: "Weapons cannot cut it nor can fire burn it; water cannot wet it nor can wind dry it:"[2] Thus the soul survives bodily death.

6. In continuation of its belief in the immortality of the human soul Hinduism believes in the transmigration of the soul from one body to another, from the old to a new one. This is more popularly known as the doctrine of rebirth in Hinduism. The death of a body simply means soul's casting off that body in order to put on another one so as to begin a fresh worldly life. The Bhagavadgītā characterises this transmigration of the soul from one body to another as follows: "As a man by shedding worn-out garments, takes the other new ones, likewise the embodied soul, by casting off worn-out bodies, enters into others which are the new ones."[3]

7. This transmigration of soul from one body to another, *i.e.*, rebirth, is not, however, taken as something desirable in Hinduism. It is a sign of soul's bondage which begets continued suffering. Rebirth, therefore, is not a boon, but a curse which must be got rid of.

8. What causes this chain of birth and rebirth and the consequent bondage and suffering is man's own action (*karma*). Hinduism firmly believes in what is called the law of *karma*. This law implies that no action done by any man

---

2. Nainam chindanti śastrāṇi nainam dahati pāvakaḥ na cainam kledayantyāpo na śoṣayati marutaḥ.

– *The Bhagvadgītā*, II.23.

3. Vasāṃsi jīrṇāni yathā vihāya navāni gṛhnāti naro'parāṇi tathā śarīrāṇi vihāya jīrṇānyanyāni saṃyāti navāni dehī.

– *Ibid.*, II.22.

goes in vain. It necessarily bears its fruits and the man doing the action has to reap the fruits of his action. That is, the man doing the action has necessarily to undergo the consequences of his action; he has to bear the burden of the good or bad results that his good or bad actions produce. No one can escape the results of his actions. If one does not exhaust the good or bad consequences of his actions in the present life, he has to take another birth for bearing the burden of his remaining actions. Thus, rebirth is the result of one's own past *karmas*.

But again all sorts of actions done by someone do not cause rebirth or bondage. The actions which generate fruits and which cause rebirth are known as attached actions (*sakāma karmas*). Such actions are actions done with a sense of attachment, i.e., with some narrow egoistic passion or desire. Actions opposed to these, i.e., actions done with a sense of non-attachment are known as non-attached actions (*niṣkāma karmas*). Such actions are like fried seeds which do not generate any fruits and consequently do not cause rebirth or bondage.

9. Thus action done with a sense of attachment (*kāma*) is the root cause of man's continued involvement in the chain of birth and rebirth. *Karma* and *Saṃsāra,* therefore, go hand in hand. If one wants to be liberated from the chain of *Saṃsāra,* he will have to be free from karmas, i.e., from attached, egoistic actions.

10. As indicated above, release from the chain of birth and rebirth is possible. This continuing chain is not the destiny of man. The destiny, according to Hinduism, is Moksha, which is life eternal, a life of pure spirituality. In this life the soul becomes free from all worldly suffering and attains its original pure spiritual nature. This is state of eternal bliss. In this state, the soul attains its real immortal nature.

11. Moksha is attainable by the adoption of any of the following three paths – the path of knowledge, the path of

actions and the path of devotion to God. The path of knowledge is the path of attaining true knowledge about the nature of reality by direct realization. The path of action is really the path of disinterested or non-attached actions (*niṣkāma karmas*) and the path of devotion to God is the path of worship and prayer with full sincerity and with a sense of total submission and surrender to God.

Besides these, there are a host of other beliefs and practices which an average Hindu seems to entertain and follow, but they are not very pervasive and most of them are only regional or locational in nature. We need not, therefore, mention them here.

3. God

We have said above that one can be a good Hindu without having any belief in any god or goddess. There is a full-fledged, rather highly esteemed, system of Hindu philosophy, known as the Samkhya system, which is clearly atheistic. Thus in one sense it may look rather odd or irrelevant to talk of Hindu conception of God. But really it is not so. An average Hindu seems to be a firm believer in God – either in one God or in several gods and goddesses. Hindu belief in God ranges from polytheism through abstract monism to a concrete monotheism. Vedas are regarded as the most original source of Hindu faith and they are clearly polytheistic in nature. They abound in various gods and goddesses of whom Varuna, Mitra, Agni, Indra etc. seem to be prominent. Although in later Hinduism, these gods have hardly any hold on the common mass, still polytheism having other gods and goddesses such as, Ganesh, Hanumān, Durgā, Kāli, etc. seems to be the dominant faith of the average Hindu. An average Hindu even now worships some or all of these gods and goddesses on different occasions. But a monotheistic tendency seems to be present in Hinduism right from the age of the Vedas themselves. Although apparently the Vedas speak of a host of gods and goddesses, there is always a tendency towards monotheism involved therein. This may be seen in the fact that whenever there is a praise in favour of any god or goddess in the Vedas, it is so construed as if the god or goddess in praise reigns supreme over all and others are just his various forms. There is a clear indication towards monotheism also when the Vedas declare that the same one reality is called by various names (*Ekam sadviprā bahudhā vadanti*). This tendency of the Vedic polythiesm towards monotheism is amply characterised by Maxmuller as henotheism. Although, as we have said above, an average Hindu even now worships a host of gods and goddesses such as Viṣṇu, Śiva, Gaṇeśa, Kārtikeya, Hanumāna, Pārvatī, Durgā, Kālī, Saraswatī, Lakṣmī etc. (there are said to be 33 crore gods and goddesses in Hindu pantheon), there is an inherent faith in even the most illiterate of Hindus that at bottom there is only one God and the various gods and goddesses are just his various forms or manifestations.

Anyway, when we come to the stage of the Upaniṣads, the Vedic polytheism (and the associated ritualism) seems to be converted here into a philosophic monism. As a matter of fact, in the Upaniṣads there are two trends of which the drift towards monism is the one. The other trend gives vent to monotheism. It is really these two different trends present in the Upaniṣads which give rise to two equally important Hindu philosophic systems of Samkar's Advaita and Ramanuja's Visiṣṭādvaita, the former being an exquisite example of absolute monism and the latter of a full-fledged theism. These two philosophies based upon the Upaniṣads have really both captured the Hindu religious mind, although it is the former which is more well known amongst the Westerners as the characteristic Hindu philosophy and religion. The former speaks of God as an attributeless Absolute (*Nirguna Brahma*), while the latter takes God as the Lord, the 'Inner controller' who indwells the entire cosmos. This God is not *a* god of the Vedas, but *the* God, the only supreme being, omnipotent, omniscient etc. and the ruler of the entire universe. This God is called here the *saguṇa* Brahma. It is the latter view assisted by the theism of the Rāmāyaṇa, the Mahābhārata and the Bhagavadgītā which has a mass impact and has captured the minds of the popular Hindu milleau. The former has proved to be great Hindu philosophy, but as a religion the latter has gained more ground. We shall therefore try to expound here in brief the conception of God as envisaged in the theism of Ramanuja and the Bhagạvadgītā.

God is *Antaryāmi*, the inward dweller, the inner soul of the entire universe. He is infinite, eternal and all-pervading. He is omnipotent, omniscient and omnipresent. He is the supreme value also and is endowed with infinite auspicious qualities such as truthfulness, knowledge, bliss, tenderness, compassion etc. He is the creator, preserver and destroyer of the world. He creates the world not out of nothing (as Judaism and Christianity seem to believe in), but out of the material of his own being. He has within his being two aspects of *cit* (Consciousness) and *acit* (Matter) (*Para* and *Apara* in the language of the Bhagavadgītā) and he creates the entire universe of material objects and conscious beings out of these two aspects. The objects of the world are the real expressions or modifications of these two aspects. God is thus both the efficient (*Nimitta*) and the material (*Ūpādāna*) cause of the universe. (Here it should be remembered that the Nyaya regards God as only the efficient cause and not the material cause). He is both immanent in the world as its indwelling sustainer as well as transcendent to it as its creator. He is the inner soul of the world, which, as if, constitutes his body. Just as the soul is unaffected by the changes in the body, similarly God remains unaffected by the changes in the world. He is changeless in his nature. He is also unaffected by the impurities of the world. He is supreme goodness. That the entire universe is God's body and that nothing is outside him are as much the theme of the Gita conception of God as that of Ramanuja's. In the body of God, Arjuna beholds all the beings of heaven and earth but still he does not visualise the beginning, the middle or the end of the Lord.[4] God is regarded as the Purusottama in the Bhagavadgītā and as Nārāyaṇa and Vāsudeva by Ramanuja. He is neither personal nor impersonal but super-personal. Ramanuja also takes God as Viṣṇu, who at the time of creation projects the whole world from within him at the time of dissolution withdraws everything within him.

Although the above conception of God as envisaged in the Bhagavadgītā and in the philosophy of Ramanuja is very much acceptable to a Hindu, an average, unsophisticated Hindu conceives God in a way which seems very much based on the Purāṇas. The average Hindu in his own unsophisticated manner believes that God has no definite shape and form. He is *nirākāra*. He is above time and space and is eternal and infinite. But he has three aspects within him – the creative, the preservative and destructive. His creative aspect is personified as Brahmā, the perspective aspect as Viṣṇu and the destructive aspect as Shiva. These three aspects are so often taken as the three deities, although within the one supreme Lord. Brahmā, Viṣṇu and Shiva (Mahesh) therefore constitute what may be called the Hindu Trinity. The one basic reality of which the three are taken as the inseparable aspects is himself known as Viṣṇu. He is conceived as essentially loving, compassionate, kind and good. He is further conceived as eternally sleeping on his couch, unless disturbed by the supplication of other gods who on occasions require his intervention for the

4. *The Bhagavadgītā*, XII, pp. 15-16.

preservation of righteousness and good in the world. It is believed that whenever unrighteousness reigns supreme on the earth, Viṣṇu incarnates himself in the world and does away with all evil. So far he has incarnated nine times in different forms in the forms of a fish, a tortoise, a bear, a man-lion (*Nṛsiṃha*), a dwarf (*Vāmana*) and four times in human forms as those of Parasurama, Rama, Krishna, the Buddha and the tenth is due in near future.

Brahmā is regarded as the author of all creation. He, however, is not worshipped by the Hindus as a principal deity. It seems that Brahmā-worship was once popular, but was over-thrown by the worshippers of Viṣṇu and Shiva. Brahmā is mythologically known to have taken birth out of the navel of Viṣṇu while he keeps asleep with his consort Lakshmi at the time of the equilibrium of the world. This is symbolic of the creative aspect of Viṣṇu.

The worship of Shiva, the third deity of Hindu Trinity, is the most popular amongst the Hindus. Although Shiva is primarily regarded as a god of destruction, the average Hindu worships him as a very kind and beneficent deity. He is regarded as the god of regeneration and is believed to be pleased by little of prayer and devotion. He is equally the god of the ascetics as well as of the Hindus leading an ordinary domestic life.

4. World

There is no definite theory of creation in Hinduism. Even this is not clear whether the world is an act of creation at all. There is at least one Hindu system of thought – the Samkhya system which believes that the world is a product of evolution. Samkhya is an atheistic Hindu system and therefore for it there is no question of creation. In the absence of any creator God, the question of creation does not arise. The world arises out of an evolution of *Prakṛti*, the primordial matter, with the help and co-operation of *Puruṣa*, the non-changing primordial consciousness. Even those systems which take the world as an act of creation do not take it created all at once at a definite period of time in a well defined manner in the fashion of Judaeo-Christian belief. It seems the world is somehow taken as created from all eternity and the acts of creation and destruction go on infinitely in a cyclic order. There are, of course, various mythical stories about creation in the various religious texts of the Hindus, but for the most part creation seems to be a mystery and it is not very clear when and how it was exactly done. The following hymns of the Ṛg Veda clearly paint creation as a mystery. "Then was not non-existent nor existent: there was no realm of air, no sky beyond it. What covered in, and where? and what gave shelter? Was water there, unfathomed depth of water? Death was not then, nor was there aught immortal: no sign was there, the day's and night's divide. That one thing, breathless, breathed by its own nature: apart from it was nothing whatsoever. Darkness there was: at first concealed in darkness, this all was indiscriminated chaos. All that existed then was void and formless: by the great power of warmth was born that unit. Thereafter rose desire in the beginning, Desire, the primal seed and germ of spirit. Sages who searched with their heart's thought discovered the existent's kinship in the non-existent.

Transversely was their severing line extended. What was above it then and what below it? There were begetters, there were mighty forces, free action here and energy up yonder. *Who verily knows and who can here declare it, whence it was born and whence came this creation? The gods are later than this world's production. Who knows, then, whence it first came into being?*
He, the first origin of this creation, whether he formed it all or did not form it.
Whose eye controls this world in highest heaven, he verily knows it, or *perhaps he knows not.*"[5]

---

5. *Ṛg Veda*, X, 129.

There are mythical narratives regarding the creation of the world in the Viṣṇu Purāṇa, the Manusmriti and such other texts also. Much of the details contained in these texts tallies with each other, but there are differences too. The details of the creation myth as contained in Ṛg Veda and the Manusmriti very much agree with each other. In one of the hymns of the Ṛg Veda (X.121) Brahmā, as *Hiranyagarbha*, appears to be the seed of all creation. This golden seed of all creation comes from Viṣṇu himself, who is lying in the fathomless water. The hymn says, "In the beginning was the Golden seed: once born he was the one Lord of all that is." The golden seed is *Prajāpati* the Lord of creations, who is both the transcendent God and the immanent spirit of everything. This story of creation out of the golden seed is the most popular amongst Hindus. There are other myths also (as in Viṣṇu Purāṇa) which relate that the world came out of an egg which was cut by God himself. Of these various creation myths of Hinduism, Sir Charles Eliot says, "Hindu cosmogenies are various and discordant in details, but usually start with the evolution or emanation of living beings from the Divinity and often a reproductive act forms part of the process such as the hatching of an egg or the division of a divinity into male and female halves. But every thing in these creation stories is figurative."[6]

Apart from the authenticity and literal reality of any of the stories of creation present in Hindu religious texts, one thing is clear and that is that, those who believe that the world is an act of creation believe that God has not created the world *ex nihilo*. He has created it either out of certain elements existing eternally (as the Nyāya-Vaiśeṣika system believes that God has created the world in space and time out of the eternal material atoms in accordance with the previous karmas of people) or out of the materials of his own being (as the Bhagavadgītā and the system of

6. Sir Charles Eliot, *Hinduism & Buddhism*, Book II, p. 43.

Ramanuja have it). In all these theistic systems, however, the world is taken as totally dependent upon God. Even though God creates the world with pre-existing materials, as according to the Nyāya-Vaiśeṣika, still nothing in the world is independent of God. The popular Hindu belief also is very much in favour of world's absolute dependence upon God. This belief is well contained in the Hindu idea of Trinity of Brahmā, Viṣṇu and Mahesh. This Trinity signifies that God in his different aspects is responsible for all the three acts of creating, sustaining and dissolving or destroying the world.

God as the creator of the world is regarded as transcendent to it but as its inner sustainer and controller he is also regarded as immanent into it. Even if God creates the world out of the material his own being, he is not fully exhausted in this world. This is clear from the following extract from the Pūruṣa Sūkta of the Ṛg Veda which speaks in a figurative way about the fact that although God is present everywhere in the world, he is not exhausted into it – "Thousand headed is Puruṣa, thousand eyed and thousand footed. Enveloping the earth on every side he exceeds it by ten fingers breadth. Puruṣa is indeed this All, what has been and yet to come and he is the Lord of immortality (and) of what grows by (eating) food. ...One quarter of Him is all contingent beings, three-quarters of Him is what is immortal in heaven. With three-quarters Puruṣa ascended, one quarter of Him came into existence again (down) here. Thence did he stride form on every side among all that eats and does not eat."[7]

As to the nature and status of the world, the general Hindu belief is that, although the world is dependent upon God, it is nevertheless real. It is a real creation of God and is a ground for human action by which his future life will be

---

7. *Ṛg Veda*, Puruṣa Sūkta. X, 90.

determined. Only Śaṃkara Vedanta takes the world as *māyā* or illusion and it is a fact that a great majority of Hindu belief is affected by this view. The westerners take Śaṃkara's view of world as characteristic of Hindu religion and philosophy and this is why they so often level the charge against Hinduism that its attitude is world-negating. But this is hardly a correct assessment of the Hindu view of world. Firstly it is to be very clearly kept in mind that Śaṃsara's view about the world is only one of the several views that the Indian tradition and philosophy have within them. Moreover, even Śaṃkara regards this world as *māyā* not in the sense that it s a phantom or a dream. On the other hand, by calling the world *māyā* he simply wants to direct our attention to a more fundamental spiritual reality underlying the world. This aspect of Samkara's thought has been times without number highlighted and emphasised by modern interpreters of Advaita Vedānta such as Vivekanand, Radhakrishnan, etc. Samkara himself quite unambiguously says that although on the ultimate level, the world is not real and what is real is Brahman and Brahman alone, on the practical level the world is fully real and all its activities have a real significance.

As to the problem, why the world at all came about or what made the Lord create it, the general Hindu answer is that the world is the *lilā* or play of God. It is the spontaneous overflow of God's exuberance (*Ānanda*). Sometimes, as in the Nyāya-Vaiśeṣika, the world is regarded as the product of God's desire (*Ichhā*). But the word 'desire' does not imply here that God has created this world to fulfil some of his needs. God has no need to accomplish. He creates the world only in accordance with the requirements of the law of karma.

5. Man

In Hinduism man has been given a very high status. He is not only the highest creature of the world; he is often given a status equal to God. The concept of *Nar-Nārāyaṇa* (Man-God) in Hinduism amply speaks of the Godly status that man has been given. Śaṃkara's identification of human self with Brahman is also an indication of this truth. Although outwardly man is a psycho-physical being, in the inner core of his being, there is a soul which is really the spark of the Divine within him. So man is essentially divine in nature. This soul in man is immortal. Nothing can destroy it. Even death can do nothing to it. The famous Gītā saying in this regard amply characterises soul as immune to any destructive agency, "It (the *Ātman*) is never born, nor does it die at any time, nor having once come to be will it ever cease to be. It is unborn, eternal, permanent and primeaval. It is not slain when the body is slain."[8] Then again "Weapons do not cleave this self, fire does not burn it, water does not make it wet, nor does the wind make it dry. It is uncleavable, it cannot be burnt. It can be neither wetted nor dried. It is eternal, all-pervading, unchanging and immovable. It is the same for ever."[9] This Ātman or soul constitutes the real being of man and it is really the infinite within the apparently finite man. Man is therefore regarded finite-infinite (i. e. infinite within the finite) in nature. Tagore has recently very much emphasised this infinite aspect of man's nature in his book *Religion of Man*.

However, despite his essential greatness, man, as he stands here in this world, is a victim of ignorance (*Ajñāna*) and is in bondage. The potential greatness and infinity of the soul are overshadowed by its attachment with the material and the sensuous. And this sense of attachment is generated by *Avidyā* or *Ajñāna*, which according to the Hindu belief is *Anādi* (Beginningless). This beginningless *Avidyā* with which man is condemned to be born may, to some extent, be compared with the Christian idea of

---

8. Bhagavadgītā, II, 20.
9. *Ibid.*, II, 23-24.

Original Sin with which man is vitiated from his very origin. This *Avidyā*, however, is not endless. It can be won over and freedom from it can be achieved. Freedom from ignorance, and consequently from bondage, is known in Hinduism as *Moksa* (Salvation). Every man is capable of salvation. As ignorance is the root cause of bondage, the natural cure is knowledge (*Jñāna*). By knowledge man can get rid of *Avidyā* and attain liberation. However, knowledge does not mean here only intellectual knowledge. It means wisdom, which can be attained by direct realisation, direct experience, of what is real and what is unreal. In liberation, man does not get anything new; he simply recognises his true, original nature. He regains his soul and nothing else. Man is so great potentially that he has to get nothing more than himself.

That man can liberate himself from his state of bondage amply speaks of the fact that man is free. If he is bound at all, he is bound by his own karmas. Man is the maker of his own destiny. As he will sow, so he will reap. Hinduism firmly believes in the law of *karma*, which implies that the only factor which shapes a man's destiny in his own actions. If he performs non-attached actions for the sake of humanity at large, he is destined to be free from all suffering and ultimately from all bondage. But if he performs selfish actions by being involved into sensuous and worldly attractions he will have to reap the consequences by being bound into a continuous chain of birth and rebirth.

That Hinduism allows freedom to man is sometimes disputed. It is said that the law of *karma* is not a symbol of man's freedom; rather it is a mark of just the opposite. A man's present life is absolutely bound by his past karmas and therefore where is the scope for the exercise of his own freedom? But this is a wrong interpretation of the law of *karma*. This law is a perfect guarantee to man to shape his future according to his own will and action. If there were no freedom of will and action in Hinduism, then there could be no question of reward or punishment to man (in terms of salvation or rebirth) in accordance with his actions. The maxim 'As one will sow, so will he reap' clearly shows that the future of a man fully depends upon his own actions, that man himself is fully responsible for what he is at present and what he will be in future. There can be no greater guarantee for the freedom of man than this. Man is thus free and everything depends upon what he wills and does.

6. Evil and suffering

Hindu approach to suffering is more practical than theoretical, and, according to it, for the most part, suffering is attributed to one's own past karmas rather than to any other agency. The main problem is to get rid of this suffering rather than to explain it. Again, suffering is not any specific feature of life, it is life or existence itself. To take birth and to be in the world is by itself a suffering and we have to get rid of it. What are taken as specific examples of suffering are just the consequences of coming into worldly existence. As a matter of fact, *saṃsāra* itself is suffering. Our own past karmas are responsible for our birth and all consequent suffering. So no one else can be held responsible for that. Even if God be taken as the creator of this world, as it is taken by the theistic systems, God can not be held responsible for our suffering, because he creates this world strictly in accordance with the karmas done by people in their previous lives. God never bypasses the law of *karma*; rather he works in accordance with it. The law of *karma* acts in Hinduism unfettered and unmitigated. Karmas are all due to attachment (*Kāma*) and attachment is due to ignorance (*Avidyā*) which is beginningless (*Anādi*). Thus ignorance is the root cause of all suffering.

The above is a very general outline of the problem of suffering in Hinduism. However, if we refer to the ancient sacred texts like the Vedas and the Upaniṣads, we shall find somewhat different forms of the understanding of the problem. The Vedas seem to take the problem quite directly and straightforwardly. Suffering of a man is taken there as a consequence of some activity of a god. Therefore, it could be dealt with only by an appropriate relationship with the god, which is frequently expressed in ritual terms. However, even in the Vedas, all suffering is not taken to be the consequence of some arbitrary action on the part of the gods. On the contrary, the concept of karma, in some form or other, seems to be present even there. The god Varuṇa seems to be either the custodian of the law of *karma* or himself the personification of *karma*. Hence, suffering, for the most part, is attributed to one's own karmas in the Vedas too.

The above may be taken as an explanation of individual suffering. But the Vedas also seem to account for evil as a cosmic problem. Evil is due to certain forces which are called demons or anti-gods (*Ȧsura*). These forces always act against the forces of good, the devas or the gods. There is a constant strife between these two forces in which ultimately the forces of good prove victorious. This strife between the two forces and the ultimate victory of the forces of good are symbolised in the Vedas in form of the mythological story of the *Devāsura Sangrāma* (The battle between the gods and the demons), in which the Devas have ultimately proved victorious. This understanding of the problem of evil by the Vedas tallies to some extent with the Zoroastrian understanding of the same.

However, the above kind of understanding of the problem does not imply a basic dualism in Hindu Godhead, as it seems to suggest. The conflict takes place within the same frame, and what appear to be two principles are in reality aspects of a single entity viewed from two different sides or angles. The clearest illustration of this lies in the fact that in Hinduism all the gods who represent evil also represent the opposite quality, good. It all depends upon how one looks at them. Yama, the Lord of death, is dreadful in appearance, but he is at the same time handsome too. As is said in the Padma-Purāṇa: "To the upright man Yama appears gracious, to the evil doer he looks ferocious." It all depends upon how one looks at death or what type of person one is. Exactly the same is true of many other gods. Śiva, for example, is fearful and is regarded as the destroyer of the world, but he is at the same time very auspicious and kind too. Kāli also has this dual aspect. She is to be feared but only from the point of view of attachment.

The Vedas thus seem to have rather a complex understanding of suffering. Suffering is basically an experience and it depends more on how one takes life. It is an instrument which cuts human beings off the objects of attachment and induces them to good actions. It is thus instrumental in inducing dissatisfaction from worldly attachment and initiating quest for *Moksha*.

According to the Upaniṣads, the root cause of suffering is ignorance regarding the true nature of reality. Reality is basically one, but due to ignorance, we create duality or multiplicity in it. Breaking up this basic unity into duality or multiplicity is the root cause of all tension, conflict and suffering. The Bṛhadāranyaka and Chāndogya Upaniṣads refer to the conflict between the devas (gods) and asuras (demons), both being the sons of Prajāpati himself. This symbolises the fact that suffering is only relative. It exits only so long as we are involved in duality. The moment we realise the basic unity, there is no suffering.

Thus, on the whole, suffering is due to ignorance about the true nature of reality. It is due to this ignorance that man performs attached actions and invites rebirth which marks the origin of all suffering. The moment ignorance is removed, suffering ceases to be a reality. Hindu solution of the problem of suffering, therefore, mainly consists in holding that man himself, and not God, is responsible for his suffering and he can remove it by his own efforts.

7. Life after death

Like all other religions, Hinduism also believes that life of man does not end with his physical death. The immortal soul of man endures even after the death of his body. But what happens to the soul after the death of the body? In what form or state does it endure after the physical death of man? To these questions, Hinduism has an answer which is very different from the answer given by Semitic religions. Here Hinduism has a story to say which very sharply distinguishes its nature from the religions of Semitic origin. And this story is the story of transmigration or rebirth. According to the Hindu faith, the soul, after the death of the present body, has to enter into some other new body in accordance with its past deeds. It undergoes transmigration from the old body to a new one. It has to be reborn. The famous Gītā saying in this regard is as follows: "Just as a person casts off worn-out garments and puts on others that are new, even so does the embodied souls cast off worn-out bodies and take on others that are new."[10] This doctrine of rebirth is really a very important feature of Hinduism. Zaehner takes it as a distinguishing feature of Hinduism when he says, "What most sharply distinguishes Hinduism, like its off-shoot Buddhism, from the religions of Semitic origins, is its unquestioning acceptance of the doctrine of rebirth, reincarnation or the transmigration of souls."[11]

The idea of rebirth in Hindu faith is essentially bound up with the idea of *karma*. Belief in *karma* implies that, as one sows, so he reaps. One has essentially to undergo the consequences of whatever actions one performs. No action goes waste or undone. It does produce its fruit sooner or later and the performer has to reap the fruits without fail. If one does not undergo the consequences of his actions in this life he has to undergo them in a life after death. Rebirth is, therefore, a necessary consequence of the actions done in one's previous life, the consequences of which he has not been able to undergo. So long as one does not exhaust

10. The *Bhagavadgītā,* II, 22.
11. R.C. Zaehner, *Hinduism* (Oxford University Press, 1962) p. 55

the fruits of his actions, he has to be bound in a continuous chain of birth and rebirth. Karmas generate samskāras which force a soul to be born. The soul migrates from one body to another with all the samskāras of his past karmas. And the state of rebirth is conditioned by the nature of actions one has done in his past life. The happy or undesirable life that one has in his present birth is to be a explained in terms of the good or bad actions performed by him in his past life. Only *niṣkāma karma* (Action done without attachment) does not generate any *samskāra* and therefore a performer of these actions has not to take rebirth. He attains *Moksha* or release which is a pure spiritual state of perfection. All actions done with attachment cause the soul to migrate from one body to another and the chain continues so long as one is engaged in such actions. Only when one fully exhausts the fruits of one's such karmas that one becomes free from the chain of birth and rebirth and attains the final release.

However, there hardly seems any trace of idea of rebirth in the Vedas. The Vedas seem to imbibe the idea of heaven and hell, but not of rebirth. It is only when we come to the Upaniṣads that we meet with this doctrine of rebirth which was to become so central to Hinduism. The Vedas believe that after death the spirit of man is sent to heaven or hell in consequence of good or bad actions done by him on earth. However, little is said about the miseries of the hell in the Vedas. Much is spoken of heaven and its pleasures. The joys of heaven are conceived mostly in material terms. The soul receives there a new, more subtle body and is freed from all imperfections. There is eating and drinking of heavenly food and drink. There is the delight of unrestricted movement, soft, cool breezes, refreshing water, streams of milk etc. Everything seems to be there in plenty and nothing is in dearth. There are neither sick, nor old nor deformed there. Every one is in perfect happiness and pleasure.

The idea of post-mortem judgment, which we very

prominently find in the Semitic religions, appears for the first time in the Brāhmaṇas. It is pointed out here that man's deeds are weighed in a balance and people are rewarded or punished in accordance with the balance of their good or bad deeds over each other (*i.e.* of good deeds over the bad ones or of bad deeds over the good ones respectively). Righteous are separated from the unrighteous in the presence of the *Yama* (the king of the land of dead) and while the former are sent to heaven, the latter have to go to hell.

The doctrine of rebirth can be met with for the first time in the Hindu tradition in the Bṛhadāraṇyaka Upaniṣad where three classes of soul are distinguished – those that have faith in the eternity of the *Ātman*, those that perform their Vedic duties of sacrifice etc. in a proper manner and those that are devoid of both these ways. The first are liberated from the round of birth and death, the second are reborn in human form, and the third are condemned to the life of worms and insects. However, we also find here a description of the various places where the soul has to wander before taking rebirth. The description is as follows: The first kind of soul purified by the fire that has consumed its gross body passes on into the flame, the day, the world of the gods and thence into the lightening. A spiritual person conducts him to the worlds of *Brahma i.e.* to Brahma-loka. Of him there is no return. The second kind of soul, however, passes into smoke, the night, the world of fathers and finally into the moon. There it becomes the food of the gods, but when it passes away from them, it descends into space, from space into the air, from the air into the rain and from rain onto the earth. But those who do not know these two ways become worms, moths and biting serpents.[12] How far these details are really significant and true may be a matter of controversy. But apart from any such

12. *Bṛhadāraṇyaka Upaniṣad* 6. 2, pp. 15-16.

controversy, it may be said safely that here there is a clear idea of rebirth.

Thus from the stage of the Upaniṣads onwards, Hindu eschatology mainly consists of the belief in the transmigration of souls from one body to another. However, in popular Hindu belief ideas of heaven and hell are also present and it is not very clear how the Hindus relate the ideas of heaven and hell with the idea of rebirth.

8. Human destiny

Generally speaking, the destiny of man according to Hinduism is the attainment of *Moksha*, although the idea of Heaven or Hell as the final abode of man is not totally absent from it. By attaining *Moksha*, man becomes free from the cycle of the birth and death and attains a purely spiritual status. *Moksha* means release or liberation which is opposed to *Bandhan* or bondage. Bondage consists in being chained in the constant cycle of birth and rebirth and therefore freedom from this cycle is release or liberation. What exact status man actually attains after attaining liberation or what exactly is the nature of *Moksha* is not very clearly and uniformly maintained in the different trends of Hindu tradition. It is so often said that the nature or status of *Moksha* is such which cannot be expressed in language. It is unique in its nature and can only be known by direct experience. However, this much is maintained by almost all the systems of Hindu thought that negatively, it is release from all sorts of worldly bonds and positively, it is the attainment of a purely spiritual status which is beyond the limitations of space and time and which is a status of perfect peace, tranquility, equanimity etc. It is the attainment of a free, eternal, immortal spiritual life. We know that according to Hindu belief every man has within the inner core of his being a soul which is, as if, a divine spark within him. The soul is potentially perfect in all respects and free from all limitations. It is due to ignorance that the soul misses its real divine nature of perfection and falls in bondage. But when release from worldly bondage is attained, the soul once again realises its true nature and obtains its inherent perfection. This attainment of perfection, according to some, is really the attainment of infinitude. Śaṃkara, for example, takes the soul identical with the infinite Brahman and therefore, according to him, when the soul attains its real nature after liberation, it really attains its original infinite status. But again according to some, as according to Ramanuja, man's soul is always finite in relation to Brahman or God and therefore even after liberation the soul does not become infinite like God. Qualitatively, of course, it attains a status similar to that of God, but it never becomes identical with or equal to God. In Ramanuja's or Bhagavadgītā's conception of *Moksha*, we may find something like the Christian conception of eternal communion with God. The soul after liberation attains a similarity or likeness of nature with God and lives in eternal nearness to or communion with him.

Liberation in Hinduism, of course, means freedom from all sorts of worldly bonds, specifically freedom from the cycle of birth and rebirth. But it does not necessarily imply immediate cessation of the physical body. Hinduism along with its off-shoot Buddhism, believes in what is called *Jīvan-mukti*, i.e., liberation in this life itself. The moment one becomes passionless, i.e., devoid of all worldly attractions (*Niṣkāma*), even in spite of his being present in this world with his physical body, he virtually becomes a man of a different world, a spiritual world so to say, and he is liberated. Liberation does not necessarily mean release from the body. It means release from the passions and desires. In that case, man, in spite of his being in this world, no longer remains a being of this world. Hence, although in the final analysis, liberation in Hinduism means redemption from the bonds of the world (*saṃsāra*), it does not necessarily imply an immediate giving up of this world. What is required is detachment, and not escape, from this world.

As we have said above, bondage in Hinduism is due to ignorance (*Avidyā*) and therefore naturally liberation is the fruit of knowledge (*Jñāna*). In the context of some of the Hindu systems, however, even this saying that *Moksha* is a *result* or *fruit* of Jñāna will be regarded as misstatement. According to them Jñāna itself is *Moksha*, because *Moksha* is nothing other than the realisation of the true nature of one's self. In a sense, by attaining *Moksha* one does not get anything new. He is simply in possession of what he always had with himself. *Moksha* is like detecting the presence of one's necklace on one's neck itself. Anyway, it is by removing ignorance, consequently by attaining knowledge that one attains *Moksha*. Nevertheless, the role of moral actions and devotion to God in attaining liberation is not simply ruled out in Hinduism. It rather prescribes and recognises the importance and efficacy of all the three ways – *Jñāna* (knowledge), *Bhakti* (Devotion to God) and *karma* (Moral actions) – in the realisation of *Moksha*. The famous Hindu sacred text, *Bhagavadgītā*, repeatedly emphasises the role of *niṣkāma karma* in the attainment of *Moksha*. It also speaks of the immense importance of one's surrendering devotion to God for his liberation. Ramanuja takes the grace of God, which can be won only by devotion to God, as a necessary condition for one's attainment of *Moksha*. Even Śaṃkara who takes Jñāna as the only way to *Moksha* does not rule out the importance of moral actions and devotion to God in this respect. He rather recognises their importance in paving the way for Jñāna.

Here in the light of whatever we have said about Hindu concept of bondage and liberation, one may mark an obvious contrast between the Hindu concept and the Christian one. Hinduism takes ignorance to be the cause of bondage and knowledge to be the essential nature of or pathway to liberation. But in Christianity, it is the knowledge (the eating of the fruit of knowledge by Adam despite God's forbidding) which is the root cause of the

Fall of man. But this difference should not mar the essential similarity between the two faiths. Christianity's taking knowledge to be the cause of man's Fall does not imply that human salvation consists in going back to a state of ignorance. Here the important point in man's Fall or bondage lies in his disobedience of God's will rather than in his eating of the fruit of knowledge. Salvation, therefore, consists in pleasing God and winning his grace by doing moral acts of love and kindness as well as by sincere devotion to God. In Hinduism also, these moral and devotional paths are prescribed for salvation, because in essence, bondage here is due to man's missing his true nature as divine and spiritual. In a way, in both Hinduism and Christianity, creating an unnecessary and unwanted chasm between man and God is the real nature of man's bondage and that can be filled in by true knowledge of things, by moral acts of love and kindness and by prayers and devotion directed towards God.

9. Hindu ethics, ways of prayer, rituals etc.

As ignorance is the root cause of bondage in Hinduism, naturally knowledge is regarded as the means to liberation. In some cases, as we have said earlier, knowledge itself is taken as *Moksha,* and not that it is a means to *Moksha*. In any case, knowledge seems necessary for *Moksha*. It is the karmas (actions) which bind, and therefore, they must be checked. Ethics, therefore, cannot have any place in Hinduism as a means to liberation. For liberation, all sorts of karmas must be renounced. But this is not the case. Like all other religions, Hinduism also deals with many ethical virtues and duties and regards ethical life as a means to liberation. *Dharma* leads to *Moksha* in Hinduism. Only actions done with passion, with gross selfish interest, bind; actions done without egoistic passions do not bind. Selfless actions or actions done for the benefit of others pave the way for liberation. In fact Hinduism recognises three paths for liberation – the path of knowledge (*Jñāna Mārga*), the path of action (*Karma Mārga*) and the path of devotion (*Bhakti Mārga*).The adoption of anyone of these with sincerity and earnestness may lead to the ultimate goal of liberation. The paths are not totally independent of each other. They are rather interdependent, and one implies the other. But nevertheless adoption of any one of them in accordance with one's attitude or temperament leads one to his spiritual goal of *Moksha*. The Bhagavadgītā clearly envisages that either by following the path of knowledge or by following the path of selfless actions or again by following the path of dedicated devotion to the Lord, one can attain liberation. All the three paths lead to the same goal. The path of knowledge is the path of inner realisation, the realisation of the immortality of the soul and of the identity of one's own inner being with all others; the path of action is the path of performing selfless, non-attached actions (*Niṣkāma karma*) and the path of devotion is the path of sincere worship and prayer of God. For the attainment of true knowledge, i.e., for the attainment of the inner realisation of truth, Hinduism prescribes the various disciplines of Yoga, Sādhanā or meditation. The famous *Astāngika Yoga-mārga* as envisaged in the Yoga-system of Indian philosophy may be cited in this connection. Many Hindu Yogis or Sādhus renounce the world, go to the jungles or mountain-caves and practise this path of meditation for *Moksha*. This is the path of *Nivṛtti*. But those who cannot leave the world are advised to take the path of *niṣkāma karma* which is really the path of morality. The Bhagavadgītā has laid utmost emphasis upon this path of *niṣkāma karma* as a means to liberation. As against the path of *Nivṛtti*, this may be called the path of *Pravṛtti*.

Hindu morality has its roots in the Vedas and the Upaniṣads themselves, although Vedas are generally regarded as a treatise of rituals and the Upaniṣads as a treatise of Jñāna – *Brahma*-or *Ātma-Jñāna*. The conception of the *Ṛta*, which is the central concept of Hindu morality, comes from the *Ṛg* Veda itself. Furthermore, the virtues like truth, charity, liberality etc. are much emphasised, in the Vedas themselves. In the Upaniṣads, several references can be found, where the teacher after giving the lesson of Jñāna to his pupil instructs him to practise virtue, to speak the truth, to cultivate modesty, humility etc., without which, it is emphasised, no release is possible. The Dharma Shāstras abound in the analysis and description of ethical virtues and duties. Two kinds of duties (dharmas) have generally been distinguished in the Dharma Shāstras in particular and in Hinduism in general – (1) *Varnāshrama Dharma* and (2) *Sādhārana Dharma*. It is well known that Hindu society has been divided into four broad classes – Brāhmaṇa, Kshatriya, Vaiśya and Sūdra. Duties of each class are well-defined and every individual is expected to perform duties of the class to which he belongs. Such duties of the individual are known as his *Varṇa Dharma*. The Bhagavadgītā gives the following list of duties for each class separately –

(1) For a Brāhmin – Self-control, austerity, purity, forbearance, uprightness, wisdom, knowledge, and faith in religion.

(2) For a Kshatriya – Heroism, Vigour, steadiness, resourcefulness, not fleeing from the battle ground, generosity and leadership.

(3) For a Vaiśya – Agriculture, tending cattle and trade.

(4) For a Sūdra – Service to all the above classes.

Then there are *Āshrama Dharmas*, duties assigned to each individual in accordance with the stage of life which he is crossing at a particular time. Life of each individual in Hinduism has been divided into four gradual stages – (1) the stage of *Brahmacarya* (2) the stage of *Gārhasthya*, (3) the stage of *Vānaprastha* and (4) the stage of *Sannyāsa*. At the stage of *Brahmacharya*, one is to lead strictly the life of a student keeping completely apart from sensuous enjoyments. At the stage of *Gārhasthya*, he is to lead the life of a household by marrying and producing children. The two other stages are the stages of gradually renouncing the world completely and becoming a creature of a different world even in spite of living in this world.

The *Sādhāraṇa dharmas, i.e.*, the general duties to be performed by everyone irrespective of his *varna* or *āshrama*, are differently conceived by different thinkers, although there is an air of affinity about many of them. According to Manu they are the following ten – steadfastness (*Dhṛti*), Forgiveness (*Kshamā*), Application (*Dama*), Non-stealing (*Asteya*), Cleanliness (*Saucha*), Restraint on the sense-organs (*Indriya-Nigraha*), Wisdom (*Dhi*), Learning (*Vidyā*)., Truth (*Satya*). Freedom from anger (*Akrodha*). It can be easily seen that this list is a combination of virtues and duties both. Later on, these ten virtues and duties were abridged into the following five only by Manu himself – Nonviolence (*Ahimsā*), Truth, Non-stealing, Cleanliness and Restraint of senses. Yajnavalkya substituted Celibacy (*Brahmacharya*) for Cleanliness and Non-attachment (*Aparigraha*) for restraint of the senses and thenceforward *Ahimsā, Satya, Asteya, Brahmacharya* and *Aparigraha* were recognised to be the most basic virtues or duties that a Hindu must cultivate in all dealings of his life. The *Panchamahāvrata* of Jainism and the *Panchaśīla* of Buddhism are the symbols of exactly these virtues. *Ahimsā* negatively refers to abstention from injury or harm to any living being in any form, but positively, it refers to the virtues of love, kindness and compassion towards all beings. *Satya* refers to abstention from telling a lie or speaking harsh and unpalatable language. *Asteya* implies abstention from taking away anybody's property without his consent. Taking undue profit in business, restraining someone from earning the gains of his legitimate rights etc., all come under stealing and they must be avoided. *Brahmacharya* refers to a life of purity, celibacy, non-adultery etc. *Aparigraha* is a general attitude of non-attachment towards worldly objects. We have seen that attachment towards worldly objects is at the root of all vices according to Hinduism and therefore it must be avoided. Thus Hinduism, in general, emphasises the virtue of love, kindness, compassion truth, purity, celibacy, self-restraint, non-attachment etc. as virtues to be inculcated and cultivated.

Prashastapada gives a different list which includes the above five and many more – Moral earnestness or regard for *Dharma (Śraddhā)*, Non-violence (*Ahimsā*), seeking good of creatures (*Bhutahitatva*), Veracity (*Satyavachana*), Non-stealing (*Asteya*), Celibacy (*Brahmcharya*), Purity of motive (*Anupadha*), Restraint of anger (*Krodhavarjana*), Personal cleanliness (*Abhisechana*), Non-eating of impure food (*Suchidravyasevana*), Devotion to the recognised deity (*Visista-Devatā-Bhakti*), Fasting (*Upvāsa*), Moral alertness (*Apramāda*). The most attractive feature of this list perhaps consists in the inclusion of the virtue of seeking good of creatures, which gives the list a more philanthropic character. In Vatsyayan's list certain more qualities philanthropic qualities are added which make Hindu ethics more socially oriented. These qualities are – *Paritrāṇa* (Saving or defending the distressed), *Dāna* (Charity), *Paricharan* (Social service), *Dayā* (Benevolence) etc.

Thus we can see that all the individual and social virtues generally recognised in the world religions are recognised and asked to be followed in Hinduism also. The inculcation of virtues and practice of ethical duties have a definite contribution towards the attainment of *Moksha*. Hinduism can not be said to be non-ethical. Something like Judaic *Imitatio Dei* or the Christian *Imitatio Christi* is also present in Hinduism in the views of the great theistic philosopher Ramanuja. He counsels men to imitate God in his qualities, because God possesses all the virtues in him in an infinite manner. Amongst the virtues that God possesses in a supreme and infinite manner and that we are to imitate, the following are important – kindness, forgiveness, tenderness, knowledge, straightforwardness, sympathy etc.

Besides the paths of knowledge and morality there is the path of devotion to God which a Hindu may adopt for the realisation of the highest goal of liberation. As a matter of fact, an average Hindu adopts the path of devotion itself in the form of prayer, worship etc. as his most important religious duty in order to please God and attain *Moksha* by his grace. In spite of his strong belief in the Law of *Karma*, an average Hindu believes in the grace of God and worships him to secure his grace. Even in theoretical Hinduism, Ramanuja and the Bhagavadgītā have much emphasised the role of *bhakti* in man's realisation of his highest ideal. *Bhakti* begets 'God's grace, which is a necessary factor in release. Speaking rather more honestly, one may say that an average Hindu adopts in his religious life a combined path of God's prayer and worship and of practising the ethical virtues of charity, liberality, kindness, honesty, truth etc.

There are no hard and fast rules of Hindu worship and prayer. Each one adopts a method that suits him best. These prayers and worships are mostly individual rather than congregational, although on certain special occasions the latter are also adopted and observed. Mostly Hindu worship consists in sitting or standing before some idol of a god after taking bath and offering sacred water, flowers, some feeding material, some scented flames etc. to it with utmost love and devotion. After *pūjā* (worship), the individual takes back the feeding materials with him and eats it along with his family members and others with utmost sense of sacredness as God's *prasāda*. This idol worship is done either in one's own house or in a temple. Temples are numerous in villages and towns alike. Some important temples at selected places are the places of pilgrimage where on special occasions lakhs of Hindus assemble to offer *pūjā*. to the concerned god or goddess. Most of the temples have Brahmin priests within them who help the worshippers in giving their offerings to the God or gods in the temple. These priests are also concerned with cleansing the idol at times from the load of offerings, dressing it with sacred clothes etc.

Hindu prayer mostly consists of the silent recitation of mantras which are repeated for long hours. Sometimes, simple repeating of the name of God, such as, Rāṃ! Rām! or Kṛṣṇa! Kṛṣṇa! constitutes the prayer of God. Sometimes, a group of people stand together before the image of a god and sing song in praise of that God. Sometimes, mere study of scriptures and sacred books like the Rāmāyaṇa, the Gītā etc. or reciting passages from them are taken as sacred works of prayer or worship.

Besides, on certain occasions, collective prayers are done by organising *Hari-Kīrtan* (Song of God) or *Yajñā* (paying sacred offerings to flames in the form of sandlewood etc.). On special occasions such as those of birth, marriage, death, etc, elaborate procedures of *pūjā* are carried on with the help of elaborate rites and rituals, a complete description of which is not possible here.

10. Principal sects

As has been quite usual with all the religions of the world, Hinduism is also divided into certain sects. However, the Hindu sects have never been set completely apart from each other and there is a perfect understanding between them. As a matter of fact, a sense of mutual penetration and brotherhood exits between them. In a way, there have been only two sects in Hinduism. Śaivism and Vaishnavism, but generally speaking, one more sect – Sāktism has also been recognised in it. In a sense, this sect may be regarded as an offshoot of Śaivism itself.

Śaivism is the name given to that Hindu sect which takes Śiva-worship as its principal religious duty. Śiva-worship was first of all popularised by Shankara, the great Vedantist, in his effort to fight against the spread of Buddhism in India. Later on, Kumarila took over the task upon his shoulder. Both Shankara and Kumarila tried to popularise Śiva-worship in a bid to render Hinduism appealing to the general mass.

Śiva as a god seems to be developed out of the Vedic god Rudra (the terrible). He may well be taken as very ancient pre-Aryan deity too. He is generally regarded as the god of fertility and destruction. For the Śaivites (followers of Saivism) he is the Śupreme Deity possessing all the supreme qualities and powers. He is generally depicted in a form which generates fear and which speaks of his being a god of wild people. He is represented as wearing the skin of a tiger in his waiste, a garland of human skulls or living snakes in his neck, the whole body besmeared with ashes and with long matted hair on the head. This really gives an appearance of terror which is very much fitting with the god of destruction. But quite contradictorily, Śiva is regarded as a very kind and benevolent god too who is pleased with very little of devotion and worship and bestows upon his worshippers the best of gifts. Śiva is also depicted as dancing god with four arms, the dance symbolising the acting of the creative force. Perhaps this is the best depiction of Śiva as the terrible wielder of the forces of life and death and as the giver of sexual fertility. Śiva is most commonly represented by means of an elongated piece of stone, the *lingam*, which is the symbol of male sex-organ. Śiva worship is mostly prevalent in Hinduism in the form of this *linga*-worship. The Lingayats, Hindus belonging to a special sect within Śaivism, also wear this *linga* as a sign of their specific sectarian distinction. Śiva represented in the form of this *linga* specifically speaks of his being a god of sexual fertility. However, this specific *linga*-symbol is not a symbol of sexual license to the Śaivites. Quite contrarily, they are very pure, decent and morally perfect sort of people. The erotic element associated with the *linga-rupa* of Śiva is largely conspicuous in the religious activities of the Saktas, but they are also highly reputed for their pure moral behaviour outside the bounds of their religious activities.

Śaivism is also very greatly associated with asceticism. The Lord Śiva is so often represented as the great Yogi sitting with naked body besmeared with ashes in an age-long mood of meditation and self-mortification. He is the great sage, the *Mahāyogi*, constantly engaged in the act of *Sādhanā* and *Tapasyā*. This representation of Śiva stands as a symbol for the Śaivites to lead a life of ascetcism and self-modification. Sometimes the Śaivas take to very extreme sort of ascetism in which they spend their days and nights on beds of spikes, keep their arms always raised above their heads and plant hooks into their flesh. The last one is clearly a crude symbol of the mortification of the flesh for the cause of the spirit.

The other great sect is that of the Vaishnavas. This sect is very little associated with asceticism or other such other-worldly practices. It is very much a sect of the common religious people who believe in the supremacy of a kind and loving God who sometimes also incarnates himself on earth in human form to take people out of their miseries brought about by the activities of the demons. Ram and Krishna are the two very popular incarnation of Viṣṇu, who are very widely reverred throughout India in various forms. The two great epics – Rāmāyaṇa and Mahābhārata – are associated with these two God-incarnate personalities.

Vaishnavism was first popularised by Ramanuja and then by his successor Madhva. Then there have been various Vaishnava poets like Ramananda, Chaitanya etc. who have added much in popularising Vaishnavism. In Vaishnavism Vishnu is taken as the Supreme Deity who is all-inclusive, all-pervasive and all-comprehensive. All other deities are regarded as his manifestations. During the Vedic times, Vishnu seems merely to be a god amongst gods, but later on he assumes the status of the God and becomes all-inclusive, all-pervasive and all-powerful. Besides these, Vishnu is regarded as kind, benevolent and all-good.

Although in the Hindu *Trimurti*, Vishnu forms only one godhead, the other, two being Brahmā and Śiva, but really speaking, Vishnu is treated as the Supreme God, and Brahmā and Śiva as his mere manifestation. Thus although in the *Trimurti* Vishnu represents merely the sustaining and maintaining aspect (*i.e.*, that aspect which sustains and maintains the world) of the Supreme Deity, as a matter of fact, he himself is taken as representing the creative, preservative and destructive – all the three – aspects. He is thus the Supreme Lord, the creator, sustainer and destroyer of the world. He is depicted as sleeping on his couch on the surface of the ocean with his consort Lakshmi. He continues in his sleep unless he is disturbed by other gods who sometimes require his intervention in the affairs of the world. Brahmā, the creative aspect, is depicted as taking birth out of the navel of Vishnu.

The Vaishnavas take devotion to Vishnu as their principal religious duty. This devotion they express chiefly by reciting passages from Rāmāyaṇa and Mahābhārarta, mainly from 'that part of the latter which is known as the Bhagavadgītā, or by performing Ramlilas and Krishanalilas or else by performing kirtans and bhajans in the name of Rama and Krishna. Also the images of Rama and Krishna are worshipped by the Vaishnavas and many temples in India are specifically dedicated to them. Krishna has proved to be more popular *avtāra* of Vishnu than Rama and Vaishnava *bhakti*-cults centre more around Krishna than around Rama. Direct worship of Vishnu in his original image is less popular. More popularly, Vishnu is worshipped and reverred through various cults centering round his two incarnations, Rama and Krishna.

The third Hindu sect is that of the Saktas, i.e., of such Hindus who worship the *Sakti* (the female part) of the gods. The consorts of these gods are taken, as the personified forms of these saktis. Śiva's *sakti*, mostly in the form of Durgā or Kāli, is particularly the object of adoration for the Saktas.

However, the way in which the Saktas perform their acts of adoration or worship is very mysterious, full of rites and rituals and in a sense very filthy and obnoxious. They take wine and perform the worship of female sex-organ (*yoni*) through various filthy rites. This *yoni*-worship of the Saktas is very conspicuously depicted in the famous Kāmākhyā temple of Assam, where in the name of the goddess kāmākhyā, a mere cleft in a rock is adored as the *yoni* of the *Sakti*. However, although the Saktas perform *yoni*-worship and sometimes the proceedings of their religious rites develop into an orgy of drinking and sexual license, still outside the bounds of their temples, they are very much reputed for their pure moral behaviour. Prostitution is unknown among them and women are taken in very high esteem. Sāktism seems based on the idea that the passions of the flesh may be best regulated and sublimated by making a complete exhaustion of them in religious rites. Sex is not to be suppressed, rather it is to be given the most elaborate expression and satisfaction.

The sect mark of the saktas is the *Tripundra*, which has a sexual significance. Men and women of all castes are admitted into Sāktism and widow-marriage is allowed.

As we have said earlier, Saktism may be taken as an offshoot of Śaivism itself. It is the *Sakti* of Śiva which is adored in Sāktism. Śiva himself represents in his body both a male and a female organ. He is represented as having a female breast and male sex-organ. His symbol also, as is contained in most of the temples, is a combination of male sex organ (*lingam*) and the female *yoni*. To show the oneness of the reproductive principle, Śiva is depicted as a half-man, half-woman. Thus *Sakti-pūjā* is in a sense the adoration of Śiva himself in a specific form. His *Sakti* takes different forms – sometimes Pārvati, sometimes Durgā, sometimes Kālī and sometimes Umā.

There are two types of Saktas with some amount of difference in their rites. There are *Dakshināchari* Saktas and

Vāmāchāri Saktas. The former are in greater majority and they worship the *lingam* and the *yoni* as more or less symbolical. The latter perform what is known as *Chakra-pūjā*. This sort of *pūjā* is group-worship carried on at midnight. The rites of this *pūjā* require the five M's (*Panchamakāra*) – the wine (*Madya*), meat (*Mānsa*) , fish (*Matsya*), parched com (*Mudra*) and copulation (*Maithuna*). A beautiful naked girl, hypnotized in a trance, is placed in the midst and *yoni-parast* is practised. In its appearance, the practice may seem very vulgar, but it is symbolic of the worship of he reproductive principal of Deity. The Saktas perform all these apparently filthy rites, but in their essential character they are very elevated people.

In modern times, certain social and religious reformers have been able to attract certain Hindus around them to form new groups within Hinduism. It is not very clear whether these groups can be called new sects of Hinduism, but this much is definite that persons belonging to these groups have certain specific principles in their faith and belief which distinguish them from the common mass of Hindus. Two of such groups are important and they are known by the names of Brahmo-Samāj and Ārya-Samāj. The former was founded by Ram Mohan Roy and the latter by Dayanand Saraswati. The two really mark two important reform movements under Hinduism. Both aim in their own ways to take back Hinduism to its essentials instead of the many encumbrances by which the founders of these movements felt Hinduism surrounded. Ram Mohan Roy mainly preached the return of Hinduism to strict monotheism, to the worship and adoration of one and only one supreme, eternal, immutable and infinite God, who is the creator and the preserver of the world. Brahmo-Samāj, thus is a society of Hindus believing strictly in one Supreme Deity. Roy pointed out that every religion had certain fundamental principles and only those were to be believed in and followed. The inessentials were not to be given much weight. Hinduism had for its essentials, believing in one and only one supreme God who had never incarnated himself on earth in human form, in the immortality of soul and in salvation by repentance and good works as well as by sincere, heartful devotion to God. Roy therefore, advised Hindus to observe only these beliefs and practices. He fully decried and discouraged pilgrimage, sacrifices and various rites and ceremonies.

The watchword of Ārya-Samāj has been 'Back to the Vedas' which it takes as the purest revelation of God and as the books of true knowledge. It is the duty of every Hindu (Ārya) to read the Vedas or at least hear them read and preach their truth to others. Like Brahmo-Samāj, the Ārya-Samāj also seems to believe in the strict oneness of God, although its call to be back to the Vedas could well imply a faith in polytheism. The Samāj is totally opposed to idolatory and caste-distinction but favours remarriage of widows. It also seems to have strong opposition to Islam and Chritianity. It is out and out a Hindu theistic sect strictly loyal to the pure and essential principles of Hinduism. It always emphasises to distinguish between truth and falsehood and adore the former. It is strictly moral and thoroughly humanistic in its outlook. It labours to improve the physical, spiritual and social conditions of man.

The followers of Ārya-Samāj observe certain rituals in their own ways. They assemble at one place on Sunday mornings and perform these rites. The rites consist of burning of incense on the alter of Vedic fire, offering prayers, exposition of Dayanand's views and ideas, reciting hymns of the Vedas etc. There is no official priest and all members are treated as equal.

There have been certain other reform movements also giving rise to specific congregations of Hindus around them. However, it is not very clear whether all such congregations are to be treated as forming various sects. One such important movement effecting a specific congregation has been brought about by the famous saint Ram Krishana. Ram Krishna tried to make a revival of Advaita Vedanta in real Hindu practice. Vivekanand proved to be his famous and most effective mouth piece. The Ram Krishna missions spreading all over India and also abroad are like the Churches of all such Hindus who are the followers of Ram Krishna. These missions have really been serving missionary purposes by spreading the lessons of Vedānta all over the world and bringing people under its fold.

3

Buddhism

1. Introductory

Buddhism, like Jainism, is an offshoot of Hinduism. Although Buddhism denies the authority of the Vedas, there are obvious signs of the influence of the Vedas and the Upanisads on it. It hardly becomes able to divest itself of the essentials of the Hindu religious, ethical and cultural traditions, although it succeeds in presenting itself as a pure ethical and spiritual religion against the extreme polytheism and ritualism of the Vedic tradition. However, Hinduism has never been only ritualism. It has its own spiritual foundation and has always abounded in a pure spiritualistic ethics. This aspect of Hinduism has influenced Buddhism to an extent which did not allow the latter to maintain its completely separate identity for a long time in India. Nevertheless, Buddhism is indisputably a separate religion and Philosophy, which has exerted immense influence over the religious and philosophical thinking of the world. It has a greater following in the world than Hinduism has, and is deemed by most of the western thinkers as a universal religion, rather than a national one, which is taken by them as characteristic of Hinduism.

Like Islam and Christianity, Buddhism has a definite origin in a definite founder, Gotama, the Buddha. Gotama was born in a royal Hindu family, but from his very childhood he seemed to have no attraction for his princely life and was always found in a pensive and despondent mood. He was very much concerned about the unabated suffering of man throughout his life-time. Birth, various diseases, old age and death – all are signs of suffering and Gotama wanted to find out a permanent cure to all these sufferings of man. Being overpressed by such concern, one night while all were engaged in rejoice connected with the birth of a son to Gotama's wife Yashodharā, he himself left his house forever and went out in search of real knowledge – *Bodhi* or *Prajñā* – with the help of which people could be saved. It is said, he got such intuitive light or *Bodhi* while he was in a *Samādhi* beneath a tree (now called Bodhi-tree) in Bodh-Gaya. Thenceforward, he was begun to be called the *Buddha*, the Enlightened one. After attaining this enlightenment, Buddha did not sit idle, rather he worked day and night to instruct people regarding the path through which they could save themselves from the pangs of worldly suffering. Buddha pointed out that birth was at the root of all suffering and therefore it was to be avoided. As a matter of fact, man was bound in a constant cycle of birth and death and this cycle was to be brought to a permanent halt. Otherwise, there could be no permanent end to human suffering. The way how people generally lived and worked in the world was a sign of their ignorance regarding the real nature of the world. All their works were guided by attachment to the world which was only impermanent and fleeting. This attachment was the real cause behind man's suffering and this in turn was the result of ignorance (*Ajñāna)*. If this ignorance could be removed, man could attain a state which was called the state of *Nirvāṇa*. This state was negatively a state of the permanent cessation of all suffering and positively a state of perfect peace and equanimity. This was a perfectly spiritual state having no cause for any future birth and rebirth. For the attainment of this state and removal of ignorance, Buddha pointed to an eight-fold path (*Astāngika mārga*) to be followed by each and every man. This eight-fold path was neither one of complete indulgence nor one of complete asceticism. It was a middle path (*Majjhima nikāya*) which consisted in the following eight disciplines – Right understanding (*Samyaka dṛṣti*), Right thought (*Samyaka sankalpa*), Right speech (*Samyaka vāka*), Right action (*Samyaka karmānta*), Right livelihood (*Samyaka ājiva*), Right effort (*Samyaka Vyāyāma*), Right mindfulness (*Samyaka smṛti*) and Right concentration (*Samyaka Samādhi*).

Buddhism is thus, at least in its original form, a practical religion of pure ethical discipline. It does not believe in any God and therefore no ritualistic acts find any place in it. It is out and out a man-centered religion, totally humanistic in its outlook, approach and aim. It concerns itself with human life as it stands here and now, and puts forth ways and means so as to tide over the present problems of conditioned existence. In its essence, therefore, Buddhism gives us a way of life intended not for persons belonging to any particular caste or nationality but universally for all. It firmly believes that by following the eightfold path as mentioned above every man for himself can transcend his present miserable condition and attain to a life which is completely free from all kinds of suffering. Every man can be a light unto himself (*Ātma Dipo Bhava*), a saviour of himself. The present miserable state of human life can be transcended and that is by sincere efforts of man himself. Man is not to seek the grace of any power superior to him. He is himself sufficient for improving his condition and that is by the adoption of the above mentioned eightfold path, the middle path.

Although Buddhism does not believe in any God until later on Buddha himself was begun to be venerated like God, Buddhists from the very beginning have entertained and shown a sense of veneration towards Buddha as a teacher, guide and protector. Of the three valued components of Buddhism, known as the three jewels (*Triratna)*, Buddha is the first one, whose refuge, or shelter every Buddhist seeks with a deep sense of respect and veneration (*Buddham śaraṇam gachhāmi* – I seek the refuge of the Buddha, or, more literally, I go to the Buddha for refuge). The other two valued components are – the *Dhamma* (or *Dharma*) and the *sangha*, whose shelter also is sought by every Buddhist (*Dhammam śaraṇam gachhāmi*, *Sangham śaraṇam gachhāmi)*. As a matter of fact, everybody who is to be admitted under the fold of Buddhist religion has to repeat the above three lines concerning refuges under the three jewels. Moreover, the three sentences are also repeated at the time of opening of the every Buddhist meeting. *Dhamma* or *Dharma* is the order, the law or the doctrine taught by the Buddha and *Sangha* is the community of the Buddhist monks (*Bhikkhus*). The three components (Jewels) are thus interconnected and they all basically represent a deep sense of respect, dependence and love for the Buddha. This veneration and love for the Buddha is clearly expressed through the following Pāli text which precedes the repetition of the above three sentences concerning refuge under the three jewels – "*Namo tasso Bhagvato Arahato Sammasambuddhassā*," (I bow the head to the Blessed one, the Enlightened one, the perfectly Enlightened one). The repetition of the above *Trisaranaga-mana* formula by every Bhuddhist represents an act of veneration, resolution and elementary training – all at the same time on the part of the Buddhist.

As stated earlier, Buddhism in its original form was a purely ethical religion believing in no god and no rituals. Allegiance to *Dhamma* consisted in believing in the four noble truths and some of the doctrines like *Pratitya-samutpāda, Anātmavād, Karma* etc. as well as in practising certain ethical virtues. But later one Buddhism – at least one sect of it, called *Mahāyāna* – lapsed into a kind of theism, or even polytheism, which found place for all sorts of rituals etc. and gave birth to an elaborate organisation of shrines, monastries and temples. Buddha himself was begun to be treated as God and was believed to have incarnated himself on earth several times, even earlier. Alongwith the Buddha, several other Bodhisattvas, who were believed to have taken the final step into *Nirvāṇa,* were begun to be prayed and worshipped much in the same fashions in which the gods of Hinduism were prayed and worshipped. However, the other sect, called *Hīnayāna,* kept itself strictly adhered to the original doctrine taught by the Buddha and maintained its purely ethical character. Several sects or schools of Buddhism were formed on the philosophical or metaphysical side also. As is well known, Buddha himself remained silent on metaphysical questions, but later on his followers began to develop metaphysical theories on the basis of the hints imbibed in Buddha's thoughts and ideas. At least four philosophical schools – Yogāchara school of *Vijñānavāda,* Mādhyamika school of *Shunyavāda,* Sauntrantic school and Vaibhāṣika school – came into existence deciphering totally different but very important metaphysical and epistemological views.

The range of Buddhist literature is very vast and it is difficult to give an account of it here. However, our knowledge of early Buddhism mostly comes from the Pāli scriptures, the monastic rules and the discourses of Buddha (Suttas). The Pāli scriptures consist of three pitakas (baskets) known together as *Tripitaka.* They are the *Vinaya,* the *Dhamma* or the *Sutta,* and the *Abhidhamma.* The *Vinaya Pitaka* is concerned with the rules for the monks. The *Dhamma* or the *Sutta Pitaka* is the chief authority regarding the Doctrine taught by the Buddha – the four noble Truths including the doctrine of *Nirvāṇa* and the eightfold path, the doctrine of *Pratityasamutpāda* and no soul, the theory of *karma* etc. The *Abhidhamma Piṭaka* consists of more advanced doctrines than the Suttas. It is comprised of seven works produced in the course of centuries in the academics of Buddhist monastries. Besides the Pitakas, there is also a collection of stories in Pāli, called *Jātaka*. These stories relate with the birth tales of Gotama Buddha, giving an account of his 547 previous births (incarnations).

2. Basic features of Buddhism as a religion

(1) Buddhism is primarily a religion without God. Buddha taught a purely humanistic religion, whose sole concern was the liberation of the suffering man. Man's only religious obligation is to free himself from the bonds of worldly suffering by following the eightfold discipline. Of course, in later Buddhism, Buddha himself is treated much like a God, but even in that form Buddhism cannot be regarded as a theistic religion, because Buddha is hardly treated as the creator, destroyer etc. of the world. Moreover, even in this phase the following of the eightfold discipline for the attainment of Nirvāṇa is taken to be the essence of Buddhist religion.

(2) Buddhism is totally opposed to the Hindu belief in the authority of the Vedas and Vedic ritualism. It is also opposed to the Hindu *varṇa vyavasthā*. It is really these oppositions which distinguish Buddhism sharply from Hinduism. Otherwise, in most of the essential points, Buddhism shares Hindu beliefs.

(3) As early Buddhism has been very much opposed to the Vedic ritualism, it proves to be a purely ethical religion free from all sorts of ritualism and ceremonialism. But later Buddhism, at least in the form of the Mahāyāna, gives vent to various ritualistic practices.

(4) Belief in the four noble truths (*Chatvāri ārya satyāni*) and the pursuit of the eightfold discipline (*aṣṭāngika mārga*) seem to be the essence of Buddhism. The four noble truths are: (i) *Dukha-Ārya-Satya* (The noble truth concerning the nature of suffering), (ii) *Dukh-Samudaya-Ārya-Satya* (the Noble-truth concerning the origin of suffering), (iii) *Dukha-Nirodha-Ārya-Satya* (The noble truth concerning the

removal of suffering and the realisation of the state of Nirvāṇa, (iv) *Dukh-Nirodha-Gāmini-Pratipad-Ārya-Satya* (The noble truth concerning the path leading to the removal of suffering and the attainment of the state of Nirvāṇa). In simple language, the four noble truths are: (i) There is suffering all around in the world (*sarvam-dukham*), (ii) The suffering may be referred back to a twelvefold chain of causation (*Dvādas-Nidāna*), (iii) The chain of causation can be removed and cessation of suffering is possible (Nirvāṇa), and (iv) There are definite ways to remove the chain of suffering (*Aṣtāngika-Mārga*). The pursuit of the eightfold discipline consists in following the consecutive paths of Right understanding, Right thought, Right speech, Right action, Right livelihood, Right effort, Right mindfulness and Right concentration.

(5) Two of the very characteristic beliefs of Buddhism are its belief in the theory of momentariness (*Kshaṇika-vāda*) and in the doctrine of no-soul (*Anātmavāda*). *Sarvam Kshanikam* (Everything is momentary) is a very important part of Buddhist faith. Buddhism believes that nothing is permanent, nothing endures for more than a moment. Its theory of momentariness is based on a more comprehensive theory of Dependent Origination (Pratityasamutpāda), according to which everything owes its origin to an antecedent condition which ceases after giving birth to its consequent. The world is, therefore, a chain of interdependent momentary events.

Quite in consonance with its theory of momentariness, Buddhism believes in the doctrine of no-soul, which does not totally deny like the Charvakas the existence of soul, but denies the existence of a permanent, non-changing soul-substance. Because everything is momentary, so the soul also cannot be an unchanging something. It is also in a state of continuous flux. As a matter of fact, the soul is not a substance at all, it is a stream of consciousness and nothing more. Every subsequent moment of consciousness is, of course, a product of the continuous flux of the antecedent moments, but every moment vanishes immediately by giving birth to its subsequent moment.

This emphasis on the momentary nature of everything, including bits of consciousness, equips Buddhism with a kind of metaphysical weapon by the help of which it becomes able to preach in an effective manner its theory of non-attachment (*Aparigraha*). Attachment with the momentary, vanishing objects of this world is the cause of our suffering. We attach ourselves with the objects by taking them enduring, but when we find them decaying or being destroyed, we feel pain. Once we understand their evanescent nature, we will not be attracted towards them. Only the spiritual state of *Nirvāna* is eternal and once we understand it, we will be attracted towards *Nirvāna* and *Nirvāna* alone. We will give up clinging to the momentary objects, because they bring only hopelessness, despair and suffering.

(6) One very important feature of Buddhism which helps it maintaining its oriental character and which brings it very close to Hinduism is its belief in the law of *karma* and rebirth. Everyone has to reap the fruits of his action either in this life or in a life after death. If one does not exhaust the fruits of one's action in this life, he has to take birth again. And the nature of this rebirth is strictly conditioned by the actions one has done in the present life. Exhaustion of the fruits of the past karmas is a necessary condition of *Nirvāṇa*.

(7) Although actions bind and are the root cause of suffering, only the attached actions are of this kind. Non-attached actions (*Niṣkāma karma*) do not bind. Therefore, Buddhism does not teach inaction, it rather teaches to perform non-attached actions.

(8) According to Buddhism the final destiny of man is the attainment of *Nirvāṇa* – a state of spiritual freedom and perfection. This state of *Nirvāṇa* may be attained in this life also and therefore cessation of the present life is not necessary for the attainment of *Nirvāṇa*. If one becomes able in blowing

off all sorts of worldly passions completely by the observance of the eightfold discipline, he has attained *Nirvāṇa* even in spite of his physical body.

(9) Buddhism teaches the avoidance of extremes and the adoption of the Middle path in every sphere – in metaphysics, in ethics, in general practice and everywhere. Buddha is as much famous for his teaching of *Majjhima Nikāya* as for any of his other teachings.

(10) Buddhism, like existentialism, teaches self-help and self-reliance as the most effective means of attaining perfection (*Ātma dipo bhava*), although unlike existentialism it also believes in the humanistic virtues of interdependence, mutual help, universal service and brotherhood.

(11) Quite in conformity with its humanistic ethics, Buddhism believes in the doctrine of Universal Salvation. It teaches that it is not sufficient for anyone to attain his own salvation. After achieving his own *Nirvāṇa,* one must work for the *Nirvāṇa* of others. The ideal of *Bhodhisattva* in Buddhism really teaches this. Buddha's own life of active service for the liberation of others is a testimony to this.

(12) Some of the ethical virtues that Buddhism repeatedly emphasises are those of non-violence (*Ahimsā*), truth (*Satya),* kindness to all beings, self-restraint, nobleness, chastity etc. Of these, *ahimsā* is most emphasised.

(13) The three refuges in the three jewels seem to represent the basic creed of Buddhism – *Buddham śaraṇam gachhāmi, Dhammam śaraṇam gachhāmi, Sangham śaraṇam gachhāmi.*

3. God

As stated earlier, Buddhism is primarily atheistic in nature. Buddha never spoke of any God. His only concern was the suffering man. Some may say here that Buddha was not an atheist; he was simply an agnostic. If he did not say that there was a God, he also never explicitly mentioned that there was no God. He was simply silent over such issues as whether there was a God or not. This silence could be nothing more than a pointer to the human inability in deciding such questions in a definite manner. And such an attitude is that of agnosticism, and not of atheism. Whatever may be the designation, it is clear that in early Buddhism there is no mention of God. Early Buddhism is purely man-centered, humanistic religion. It is out and out ethical in its character. If *Nirvāṇa* is taken as the state of perfection, as it must perhaps be taken, everyone who attains *Nirvāṇa* becomes a God. Each man, therefore, is a potential God. God in this sense is not given reality, rather Godhood is a status which is to be attained.

However, whatever has been said above can be taken as literally true only of early Buddhism. Later Buddhism accepts Buddha himself as God and believes in his various earlier incarnations. Modern Buddhism has a place for various Buddhist temples in which there are images of Buddha, which are worshipped and adored more or less in the fashion of the Hindu God. The *Mahāyāna* Buddhists also worship many Boddhisattvas other than the Buddha and abound in various sorts of ritualistic practices. This side of Buddhism seems very near to Hindu polytheism. Nevertheless, it is very much doubtful whether the Buddhists would be ready to give the various Bodhisattvas the same status as that of the Hindu gods and goddesses. Similarly, it is doubtful whether the Buddhists would take the Buddha as God in the same theistic sense in which God is regarded as the creator, the sustainer, the destroyer of the world. It seems that instead of taking him as the creator etc. the Buddhists for the most part worship and adore him as an embodiment of holiness and compassion and as a great spiritual leader and saviour of mankind. By worshipping him, they expect his kind helping hand for removing their suffering.

4. World

As we have said before, Buddha remained silent on metaphysical questions such as those of the origin of the world, the existence of God etc. Therefore, there is hardly any creation-story in the Buddhist scriptures. It seems the Buddhists believe that the cosmic order goes on without any beginning. As is said by Buddhaghosa "The wheel of the cosmic order goes on without maker, without beginning." But because Buddha was concerned about our present status and existence we can find imbibed in his teachings certain views regarding the nature of the world and its objects. The Buddhist doctrine of momentariness is famous in this regard. Everything is momentary (*Sarvam kshanikam*), nothing in the world is enduring and permanent. This statement is not to be treated just in a general manner to indicate that everything takes birth, grows and decays after some time. It rather affirms that nothing endures for more than a moment. Everything is merely a momentary link, a transitory phase in the constant chain of change. As a matter of fact, there is no 'thing', which changes. Only ceaseless change is there. All that is, is conditional, dependent and relative. Here the Buddhistic famous theory of Dependent Origination (*Pratitya-samutpāda*) comes in. In fact, the above theory of momentariness is the corollary of the more comprehensive theory of *Pratityasamutpāda*, which is really the Buddhistic theory of causation. The theory asserts : 'This being, that arises (*Asmin sati, idam bhavati*) 'or' Depending on the cause, anything originates'. Every object is thus necessarily relative, arising out of an antecedent condition and giving rise in its turn to a consequent. Nothing, therefore, endures for more than just a moment. It arises and goes away.

The Buddhists have tried to make their theory of universal momentariness clear by employing the simile of the flame of a lamp. The ordinary man believes that the same flame goes on burning, but as a matter of fact the 'same flame' is nothing more or less than a succession of similar flames, each flame lasting for just a moment. Just as the identity of the flame is nothing but the continuity of successive similar flames, similarly, the identity of any object of the world is nothing more than a continuity of becoming. The fleeting and evanescent nature of worldly objects can also be understood on the simile of a river current. No river is the same river next moment. Heraclitus said "you cannot bathe twice in the same river." Similarly, no object is the same object next moment. Rapidity of succession gives rise to the illusion of unity or permanence. But nothing in fact is permanent.

This theory of eternal momentariness, the Buddhists claim, avoids the two extremes of externalism and nihilism. Neither there is anything like permanent or unchanging substance in the world nor is the world a mere void or nonexistence. It is in between the two – a constant becoming, neither being nor non-being. This is the Middle Path (*Majjhima Nikāya)* which the Buddha is said to have much emphasised.

Thus Buddhism does not deny the reality of the world, but so paints the nature of its objects that it proves foolish to be attached to it. Everything is evanescent and fleeting and therefore it is sheer foolishness to run after material objects. Actually it is this passion or desire for the worldly objects which is the cause of all sufferings. Due to lack of proper knowledge about the real nature of the worldly objects, man always hankers after them. Buddhism by presenting the fleeting and elusive nature of the worldly objects tries to dissuade people from them. Once people know the real nature of the objects, they will never run madly after them. And once they are dissuaded in this manner, there will be the beginning of the end of all their sufferings.

5. Man

Man, according to Buddhism, is neither a purely physical being, as the Charvaka would say, nor he is a being with a permanent soul within him, as the other systems would insist. He is rather a combination of the physical and mental forces. According to the Hinayāna, man is a *sanghāta* (aggregate) of five skandhas – *Rupa* (Matter), *Vedanā* (Sensation or feeling), *Samjñān* (Perception), *Samskāra* (Disposition) and *Vijñāna* (Consciousness). Buddhism thus does not deny the presence of a spiritual element in man, as the Charvaka does, but then it does not also believe in the reality of a permanent soul in man. In fact, as we know, Buddhism, in accordance with its theory of momentariness, does not believe in anything permanent. Nothing endures for more than a moment. Everything is changing and therefore, there is no question of there being a permanent soul in man. What is called soul is just a passing stream of the moments of thought or consciousness. However, the different moments of consciousness do not stand apart from each other. They rather stand in a relation of unbroken continuity with each other. The series of conscious moments, although always changing, continues unbroken. Every next moment is conditioned and determined by the prior one such that all the tendencies and dispositions of the prior moment are transferred to the succeeding one. This explains the identity of the being of a man even in spite of the ceaseless becoming of the moments of his consciousness. This also explains the fact of the rebirth of a man after the expiry of the present life. Even in the absence of a permanent soul, man is in a sense immortal. He does not completely perish with the physical death. The last thought-moment of his present life transmigrates with all its tendencies and dispositions to the so-called next life and forms its first thought-moment.

Buddhism is essentially a humanistic religion which takes man as the highest being. There is no God, and therefore man is inferior to none, He himself is the central object of religion. He can himself attain Godhood, the state of perfection. Everything in the world is fleeting. What is eternal is the transcendental, spiritual status, known as

Nirvāṇa. Man is capable of attaining this highest status by his own personal effort. He does not require the grace of any superior power. Only the right effort on his part will do. But man, as he stands here and now, is in a pool of suffering. He is in bondage and is living a life of conditioned existence. Man's present miserable condition is the result of his own ignorance. Due to lack of real knowledge about the nature of things, he falls a prey to the worldly attractions and that is the root cause of his imperfection and suffering. Being attached to the world, man performs actions for egoistic ends. Such actions done with attachment bind man life after life. These actions produce samskāras which cause man to take another life after the end of the present one. We have seen that even in the absence of a soul, rebirth is possible. This rebirth, which is the cause of man's entire suffering, is a consequence of selfish, attached actions. But if man performs non-attached (*niṣkāma*) actions and does not fall a prey to sensory attractions under the spell of ignorance, he has not to take another body and he is liberated. Non-attached actions do not produce samskāras, and therefore in the absence of any driving force, there is no occasion for rebirth. Such a man attains *Nirvāṇa*, the highest status. Buddha has propounded definite ways so as to get rid of the false worldly attractions. If man follows them in right earnest, he is sure to come out of his present miserable status, and attain the highest status of *Nirvāṇa*, which is as good as attaining Godhood. So, essentially, there is no one greater than man. It is only due to ignorance that man is suffering under imperfection. If he wants to get rid of his present state, he can well do it. It is up to him to make himself a thing of highest value, or to remain bound under the wheel of *saṃsāra*.

6. Evil and suffering

The Buddhist approach to the problem of human suffering is purely practical. Quite boldly and honestly, it acknowledges the burning fact of reality that man is in the grip of constant suffering. Then in a perfectly scientific spirit it diagnoses the cause of suffering. And finally it points out ways and means so that man can effectively get rid of this bond of suffering. This practical approach finds full expression in the four noble truths (*Ārya Satyāni*) propounded by Lord Buddha – (1) The noble truth concerning the nature of suffering (*Duhkha-Ārya-Satya*), (2) The noble truth concerning the origin of suffering (*Duhkha-Samudaya-Ārya-Satya*), (3) The noble truth concerning the removal of suffering (*Duhkha-Nirodha-Ārya-Satya)* and (4) The noble truth concerning the path leading to the removal of suffering (*Duhkha-Nirodha-Gāmini-Pratipad-Ārya-Satya*). As a matter of fact, there is no scope in Buddhism for that type of theoretical approach to the problem which is generally characteristic of the theistic religions like Judaism and Christianity. Buddhism is clearly not a theistic religion and therefore no such question arises here as to why there is evil even in spite of an omnipotent and benevolent creator God behind the world. It is out and out a humanistic religion and therefore a perfectly humanistic approach to the problem of human suffering is quite natural. Its main concern is to save human beings from the infinite chain of suffering in which they are bound. Buddha always indicated that his aim was practical and he never liked being dragged into the theoretical questions. A practical, humanistic approach to the problem of suffering is, therefore, bound up with the very attitude of Lord Buddha towards the problems of human life. They were not to be analysed and discussed theoretically, rather they were to be solved practically.

Buddha's first noble truth is concerned with the nature of human suffering. Human life as a whole is full of suffering and suffering alone (*Sarvam duhkham*). Birth, different diseases, old age and death (*Jarāmaran*) constitute the nature of human suffering. Everywhere and at all stages of life, therefore, there is suffering. But this suffering is not uncaused.

Buddha's belief in the theory of dependent origination makes him able to trace back the origin of suffering finally to ignorance (*Ajñāna*) through a twelve-linked chain (*Dvādasa nidāna*), in which every consequent is dependent for its origin on the adjoining antecedent. The first (or, in a sense, the last) link in the chain is *Jarāmaraṇa*. The cause of this *Jarāmaran* is *Jāti, i.e.,* taking birth. If one does not take birth at all, there is no question of his being a victim of all sorts of suffering. So birth is the nearest and most obvious cause of suffering. But the question is, why one takes birth at all; what the cause of *Jāti* is. The cause of *Jāti,* according to the Buddha, is *Bhava, i.e.,* the will to be born. Unless one has the will to be born, he is not born, So birth is due to an inherent urge, a drive for that. But where from this urge or drive comes in? What is the cause of this Bhava? The cause of *Bhava* is *Upādāna,* i.e., one's clinging to the sensory enjoyments. This clinging, again, is due to *Tṛṣṇā,* i.e., thirst for such enjoyment. This thirst is due to *Vedanā,* i.e., actual sense-enjoyment, which in its turn, is due to *Sparsha,* i.e., sense-object contact. How, again, does this contact become possible? Clearly, it could not have been possible, unless the six sense-organs (including the mind) would have been there. So the cause of *Sparsha* is *Ṣadāyatana.* The cause of this *Ṣadāyatana* is *Nāma-Rupa,* i.e., the psycho-physical organism. This organism is again due to *Vijñāna,* i.e., initial consciousness of the embryo. This *Vijñāna* is due to the *samskāra,* i.e., forces generated by the past karmas, which again are finally due to ignorance (*Ajñāna*). Thus ignorance is at the root of all human sufferings. Suffering, therefore, even in spite of being real, is in one sense, a fact of our own creation. The world being exactly as it is, will not be a cause for our suffering, if we are above ignorance. If ignorance does not blur our vision, we will not perform actions with a sense of thirst for sense-enjoyment, i.e. we will not perform attached actions. And if we do not perform such actions, karmic samskāras will not be produced (Non-attached actions do not produce samskāras) and hence no cause for taking birth will be there and consequently, there will be no suffering. All human suffering is due to man's own lack of knowledge regarding the real nature of things. All things of the world are fleeting and momentary. Nothing is permanent. So, having desire for them, is a sheer foolishness. Nothing in the world is permanent, not even the human soul. Thus clinging to or thirst for anything in the world is a sheer foolishness and cause of suffering. So, in a sense, man himself is responsible for all his sufferings. There is a state of existence, which is free from all kinds of suffering, and that state is called *Nirvana.* Only this *Nirvāṇa,* which is a state of complete cessation of all sufferings, is eternal. The nature of this *Nirvāṇa* is contained in the third noble truth of the Buddha. This *Nirvāṇa* is not a fiction or dream. There are concrete ways of attaining it and the ways are contained in the fourth noble truths propounded by the Buddha. The eightfold path (as indicated above), which is a path lying in between extreme indulgence and extreme asceticism, would lead to this state of *Nirvāṇa,* if sincerely and honestly followed.

Evil and suffering, thus, according to Buddhism, are in the main products of human ignorance. Moral evils are all the direct results of attached, egoistic human actions and the various natural evils (sufferings) are also indirect consequences of these very actions. If one understands the real nature of things and does not perform such actions, the world remaining as it is, he will not be affected by it. *Nirvāṇa* is possible in this very life. What is required is to be free from all sorts of passions and desires. So, the world itself is not a place of unqualified suffering. What makes it full of evil and suffering is our own ignorance and various passions generated thereby.

7. Life after death

Like all other religions, Buddhism also believes that human life does not end with the physical death, it has a story even beyond death. But what is that story? In short, that story according to Buddhism is the story of either rebirth or *Nirvāṇa*. Buddhist eschatology, therefore, is more or less similar to that of Hinduism. According to Buddhism, as according to Hinduism, man, after the death of his present body, has to assume another body in accordance with his deeds in the present life. But only the doers of attached actions have to be reborn by assuming another body. Those who perform actions without attachment have not to take rebirth. They attain *Nirvāṇa,* a status or a state of being which is purely spiritual and which is free from all sorts of sufferings of the physical life. According to the Buddha, whatever actions one performs with a sense of attachment generate forces (Samskāras) which cause rebirth. But actions performed without attachment are like fried seeds which do not generate any plant. Consequently, there is no question of rebirth.

Thus, we see that the Buddhist eschatology is very simple, straightforward and unambiguous. Everything looks very scientific and non-mythical. Actions done with passion generate a force which causes a man to take another life so as to reap the consequences of his action. If he does not perform such actions and leads a selfless life, he is liberated from the chain of birth and rebirth. Thus man's after-life is strictly governed by a self-regulated Moral Law. There is no deity here who will judge the good and bad actions of man so as to either reward him or punish him accordingly.

But in saying all these, Buddhism has to face a very serious problem and that is that, when there is no permanent soul in man, who migrates from one body to another and who attains *Nirvāṇa*. We have seen that Buddhism presents before us a theory of no-soul (*Anātmavāda*) according to which what we call soul is nothing more than a stream of changing moments of consciousness. If such is the case, then where is the question of rebirth or salvation? Who is reborn or who gets salvation? There is also no question of the same person taking rebirth in a future life or getting *Nirvāṇa*, because in the absence of a permanent soul-substance, personal identity cannot be maintained. The Buddhist theory of momentariness does not allow a man to remain the same man even for a moment. What is the sense, then, in saying that a man is either reborn or liberated in accordance with his deeds in the present life? It seems, therefore, that the entire eschatological belief of Buddhism is simply fictional and unfounded. But Buddhism does not allow the whole thing to be a mere fiction and presents a very cogent explanation in support of the rationality of its belief in rebirth and *Nirvāṇa* even in the absence of permanent soul-substance. There is, of course, not a permanent soul-substance, and there is only a series of the changing moments of consciousness. But the series is unbroken in which every subsequent moment is caused and conditioned by the antecedent one. The series has thus got an unbroken continuity. It is like a flame that burns through the night, or like a river current which has not the same water any next moment, but still in the ever passing currents of water, there is an unbroken continuity. Just as any river is neither strictly the same river at the next moment nor is it a totally different river, similarly a person who dies and is again reborn is neither strictly the same person nor totally a different person. (*Na cha so na cha anno*). Change is there, but the continuity is there too. The last thought-moment of the present life gives birth to the first thought-moment of the next life and the continuity goes on. Just as a burning flame may lit up another flame before blowing out, similarly the last conscious moment of the present life gives rise to the first conscious moment of the next life and blows out. In this sense, the next life is nothing but a continuity of the same series and hence rebirth is possible even without a permanent soul. In the same way, the rationality of *Nirvāṇa* also may be explained. The question of self-identity is automatically solved by realising that although the soul is a stream of changing moments of consciousness, still in this stream the antecedent moment of consciousness conditions and gives rise to the next moment of consciousness and the process goes on in the fashion of an unbroken continuity. The theory of dependent origination, properly understood, solves the entire mystery.

8. Ultimate human destiny

The ultimate destiny of man according to Buddhism is *Nirvāna*, the nature of which is contained in the third noble truth of Lord Buddha. *Duhkha* is there all over, *duhkha* is conditioned by a chain of causation, but *duhkha-nirodha* is also possible and this *duhkha-nirodha* is *Nirvāṇa*. Thus *Nirvāna* is the cessation of all suffering. It is the cessation of the twelve linked wheel of causation, of the wheel of birth or death, and hence of the entire mass of suffering. But is *Nirvāṇa* a mere negative state – a state of the negation of all suffering? Is it not something positive too? Or, does it not lead to some positive state of being where not only something is negated but also something positive is achieved? This point is really controversial in Buddhism. It seems that the Hinayanists merely emphasise the negative side of the *Nirvāṇa*. But that does not appear true even in the light of the original teachings of Lord Buddha. Buddha, of course, remained silent regarding the question of the true nature of *Nirvāṇa*. But his silence does not necessarily indicate that in the positive way, *Nirvāṇa* is nothing. That simply indicates that *Nirvāṇa* is indescribable. That is actually the theme that the Shunyavadins want to convey when they treat *Nirvāṇa* as the *Shūnyata*. '*Shūnyata*' stands here for the 'Indescribable'. So, *Nirvāṇa* is definitely a positive status too, although that is not ordinarily describable. When king Milinda of Greece asked Nagsena, the famous Buddhist monk to expose the nature of *Nirvāṇa* to him, the latter told him that *Nirvāṇa* was deep like an ocean, elevated like a mountain and sweet like honey. But this description was merely to indicate the indescribable nature of *Nirvāṇa*. *Nirvāṇa*, as is generally believed and expressed by the various Buddhist monks and Boddhisattvas, is a state of perfect peace and equanimity. It is not merely a state of the cessation of all becoming and all suffering; it is also a state of perfect peace and tranquility, which in a sense is a state of bliss[1]-eternal bliss, because *Nirvāṇa* is a state of eternity. Only *Nirvāṇa* is eternal, all else is momentary. In the Pāli texts, there is a context of a talk between the venerable monks Musila and Savittha, in which the latter tells the former that "the ceasing of becoming is Nibbana", but, the truth of cessation has the characteristic of peace."[2] There are several other references in the Pali texts which emphatically repudiate the mere negative conception of *Nirvāṇa*.

The main reason of taking *Nirvāṇa* as a symbol of a mere negative status seems to be its literal meaning. *'Nirvāṇa'* literally 'means' blowing out 'or cooling down.' This blowing out, again, is taken in two senses. Sometimes it is taken in the sense of the blowing out of the existence itself, *i.e.*, in the sense of the annihilation of the body and sometimes in the sense of the blowing out or cooling down of the passions and desires. That it can never be taken in the first sense, is obviously clear by the fact that Buddha himself attained to the status of *Nirvāṇa* in this very life. There are many other Buddhist monks and Bodhisattvas who are deemed to have attained *Nirvāṇa* in this very life. In fact cessation of the present life is not necessary for the attainment of *Nirvāṇa*. Buddhism believes in *Jīvan-mukti.* A person who attains salvation in this very life is called *'Arhat'*, in Buddhism and an Arhat is the ideal man of Buddhism. He lives and works

1. *'Nibbānam Paramam Sukham'* – *Dhammapada*, 203
2. Visuddhimāgga Atthakathā (Commentary) 525; cited here from *Buddhism*, edited by Richard A. Gard, p. 122.

in the world, but still he is not attached to the world. His passions and desires have all blown out and he has now no attraction , no clinging for the earthly pleasure. So 'blowing out' can be taken in the context of Buddhist *Nirvāṇa* only in its latter sense, i.e., in the sense of the cooling down of all passions and desires. In explaining the nature of *Nirvāṇa*, the Buddhists texts so often take help of the simile of blowing out or extinction of a flame.[3] But this also refers only to the extinction of the burning passions and desires, and not of the life itself. This simile of extinction of flame adds much to the attitude of interpreting *Nirvāṇa* as a mere negative state. But that is not justified. The simile of the extinct flame, does not merely refer to the negation of the burning flame, but also to the positive state of perfect calm and equanimity that is brought thereafter. Similarly, *Nirvāṇa* stands not merely for the negative side of the blowing out of passions, but also for the positive side of being which is attained after the extinction of the passions. And that positive side of being consists in the attainment of a state of perfect peace, calm and undisturbed blessedness. This is why some have taken the mere negative conception of *Nirvāṇa* as 'a wicked heresay' a deliberate misrepresentation of fact. *Nirvāṇa* is a perfectly positive state of eternal peace and tranquility.

In this way, attainment of a state of being in which man is completely free from the chain of birth and rebirth, and hence from all consequent suffering, and where he abounds in perfect peace, equanimity and bliss, is the ultimate destiny of man according to Buddhism. This state of being is eternal and is called *Nirvāṇa* (*Nibbhāna* in Pāli).

9. Buddhist discipline

As Buddhism is basically a non-theistic religion, the religious practices of a Buddhist mainly consist in pursuing a life of

---

3. *Nibbanti dhīrā yathāyam padipo – Suttanipata.*

ethical discipline rather than in following different modes of prayer or in performing various rituals. Of course, the latter can not be completely ruled out in so far as the later developments of Buddhism are concerned. The discipline that leads to the complete cessation of suffering and attainment of *Nirvāṇa* is contained in the fourth noble truth of the Buddha. In this noble truth Buddha propounded the famous eightfold path, the Middle path as he called it. He declared that those who wished to attain the ideal of life should avoid the two extremes of self-indulgence and self-torture, because, as he said, "self indulgence is low, vulgar, ignoble and harmful, and self-mortification is painful, ignoble and harmful – both are profitless." The former retards one's spiritual progress and the latter weakens one's intellect. In fact, Buddha himself had experienced both these ways before he attained to his final Enlightenment – the first while he was a prince in his father's palace and the second while he resorted to ascetic practices for some time immediately after renouncing home. What then is that Middle path which Buddha preached his followers to follow? In Buddha's own words which he is reported to have uttered before his follower monks, it is as follows – "Verily it is this Aryan eightfold way, to wit: Right view, right thought, right speech, right action, right living, right effort, right mindfulness, right concentration. This, monks, is that middle path which giveth vision, which giveth knowledge, which causeth calm, special knowledge, enlightenment, *Nibbāna*."[4]

This eightfold discipline has been stated and explained at various places in Pāli, Sanskrit and other texts. The following statement is attributed to the Buddha himself – "And what bhikkhus, is the right view? Knowledge, bhikkhus, about the suffering, the coming to be of suffering,

4. *Samyutta Nikāya* (Trans. F.L. Woodward), Part V, p. 357.

the cessation of suffering, the way that leads to the cessation of suffering. This is what is called the right view.

And what, bhikkhus, is right thought or aim? Aim towards renunciation, benevolence, kindness. This is what is called right thought or right aim.

And what, bhikkhus , is right speech? Abstaining from lying, slander, abuse and idle talk. This is what is called right speech.

And what, bhikkhus, is right doing? Abstaining from taking life, from taking what is not given, from carnal indulgence. This is what is called right doing.

And what, bhikkhus, is right livelihood? Herein, O bhikkhus, the Aryan disciple having put away wrong livelihood, supports himself by the right livelihood.

And what, bhikkhus is the right effort? Herein, O bhikkhus a brother makes effort in bringing forth wills that evil and bad states that have not arisen within him may not arise, to that end he stirs up energy, he grips and forces his mind. That he may put away evil and bad states that have arisen within him he put forth will, he makes effort, he stirs up energy, he grips and forces his mind. That good states which have not arisen may arise he puts forth will, he makes effort, he may srip-up energy, he grips and forces his mind. The good states which have arisen may persist, may not grow blurred, may multiply, grow abundant, develop and come to perfection, he puts forth will, he makes effort, he stirs up energy, he grips and forces his mind. This is what is called right effort.

And what bhikkhus, is right mindfulness? Herein, O bhikkhus, a brother, as to the body, continues so to look upon the body, that he remains ardent, self-possessed and mindful, having overcome both the hankering and the dejection common in the world. And in the same way as to feelings, thoughts and ideas, he so looks upon each, that he remains ardent, self-possessed and mindful, having overcome the hankering and the dejection that is common in the world. This is what is called right mindfulness.

And what, bhikkhus, is right concentration? Herein, O bhikkhus, a brother, aloof from sensuous appetites, aloof from evil ideas, enters into and abides in the First Jñāna, wherein there is cogitation and deliberation, which is born of solitude and is full of joy and ease. Suppressing cogitation and deliberation, he enters into and abides in the Second Jñāna, which is self-evoked, born of concentration full of joy and ease, in that, set free from cognition and deliberation, the mind grows calm and sure, dwelling on high. And further, disenchanted with joy, he abides calmly contemplative while, mindful and self-possessed, he feels in his body that ease where of Aryans declare, 'He that is calmly contemplative and aware, he dwelleth at ease? So does he enter into and abide in the Third Jñāna. And further, by putting aside ease and by putting aside malaise, by the passing away of happiness and of the melancholy he used to feel, he enters into and abides in the Fourth Jñāna, rapture of utter purity and mindfulness and equanimity, wherein neither ease is felt nor any pain. This is what is called right concentration."[5]

The following may be taken as the further elucidation of the above stated eightfold path –

(1) *Right view or right understanding*: This primarily refers to a clear understanding of the four noble truths as propounded by the Buddha. It is also taken as referring to a clear understanding of the theories of *Pratityasmutpāda*, momentariness and non-soul as imbibed and involved in the teachings of the Buddha. Hence the beginning of the treading of the noble eightfold path consists in having a clear understanding of the above principles. In short, we must have a clear understanding of the nature of the *samsāra*.

---

5. *Dialogues of the Buddha* (Trans. T.W. Rhys Davis & C.A. Davis), pp. 343-45.

(2) *Right thought*: This second stage of the eightfold path requires that our mind should be pure, free from lust, ill will etc. Moreover, at the same time, we should be willing to give up anything that impedes our onward march. This is aiming towards or thinking for higher and purer things.

(3) *Right speech*: This consists in refraining from telling a lie, back-biting, harsh talks, and idle gossip. Moreover, our speech should be free from ill-will, selfish interests, dogmatic assertions etc. It must be commensurate with right thought.

(4) *Right action*: This generally consists in observing the five precepts (*Panchsheel*) in both their negative and positive aspects – (i) Not to kill but to practise harmlessness and compassion to all, (ii) Not to take that which is not given, but to practise charity and generosity, (iii) Not to commit sexual misconduct, but to practise chastity and self-control, (iv) Not to indulge in false speech, but to practise sincerity and honesty and (v) Not to partake of intoxicating drinks or drugs, but to practise restraint and mindfulness. Particularly, the first three constitute right action.

(5) *Right livelihood*: This counsels for a just, honestly earned and undeceitful means of livelihood which does not debar others of their just rights of the same. This includes counsel for abstaining from inclinations towards undue hoarding, unjust money-making etc. The traditional trades from which people are asked to abstain are – (i) dealing in arms, (ii) dealing in living beings, (iii) dealing in flesh, (iv) dealing in intoxicating drinks and (v) dealing in poison.

(6) *Right effort*: This consists in making sincere efforts to give up evil habits and cultivate the good ones. It, therefore, comprises of the following four constant efforts: (i) The effort to prevent the arising of evil which has not yet arisen, (ii) The effort to eradicate that evil which has already accumulated, (iii) The effort to induce good which has not yet arisen and (iv) the effort to cultivate that good which is already present. By sincerely practising these, one is expected in Buddhism to cultivate the following higher ethical virtues

which are known as the Dasparamitas – generosity, morality (*shīla*) renunciation, wisdom, energy, patience, truthfulness, determination, loving kindness, and equanimity.

(7) *Right mindfulness*: This consists in one's having a constant vigil over the body, the feelings, the mind and the ideas engenered therein so as to prevent these from going astray. Right mindfulness frees the mind of *Rāga* and *Dvesha* and prepares it for higher concentration.

(8) *Right concentration*: After practising right mindfulness, one prepares himself for the final stage, the stage of right concentration. This stage itself consists of four gradual stages. Through the three successive lower stages, mind finally reaches the fourth stage of *Samādhi*, which is really the stage of perfect rapture and equanimity and wherein neither any kind of pleasure nor pain or anguish is felt. The stage of right concentration begins with mind's effort at one pointedness (*ekāgratā*) directed towards some wholesome object and ends in mind's complete concentration, rapture and undisturbed calm.

Of the eightfold path mentioned above, the first two constitute what is called *Prajñā* in Buddhism, the next three constitute what is called *Shīla* and the last three *Samādhi*. So in one way of taking things, *Prajñā*, *Shīla* and *Samādhi* are the three broad ways through which one can achieve final salvation. Sometimes, the order is changed and the three are put as *Shīla*, *Samādhi* and *Prajñā*, which implies that after practising morality, mindfulness, and concentration, a right understanding about the nature of things arises. But it is equally correct to say that without a right understanding and right view about the nature of things, practice of true morality etc. is perhaps not possible. Hence perhaps the order is not very important, what is important to see is that components are all interrelated and they are to be practised in that light.

As requirements of morality (*Shīla*) five components have been mentioned above under 'Right action'. These five moral duties are required in Buddhism equally of a laity and a monk. But Buddhism also speaks of eight precepts (*Atthānga Śila*) and ten precepts (Daṣa Śīla) meant for those persons in the laity who are comparatively more pious and less attached to families, and specially, for the monks. The three additional precepts in the Attha Śīla are – (a) abstaining from taking untimely meals, (b) abstaining from dancing, singing, music etc. and from using garlands perfumes, cosmetics and personal adornments and (c) abstaining from using high seats. In the ten precepts, meant specially for the Samaneras (An entrant in the monkhood of Buddhism who is below the age of twenty is known as *Samanera*), the two additional are as follows – the seventh one of the Attha Śīla (2nd of the above) has been broken into two parts and the latter one is known as the eighth. So the seventh there becomes – 'Abstaining from dancing, singing, music etc.' and the eighth one – 'Abstaining from using garlands, preferences, consummatics etc.' The ninth one is the same as the eighth one in the Attha Śīla and the tenth one is 'abstaining from taking gold and silver.'

As we have indicated above, later Buddhism, besides recognising the value of the eightfold path, also abounds in prayers of Lord Buddha and in various rituals associated with him. First, Buddha was begun to be venerated as a great man, teacher, victor, lord or the blessed one, but gradually such practices of veneration developed into full-fledged Buddha-cult and Buddha was begun to be worshipped in various ways, such as, by *vandanā, i.e.*, by singing various devotional songs of praise, by the repetition of the *Tri-Saran-Gamana* formula, by offering flowers and other symbolic articles to the sculptural images of the Buddha, by relic worship of the memorial symbols or of something which he is supposed to have used etc. Various temples have now been erected at various places and these and the various stupas have become objects of pilgrimages. Specially, the temples at Bodh-Gayá attract pilgrims from all over the world. In these temples images of Buddha are installed and the pilgrims offer flowers etc. to them.

Besides these simple acts of prayer and worship of Lord Buddha, a host of ceremonial and ritualistic practices have also gathered around Buddha and his *Dharma*, specially in the Mahāyāna and the Vajrāyana traditions. The most universal and common ceremony or ritual for all Buddhists is the repetition of the *Tri-Saran-Gamana* formula, which marks the initiation of any sacred ceremony. Besides, the Mahāyānists and the devotees of Vajrāyana tradition make varied use of certain esoteric media such as the *mantra*, the *mudrā, dhāranī mandala* etc. Organisationally viewed, there has been the customary practice of maintaining and managing the *Sangha* as a monastic institution by means of special ceremonies, such as, the *Pravrajya* (initiation ceremony for novices), the *upasampadā* (ordination ceremony for monks or nuns), *Kathina* (annual ceremony in which the laity offers cotton cloth to the monks for making robes) and the *uposatha* (meetings at new moon and full moon to expound *Dhamma*), etc. Moreover, certain annual ceremonies are also observed by the Buddhists in the fashion of festival. For example, *Vaishākhi Pūjā* is observed every year on the full moon day of the month of Vaishākha according to Hindu calendar to celebrate the birth day of Lord Buddha. Even the *Dhamma* is reverred ceremoniously by organising recitations of texts. Many other rituals are also prevalent, a complete account of which is not possible here.

10. Principal sects

Two main sects can be distinguished within Buddhism – Hinayāna and Mahāyāna. The origin of the names is not very clear and certain but the distinction came to take a clear shape towards the beginning of the Christian era. *'Yāna'* means vehicle or carrier and so Hinayāna means small carrier, while Mahāyāna means the great carrier. The

Mahāyānists began to call themselves so, because they claimed that their faith was the great vehicle which could help all mankind to attain salvation and in contrast they called the faith of their opposite group small vehicle because in their opinion it was not able to do that great job. In fact, the Mahāyānists moulded the original Buddhism to a very great extent to accommodate many things which could appeal to and attract ordinary religious people. The Hinayānists on the other hand remained strictly loyal to the original principles of Lord Buddha and called themselves – *Therāvādins, i.e.* the followers of the doctrine of the Elders. Consequently, they remained small in number. Hinayāna Buddhism is sometimes called Southern Buddhism, because it has best survived in countries like Cylon, Burma and South-East Asia. In contrast Mahāyāna Buddhism has been called Northern Buddhism because it has more survived in countries like Tibet, China and Japan.

As we have said above, the Hinayāna sect of Buddhism has remained more loyal to the original teachings of Lord Buddha. It has remained atheistic to a great extent and has taken the eightfold path of attaining *Nirvāṇa,* as taught by Lord Buddha, to be only effective and real religious practice. Of course, the Hinayānists regard Buddha as an ideal and a great personality whose imitation they preach, and practise and also to some extent they adore and worship him, but nevertheless, they never take him identical with the theistic God. Moreover, they are strictly individualistic in their approach and outlook, meaning thereby that, every one's *Nirvāṇa* is possible by his own individual effort and none else can be of any real help to him in this regard. Moreover, the Hinayānists have always strictly retained their faith in doctrines such as those of momentariness, no-soul etc. which were originally preached by the Buddha.

The Mahāyāna sect, on the other hand, although not forsaking the essentials of Lord Buddha's original teachings, has lapsed into a kind of theism, even a kind of polytheism, giving place to elaborate rites and rituals. Besides the worship of Lord Buddha, it has abounded in the worship of many Boshisattvas more or less in the fashion of the worship of Hindu gods. It has also not maintained the antimetaphysical attitude of Lord Buddha and has given place to important metaphysical theories.

It is very much social in its outlook and believes that no one's salvation is complete unless he helps others in their effort to attain salvation. It is due to its simplicity, accommodativeness and humanitarianism that it has proved to be of a relatively wider appeal. This sect has given rise to various sub-sects and schools. And idea of the various sub-sects it has given rise to may be had from the account we shall give in the Appendix (1) of its spread and development in China and Japan. We shall, however, not be able to give any account of the various metaphysical schools in which it has off-shooted, because that is more a thing of philosophy than of religion.

4

Jainism

1. Introductory

Jainism, like Buddhism, may be regarded as an offshoot of Hinduism. Of course, both Jainism and Buddhism arose on the Indian soil as a reaction against excessive Vedic ritualism, but none of them could free itself from the essentials of Hinduism. Lord Mahavira, known as Vardhamana in childhood, is generally regarded as the founder of Jaina religion, although the Jainas believe that there have been twenty-three religious teachers prior to Mahavira who have contributed to the foundation and development of Jaina religion. These religious teachers are known in Jainism as Tirthankara (Perfect soul) or Jin (Conqueror or victor of passions). Risabhadeo is regarded to be the first Jaina Tirthankara and Parsuadeo to be the twenty-third one. Mahavira is the 24th and the last in the chain. However, Jainism is most prominently associated with the name of Mahavira and it is he who is regarded as the propounder of the essential Jaina principles. Mahavira, like Buddha, was a *kshatriya* by birth and was an elder contemporary of the latter. He lived for sometime the life of a household, but later on renounced everything and became a wandering ascetic in search of the light of real knowledge. After fourteen years of ascetic life he felt that he had gained enlightenment and thenceforth he devoted his life in preaching his message of human enlightenment and liberation.

Mahavira preached a non-theistic religion of moral purity and excellence in which man was at the centre and the main aim was to liberate man out of the chain of *karma* and rebirth in which he was fallen. Of the three major religions of Indian origin, i.e., of Hinduism, Jainism and Buddhism, alike, the main objective has been to liberate man out of the pool of continued suffering in which he is fallen. But in the eyes of the latter two this objective can be fulfilled not by worshipping gods and goddesses nor by performing various rituals, but simply by following the path of pure ethical conduct. Jainism finds the world eternally existing which does not need any creator God to create and sustain it. The world with all its living beings is a function of six substances and the entire working of the world is self-based and self-maintained. The moral world is governed purely by the law of *karma* and does not require any divine retributor. Man is the highest being with a most developed soul within him and he is capable of attaining godhood by himself. Jainism lays utmost emphasis upon the moral virtue of *ahimsā* (non-violence) and much upholds the life of a monk or a celibate who has renounced the world completely and is engaged in spiritual elevation.

In course of time, Jainism was divided into two sects – Digambaras and Svetambaras. There is hardly anything essentially different between the two in practice, except that, the former believe in non-possession to such an extent that they do not think it desirable to possess even a rag of wearing cloth, while the latter are not so rigid in their approach. Consequently, the Digambara monks live and move in nudity without any cloth on their body, but the Svetambaras do not believe in complete nudity and wear white clothes. There is a third sect also, known as Sthānakavāsis, limited to a very small area in Maharashtra. This sect shooted out of the Svetambaras in protest against the latter's worship of images of the Tirthankaras. They maintain a non-idolaterous worship.

Jainism did not prove to be a missionary religion like Buddhism and, therefore, it remained confined to India alone. However, these days, certain Jaina believers have become active in giving a new life to their religion by publishing literature all over the world and distributing it among people. But Jainas never make efforts to convert people, they simply publicise their faith, specially the moral virtue of *ahiṃsā*. Like Buddhism, Jainism also has no faith in the Hindu caste system, but Brahmins are given special regard and most of the Jaina temples have Brahmins as priests.

Jaina scriptures mainly consist of the teachings attributed to Mahavira. They are constituted by the Angas, the Purvas and the five Prakaranas alongwith other non-canonical literature. Besides these, there is an encyclopaedia of Jainism, known as Lokaprakāsha and compiled by Vinai-Vijai, which is also highly esteemed by the Jainas.

2. Basic features of Jainism as a religion

1. It is an atheistic religion, believing in no God behind the world-order. Of course, in its later phases, the last Tirthankara Mahāvira has been given for all practical purposes the status of God, but again he is not regarded as the creator of the world. So in the ordinary and prevalent sense of the word 'God' even later Jainism has not got any God, although Mahāvira himself is regarded as the Lord and is venerated as such.

2. As there is no creator God in Jainism, the world is taken by it as eternally existing which works by its own inherent laws. It is a function of six eternally existing substances, five material and the one spiritual. The world is, again, perfectly real according to Jainism with all its plural beings. Thus the Jaina outlook towards the world is perfectly realistic and pluralistic.

3. Jainism is a religion of moral and spiritual purity aiming at the elevation of man to the state of perfection

and Godhood. Thus although Jainism does not believe in God, it believes in Godhood, which a man can attain by following the path of moral and spiritual discipline.

4. Like Buddhism, Jainism also (at least in its early phases) is opposed to ritualism and ceremonialism. Again, quite in line with Buddhism, it also does not accept the authority of the Vedas and is opposed to Hindu *Varna Vyavastha*.

5. Man, according to Jainism, is a physico-spiritual being who has got within his physical body an eternal conscious substance known as the Jīva (soul). In fact, all living beings have souls within them. Only the soul of man is the most developed, because consciousness in it is the most manifest. Consciousness is the essential quality of the soul-substance, and it is like a light which enlightens the whole body. Man's soul is immortal and is potentially perfect. In its real and essential nature, the soul is capable of attaining infinite power, infinite knowledge, infinite faith and infinite bliss (*ananta chatuṣṭhaya*).

6. The present state of man is the state of bondage which is due to his own past *karmas*. Actions done with passion and desire work like oily substances which attract matter (*pudgala*) towards the soul and cause it to fall in bondage. Like Hinduism, Jainism believes in the transmigration of soul or rebirth. Man takes birth in accordance with his own past *karmas*. Rebirth is bondage and is the cause of all consequent suffering. Hence man suffers due to his own *karmas*, and there is no other explanation for his suffering.

7. Liberation from the chain of birth and rebirth and hence from continued bondage is possible. The state of liberation is called *Mokṣa* or *Kaivalya*, In this state of *Mokṣa* the soul is free from the association of *Pudgals* and attains its pure original status. This status may be called the status of godhood, because in this state man attains infinity – the infinity of power, the infinity of faith, the infinity of knowledge and the infinity of bliss (anantachatuṣṭhaya).

8. *Mokṣa* or *Kaivalya* can be attained not by offering rituals to gods and goddesses (because there are no such deities), but by following the path of three jewels (*triratna*) – the path of right faith, right knowledge and right conduct. Right faith is the faith in the efficacy of the moral and spiritual principles taught by the *Jins* and the *Siddhas*. Right knowledge is the knowledge of things in their real perspective. Right conduct is the conduct of total detachment which generally speaking, consists in observing the five vows – non-violence, truthfulness, non-stealing, celibacy, and non-possession (*ahiṃsa, satya, asteya, brahmacharya* and *aparigraha*). The details of these we may see in the pages which follow.

9. Jainism lays utmost emphasis on the value of moral conduct under which *Ahiṃsā* is the most emphasised virtue. Of others, purity, chastity, non-attachment, compassion, love, fellow-feeling etc. are much emphasised.

10. Jainism much extolls the life of a monk or a celebate who has renounced everything and is 'engaged in spiritual elevation by following a path of rigorous moral and spiritual discipline.

3. God

Jainism does not believe in any creator God, it rather explicitly rejects the existence of any such being. God is taken as the self-subsistent, eternal cause of the universe, but it may be asked that if the world requires a cause, why not God himself requires one. Moreover, if God can be taken as self-subsistent and eternal, why not the world itself with all its constituent forces be so taken? Physical world is governed by its own inherent laws, and no external reality like God is required for it. Similarly, the moral world is governed by the Law of *Karma,* and no God as the bestower of reward and punishment is required. There is no need to believe in God, therefore. Man himself is God, because potentially he is perfect. He is, of course, not the creator of the world, but then potentially he is all-perfect. He is capable of attaining infinite power, infinite knowledge, infinite faith and infinite bliss *(Ananta chatusthaya)*. Man, in other words, is capable of attaining Godhood. Hence, if there is God in any sense, it is man himself. The Tirthankaras, Kevalis and the Siddhas, who have attained perfection, can all be taken as God. They neither create nor destroy anything, nor do they need any such thing being done. They have conquered once for all their ignorance and passions and they do not require anything. They have attained *Kaivalya* or *Nirvāṇa*.

It is a fact that like Lord Buddha, Lord Mahavira also is treated, more or less, as God by the Jainas. There are Jaina temples at many places with the statue of Mahavira inside them and the Jainas pay their devotion and respect to it in many ways. But then it is clear and certain that Mahavira is prayed and worshipped only as a great soul, as a saviour of mankind, as a religious leader and guide, and not as an omnipotent creator God. Many other Siddhas or Jins besides Mahavira are also prayed and worshipped, but only as great souls, the qualities of whom, if properly imbibed and meditated upon, may lead one to the state of *Kaivalya*. The Jins and the Kavalis do not return the prayers nor are they expected to do so but it is believed that by a constant mental association with these ideal beings, one can imbibe their qualities and may attain *Moksha*.

4. World

As Jainism does not believe in any creator God, it has got no creation myth. In fact, the world has not come into existence at a definite moment of time. It exists eternally. It tries to explain the material world by the help of the following five substances – *Dravya* (Substance) *Dharma* (Motion), *Adharma* (Principle of rest), *Ākāsha* (space) *Kāla* (Time) and Pudgala (Matter). To explain conscious beings, it adds a sixth substance – *Jīva* (Soul). Matter is composed of atoms *(pudgal)*. These atoms form the fundamental bases material objects. Material atoms possess the qualities of touch, taste, smell and colour. Space gives room for the pudgals. It is infinite. Time effects change. *Dharma* and *Adharma* are the principles of motion and rest respectively. These two principles are peculiar to Jainism and they make the Jaina explanation of the world very scientific. It is by the principles of motion that the pudgals move and combine together to form objects. Thus motion is not imparted to objects by some external agency (like God) from without. It is an inherent, self-working principle of the world. Thus the formation of the world is a function of these five substances.

Jainism is realistic and pluralistic. It believes in the reality of the world with all the plural objects in it. Unlike Buddhism, it believes in the permanence of substances. As a matter of fact, it cuts a middle course between Vedantic eternalism and Buddhistic theory of momentariness. In one sense substances are eternal, in another sense they are changing. In its essence, every substance remains the same, but in terms of its modes it changes. To be more precise, every substance has got two sorts of qualities – Essential quality (*Guna*) and modes *(paryāya)*. The essential quality of a substance does not change and in this sense the substance is eternal. But the modes are always changing and to the extent modes change, a substance may be regarded as changing as well. Thus the world may be regarded as both permanent and changing. In its essential aspect (or aspects) the world is eternal, but in respect of its modes, it is changing.

Jainism takes the world as real, but counsels not to be unduly attached to it. It may be taken as a ground for performing moral actions, but not as a place of sensuous enjoyments. The world, of course, generally attracts one in the direction of the latter, but that is exactly what is to be guarded against. The world is a moral ground and not a place of rejoice.

5. Man

Man is given the highest status in Jainism. There is no God in the ordinary sense of the term, but if the word 'God, has any meaning, it is applicable to man himself. Potentially, man is perfect. He is capable of attaining infinitude, absolute perfection. He has a soul within him which is imbued with infinite potentialities. It is an eternal conscious substance and does not die with physical death. Consciousness is there within all living beings but it is present in the most manifest form in man. Consciousness is the essential quality of the soul (*chetanā lakshano jīvah)*, although there are other various changing qualities in it also. This soul in man is capable of attaining infinite power, infinite knowledge, infinite faith and infinite bliss, because potentially, it is all that. It is capable of attaining Godhood, so to say.

But the question is: why is man working under so many limitations then? He is obviously finite and is living and working under very miserable conditions. If he has a soul within him which is virtually infinite or potentially capable of infinitude why is man so imperfect? The Jaina answer to these questions is that man in his present state is in bondage. His present state is not his real or natural state. Being associated with *Pudgala* (which is the real nature of bondage), the soul has lost its original character. Just as the Sun's brilliance is covered by the clouds, similarly, the soul's real brilliant nature has been subdued by the cover of *pudgals* around it. The association of soul with the body is the real cause of its imperfection. This association of the soul with the body is its bondage. But why this bondage? This is basically due to ajñāna (ignorance). Due to ignorance man's soul *(Jīva)* becomes a slave of its passions and does everything under their influence. But these passions are like oily, sticky substances (Kaṣāya) which attract dust towards them. So due to its association with passions, *pudgals* are attracted towards the soul and become associated with it so as to form the bodily cover around it. This influx of matter towards the soul is known as *Āśrava* by the Jainas. This association of matter with the soul does not end with the death of one body. This goes on from one birth to another. Unless all the fruits of one's actions done with passion are completely exhausted, one has to take another body after the end of the present body. The soul migrates from one body to another in accordance with its karmas. Everything that one is or has in his present life is strictly a consequence of his own past karmas. Like Hinduism and Buddhism, Jainism also believes in the Law of *Karma.* It rather believes in it somewhat more rigorously. Man is strictly a product of his own past karmas. This speaks of a kind of determinism, but taking it as purely deterministic is not fair. Man has got freedom of will also. By his present sincere efforts, he can improve his lot and get rid of the constant chain of birth and rebirth. For this he will have to do two things – (1) Annihilate the matter which has already accumulated with the soul *(Nirjarā)* and (2) Check the further influx of matter from without *(Samvara)*. For doing these things, the Jainas point out ways and means, which we will see in the succeeding sections. In general, it may be said that attached actions, i.e., actions done out of egoistic passions, will have to be completely given up. Otherwise, *āsrava* of matter will not be checked and the chain of birth and rebirth will go on. By stopping further *āsrava* and by annihilating the accumulated matter, man will have to cleanse his soul of its dross and then only the soul will be able to regain its original character of infinitude and perfection. Thus man is capable of making himself God. It is up to him to choose between the present state of bondage and the ultimate state of perfection that he can attain.

6. **Evil and suffering**

Jaina approach to the problem of evil and suffering is practical. Being a non-theistic system, it does not have any occasion to tackle the problem in a fashion in which it is raised and answered in the context of Semitic religions. But even apart from it, it does not ask and answer the general question as to why there is evil in this world. It rather raises and tries to answer the specific question as to why a man suffers. In other words, it raises the question of suffering in a subjective context rather than in a purely objective one. Moreover, it does not simply diagnose suffering, rather it also makes out explicit ways and means so as to get rid of suffering. Its interest in the problem of suffering, therefore, is in no way purely theoretical, it is primarily practical.

The Jaina answer to the above question is that man suffers due to his own past *karmas*. Life in the world is a consequence of one's past *karmas* and in a broad sense coming to life in the world (i.e. taking birth) itself is suffering. But in a sense, life in the world may be distinguished between a happy life and a miserable one. Both are respectively due to the good and bad actions performed by someone in his past life. Besides believing in the Law of *Karma* in a general sense in which all the other Hindu and Bauddha systems believe in it, Jainism believes in the Law of *Karma* in a very specific sense also. According to it, specific *karmas* of one's past life determine separately his taking birth in a specific family, in a specific economic condition, in a specific state of bodily health etc. There are according to it *Gotrakarmāni* (i.e. *karmas* determining family of birth), *Āyusakarmāni* (i.e. *karmas* determining age), *Nāma karmāni* (i.e. *karmas* determining good or bad body-built) etc. Hence whatever suffering one has in this life, whether relating to bodily ailments or family conditions or economic status or any other such thing, is due to his own past specific *karmas*. So, none but an individual himself is responsible for all his sufferings.

As we have indicated above, life in the world may be viewed in two different perspectives. From a narrower perspective, worldly life may be either happy or miserable in accordance with the good or bad past *karmas*. But from a broader perspective, any sort of life whether seemingly happy or miserable is a symbol of suffering, because life as a whole is essentially full of limitations and imperfections and imperfection itself is the greatest evil. Hence what is to be avoided is any future birth. And for that, all sorts of actions done out of passions and desires, whether good or bad, are to be avoided. For, actions done out of passion work as sticky substances *(kasayas)* which attract matter. They are the causes for the continuance of the body and taking rebirth. So long as matter is associated with the soul, there can be no end to suffering. So, to avoid suffering completely, one has to get rid of the continuous chain of birth and rebirth. That is possible only if one gets rid of ignorance, because ignorance is at the root of all evil and suffering. And for that, attainment of knowledge and performance of only non-attached actions are required. Actions done with attachment (i.e. out of ignorance) will continue to generate saṃskāras which will cause rebirth and consequent bondage. Jainism spells out specific ways (which we shall see below) to annihilate the accumulated matter as well as to withhold the further influx of matter. If these ways are strictly and sincerely followed, then one is able to rescue the soul of the dross of *Pudgala* and consequently of all suffering. Ignorance is *anādi,* but not *ananta.* It has to end, if sincere efforts are made for that. Hence Jainism diagnoses suffering and gives out practical ways to end it. That speaks of its practical approach to the problem of suffering.

7. Life after death

The Jaina view about life after death is similar to that of the Hindu view. Man has an immortal soul within him which does not die with physical death. Immediately after the death of the physical body, the soul transmigrates into a new body. The assumption of the new body with all its circumstances depends on the *karmas* of the previous life. Everything of the new life-family, bodily conditions, economic and social status etc. is conditioned and determined by one's past *karmas.* Excessively bad *karmas* such as those done with sinful intentions, deceitfulness, sense of excessive attachment etc. lead to subhuman birth. Actions done with less of attachment and with humble and kind dispositions lead to human birth. There are Gotra-karmas and Namakarmas which determine the family of birth and the bodily built respectively. The following cause birth in a low family – speaking ill of others, self-praise, concealing the good qualities of others, proclaiming false qualities of oneself etc. Similarly, crookedness of mind and disintegrity of character lead to having a deshaped and diseased body whereas the opposite qualities lead to having good physical body. Thus Jainism goes into the details of the specific causes of specific kind of rebirth. In Jainism there are references of being born in heaven or hell also, but that perhaps simply means being born in happy or miserable conditions of life respectively. In any case, the soul, if it has left samskaras due to its passionate actions done in the previous life, it has to be reborn. The passions are the *kasayas* (sticky substances) according to Jainism which attract atoms of matter *(Pudgala),* and therefore a soul which indulges in passions and acts under their spell has to be reborn in a sub-human or human form in accordance with its deeds. Only a soul which has performed passionless karmas has followed the path of right faith, right knowledge and right conduct and has lived a life of renunciation and datachment has not to take birth again. Such a soul is liberated. Liberation is a spiritual state of perfection. In it the soul assumes its original spiritual and infinite character. It has not to be reborn and consequently being free from all suffering, it attains absolute bliss.

8. Ultimate destiny

The ultimate destiny of man according to Jainism is *Moksha* or *Kaivalya.* As bondage is the association of the soul with matter, quite naturally *Moksha* is complete dissociation of the soul from matter. This dissociation is complete only when (1) matter already accumulated with the soul is completely annihilated and (2) any further influx of matter is completely checked. Thus there seems to be no scope for what is called *Jivanmukti* in Jainism. *Moksha* in the real sense is possible only when the physical body is destroyed and there is no possibility of the soul taking another body. Negatively speaking, *Moksha* is complete cessation of birth and rebirth and of all consequent suffering, and positively speaking, it is the attainment of a status of absolute perfection and bliss. In the state of *Moksha* the soul regains its original status of infinite power, infinite knowledge etc. A *kevali* is, therefore, omnipotent and omniscient. Man, while he is in bondage, is capable of attaining only relative knowledge (Sāpeksha Jñāna), but a *kevali* attains absolute knowledge (Nirapeksha Jñāna). Just as the sun after the removal of the clouds shines in his full brilliance, similarly, the soul after attaining *Moksha* becomes completely clear of the dross of matter and shines in its original brilliance. It reassumes its original character of perfection and knowledge. It is completely free from ignorance which is the root cause of all evil. It attains the four infinites *(Ananta chatusthaya)* – infinite power, infinite knowledge, infinite faith and infinite bliss. Thus the soul attains Godhood. We can see here clearly that the Jaina conception of *Moksha* is not only negative, but clearly positive too. *Moksha* is not only the end of suffering, it is rather the attainment of infinite bliss. Jainism propounds specific ways for attaining *Moksha,* which we shall deal with in the next section. Generally speaking, it is by pursuing the paths of what it calls *Samyag darshan* (Right faith), *Samyag Jñāna* (Right knowledge) and *Samyag charitra* (Right conduct) that one can attain *Moksha.* These three are known as *Triratna* (Three Jewels) in Jainism.

9. Jaina discipline

Basically, Jainism teaches a threefold discipline, called the discipline of three jewels (Triratna), following which one can get rid of bondage and attain liberation. This threefold discipline is the discipline of Right faith, Right knowledge and Right conduct.[1] *Moksha* is a function neither only of faith, nor only of knowledge, nor again of morality alone. It is a joint product of all the three. Again the three are interconnected. Right knowledge is not possible without right faith and right conduct is not possible without right knowledge. Let us see them one by one.

Right faith

There seems to be a controversy regarding the exact connotation of right faith. Some define it as a belief in the nine Jaina categories, some define it as a belief in six substances and nine categories, some define it as faith in the *dharma* devoid of violence and in the way of life prescribed by the Jins and Kevalis, some define it as belief in Jaina scriptures and teachers and so on. Umaswami defines right faith as faith in the greatness and efficacy of knowledge. However, in general it seems to mean having a pro-attitude, a sense of respect and regard towards Jaina principles or towards what the Jaina Tirthankaras have said and advised. In following a disciplined path towards *Moksha,* the Jainas believe that the first requisite is to have a faith in the spiritual principles taught by the Jins and other Siddhas. Unless one has faith in these, he cannot proceed on the path towards liberation. At least having such beliefs as, that we are in bondage, that liberation is possible, that liberation can be had through sincere personal effort, that the saints and seers have devised and pointed

---

1. *"Samyagdarśanam samyagjñānam samyag chāritramityattritya samuditam mokshasya sakshanmārgo veditavyam".*
– Pujyapada on *Tattvārtha Sūtra,* 1.1.

to right paths, is necessary before following any path for *Moksha*. If one is sceptical about all these, no effort on his part can be successful. So before attaining right knowledge or having allegience to right conduct some faith in spiritual truths and principles is necessary. Of course, in the context of Jainism, this faith will mean faith in the spiritual truths as taught by the Jaina Tirthankaras and Jaina scriptures. But in no case, by teaching right faith, Jainism wants to teach blind faith in authority. It leaves room for personal thinking and realisation. Right knowledge, we will see, means personal realisation, and right faith and right knowledge go hand in hand. Manibhadra has particularly cautioned against taking the Jaina teaching of right faith as blind faith in authority.

The following eight essentials are given in Jainism for *Samyagdarśana* (right faith) – Absence of doubt about scriptures (*Niśśankitā*), Absence of desire for the worldly pleasures (*Niḥkānkshitā*), Absence of doubt about the attainment of spiritual path (*Nirvichikitsā*), A clear and unconfusing vision about the ideal (*Amūḍhadṛṣti*), Augmentation of spiritual qualities (*upabṛhana*), Re-establishing deviations from truth (*Sthirīkarana*), sense of affection towards the followers of right path (*vātsalya*) and preaching the importance of truth (*prabhāvanā*).

Right knowledge

Right knowledge is the knowledge of the nature of things in the real perspective. It is the proper knowledge about the real nature of the living and non-living substances.[2] We have seen that according to Jainism, there are five non-living substances and the one living one. Knowledge about the nature of these substances and also of the distinction

2. *"Yena yena prakāren Jivādayaḥ Padārthā vyavasthitasten tenāvagamaḥ samyajjñānam."*

– Pujyapada on *Tattvārtha Sūtra*, 1.1.

between the living and the non-living is regarded as the right knowledge.

Right knowledge is very essential for *Moksha* according to Jainism, because we have seen that the root cause of bondage is ignorance. It is karmas done with passion which bind, and such karmas are all the results of ignorance. So right knowledge about the true nature of things and about the distinction of the soul from the material substances is necessary. Knowledge is said to be the real *tapas* (penance) because it burns the karmas to ashes.[3] But again it must be understood that by knowledge, Jainism does not mean mere intellectual or scriptural knowledge. Knowledge means here inner realisation. Mere scriptural knowledge may check someone for sometime from attachment to the world, but a man possessed of inner knowledge sees things for himself and is therefore never in the danger of being attached again. Right knowledge is that which helps in controlling the mind and purifying the self, and this is possible only by the knowledge which is self-realised, which is attained in one's inner intuition or vision. "The wise declare knowledge to be a nectar ...a glory which does not depend on others."[4] It is self-attained and self-realised.

Right Conduct

Only right faith or right knowledge is not sufficient for liberation. Right conduct is also necessary. Generally speaking, right conduct is the conduct based on detachment.[5] Going into the details, Jainism gives a long list of actions constituting the right conduct for a householder and for a monk separately. However, the five vows mentioned below constitute the necessary ingredients of the behaviour of everyone, whether he be a householder

3. *Jñānameva budhaḥ prāhuḥ karmanām tapānattapaḥ.*
4. *Jñānaṣtaka* 6.
5. *Rāyādi Pariharanam charanam – Samayasāra.*

or a monk. These five vows are known as *panchamahavrata* in Jainism and they are as follows:–

(1) *Non-violence (Ahiṃsā)*:– It is the greatest rule of conduct in Jainism. Violence in any form is strictly prohibited in it. Emphasis on *ahiṃsā* is the distinguishing mark of Jaina religion. It is not a fact that *ahiṃsā* as a moral virtue has been recognised for the first time in Indian tradition in Jainism. The Vedas and Upaniṣads of Hinduism also recognised it as a great moral virtue. But then the Vedas did not forbid *hiṃsā* in the context of sacred rituals. It is the speciality of Jainism that it strictly forbids *hiṃsā* in any form and of any denomination. To cultivate this virtue in its strict sense and spirit, the Jainas sometimes go to the extreme of not burning light or cooking meal after sunset (because that may attract worms) and the Jaina monks walk by brushing the path with a smooth brush in their hand so that no worm etc. should come under their feet.

Again, *ahiṃsā* is understood and practised in Jainism in a very wide connotation. Violence or injury or harm caused to any living being in any form is *hiṃsā*. So *ahiṃsā* is to be practised not only in deed, but also in thought and words. Keeping ill will against someone in thought or speaking harsh words to anyone is as good an example of *hiṃsā* as inflicting any bodily injury to any body. So mere avoidance of killing somebody is not *ahiṃsā*, it is very much more than that. Even forcing some one to do something against his will or curtailing somebody's freedom is deemed as *hiṃsā* in Jainism. Causing injury to someone due to negligence is also *hiṃsā*. Negligence *(Pramāda)* implies the passions of attachment *(rāga)* and aversion *(dvesha)* and any action done under their spell is violence. So non-violence understood in this widest possible sense is the rule of conduct according to Jainism. Practising *ahiṃsā* in the Jaina sense is not something very easy. It is a kind of *tapas*. On its positive side, *ahiṃsā* implies a life of love for all.

(2) *Satya* (Truthfulness):– Generally speaking, this rule of conduct enjoins abstinence from giving false statements

or telling a lie. But mere statement of fact is not truth. Truth, if it is harmful to others, should be avoided.[6] It must be spoken with beneficent intentions. Otherwise it will offend or harm some body and that will be *hiṃsā*. Exaggeration of fact, finding fault with others, using indecent speech etc. are all examples of untruth according to Jainism therefore they must be avoided. Speaking in a noble, beneficent and balanced manner and with a peaceful mind upholds truth and hence it must be practised. According to Amritachandra, the following are the examples of falsehood and they must be avoided – (i)Denial of the existence of a thing with reference to its position, time and nature, (ii) Asserting the existence of a non-existent thing with reference to its position, time and nature, (iii) Representing a thing as something else, (iv) Reprehensible speech, (v) Sinful speech and (vi) Unpalatable *(Apriya)* speech, Jainism takes untruth as a case of violence because it harms others and therefore it must be avoided.

(3) *Asteya* (Non-stealing):– Generally speaking, this means abstention from taking a thing of some one else which is not given. But as a Jaina rule of conduct, it is much more comprehensive and includes within it the avoidance of all sorts of dishonesty and conceit. Buying a valuable article at low price, appropriating some thing that has been forgotten by someone, having greed for the property of others, taking a thing in one's possession whose ownership is doubtful etc. are all examples of stealing and they must be avoided. Jainism regards stealing as a kind of violence *(hiṃsā)*, because wealth is external vital force of a man and taking away of it without his consent offends or harms him. Even abetment of theft or purchasing of stolen property or doing any kind of illegal business would be taken as stealing according to Jainism because every one of these affects the right or property of someone.

---

6. *Satyan Vimokhavyam parpirarambhātapabhayajanakam.*

(4) *Brahmacharya* (Celibacy):– This vow has been much emphasised in Hinduism and Buddhism also, but Jainism lays much more emphasis on it, because it extols the life of a celibate or a monk much more than any other religion. This vow or rule of conduct stands for abstinence from sexual intercourse, more specifically, from all sorts of illegal sexual intercourse. Samantbhadra has therefore included within this vow renunciation of contact with any woman other than one's wife. Not only actual commitment of adultery is the violation of this vow, but also the thought thereof. In general, brahmacharya also means abstinence from excessive desire for any sort of sense- enjoyment. Too much thinking about such enjoyment is also violation of the vow.

(5) *Aparigraha* (Non-possession or non-attachment):– It stands for not only abstinence from excessive material possession but also for the aviodance of desire for such possession. So, its inner meaning is non-attachment rather than non-possession. Excessive desire for material possession is *parigraha* and therefore it must be avoided. Accumulating more than what one needs for his maintenance is *parigraha* or even *steya,* because it is depriving others of their legitimate rights. Jainism counsels that excessive desire for possession may be avoided. Attachment is generated by *moha* and it results in *himsā*. *Moha* or attraction towards worldly possession must be avoided. If not, one cannot pursue right conduct. So, *aprigraha* is one of the basic rules of conduct not only in Jainism, but also in Hinduism and Buddhism. Desire for worldly objects is the root of all evil and therefore it must be shunned.

Besides these *Mahavratas* (great vows) Jainism prescribes many more *Anuvratas* (supplementary vows) for a householder and still more for a monk. The chief supplementary vows for a householder are divided into (i) *Guṇavrata* and (ii) *Śikṣāvrata* The former again are divided into

(1) *Digvrata*, (2) *Desāvakāśikavrata* and (3) *Ānarthadanadavrata*. (The Svetambara tradition replaced *desāvakāśikavrata* by *bhogopabhaga vrata)*. The latter are subdivided into (1) *Sāmāyika vrata*, (2) *Proṣadhopavāsa vrata*, (3) *Bhogopabhoga vrata* and (4) *Atithisaṁvibhāga vrata*. (As the Svetambara tradition includes *bhogopabhoga* in the Gunavratas, so it replaces it here by *deśāvakāsika vrata)*. Let us have a brief view of these vratas below –

(1) *Digvrata* – This stands for restricting the movements of householder to specific directions so as to minimise the chances of *hiṃsā* and maximise the sense of *aparigraha*.

(2) (*Deśāvakāsikavrata)* – In its essential spirit it is the same as the Digvrata; only it refers to the area or territory of movement.

(3) *Ānarthadandavrata* – It refers to abstaining from such harmful activities which do no good to the agent himself. Pujyapada mentions the following under such acts – (a) Evil thinking, (b) Counselling for committing sins (c) Performing non-vigilant actions (d) Giving of wepons for violence and (e) Evil reading.

Śikṣāvratas

(1) *Sāmāyikavrata* – It refers to the vow of practising peace, equanimity and inner centredness of the soul. It should be performed twice or thrice a day. In so far as this *vrata* is concerned, a householder is expected to imbibe more or less the spirit of a monk. Specific types of place, bodily posture etc. are prescribed in Jainism for the observance of this vow.

(2) *Proṣadhpavāsa vrata* – This is a vow of fasting. Fasting has been recognised as a virtue in Hinduism also. Jainas are required to fast on *astami, chaturdasi* and *purnimā*. Fasting includes not only abstinence from food, but also from bath, perfumes, physical adorement, ornaments and sexual intercourse.

(3) *Bhogopabhoga vrata* – This refers to putting limit to the objects of daily use so as to minimise attachment to worldly objects. The main idea behind this *vrata* is that objects which are not necessary should be renounced, so that gradual sense of detachment from worldly objects may be developed.

(4) *Atithisamvibhāgā vrata* – This refers to the offering of *dāna* (gifts) to the needy and deserving. This has been given much importance in Vedic Hinduism also. Jainism prescribes qualities of the givers and recipients of *dāna* as well as the process through which it is to be given.

For a monk, still more stringent rules of conduct are prescribed. Jainism has much regard and respect for monkish life. It upholds the life of a celibate who renounces the world and lives a life of self-denial and purity. In accordance with the two sects in which Jainism was later on divided, there are two types of Jaina monks – Svetambaras and Digambaras. The following are the rules of conduct for a Digambara monk –

(a) Observance of the five great vows mentioned above.

(b) Observance of the fivefold path of vigilance (vigilance in movement, vigilance in speech, vigilance in taking food, vigilance in lifting and putting articles and vigilance in throwing away excrements, dust etc.)

(c) Control of five senses.

(d) Performance of six essential duties –

1. *Sāmāyika* – already explained above.
2. *Chaturviniśatistava* – offering prayers to twentyfour Tirthankaras.
3. *Vandanā* – Paying respect to the preceptors, superiors, images of the kevalis and siddhas and to those who are superior in respect of austerity, knowledge, etc.
4. *Pratikramaṇa* – Confessing transgressions of the moral conduct, censuring oneself before the *guru* etc.

This is like repentence.

5. *Pratyākhyāna* – Determination to avoid sinful activities in future.

6. *Kāyotsarga* – Cultivating bodily postures of meditation.

(e) Cutting out of the hair.
(f) Nudity.
(g) Non-bathing.
(h) Sleeping on the ground.
(i) Not cleaning the teeth.
(j) Taking food in standing posture.
(k) Eating only once in twentyfour hours.

In the Svetambara tradition, however, a monk is required to observe the following –

(a) Five great vows,
(b) Not taking meal at night,
(c) Controlling the five senses,
(d) Inner purity,
(e) Purity of possessions,
(f) Forgiveness,
(g) Detachment,
(h) Mental goodness,
(i) Good in speech,
(j) Physical goodness,
(k) Protection of living beings,
(l) Threefold discipline,
(m) Forbearance,
(n) *Sallekhanā vrata* (the *vrata* of voluntarily killing oneself through certain prescribed means under certain prescribed conditions).

Some of the qualities that a monk is required to inculcate and cultivate are the following – Forgiveness, Humility, Straightforwardness, Contentment, Truth, Restraint, Penance, Renunciation, Detachment and celibacy. Both men and women are qualified for Jaina monkhood, woman monks are rather more respected and honoured.

The above clearly shows that Jainism is a religion of strict ethical discipline which lays utmost emphasis on the qualities of purity, chastity, self-restraint, detachment, humility, love, compassion, kindness etc. However, prayer and certain ceremonies also find place in Jainism. There are Jaina temples at many places in India which contain the images of the Jins or the Tirthankaras, specially of Lord Mahavira, to which people pray and give offerings. Besides, study of Jaina scriptures is also regarded as an act of piety. The Jainas organise big processions with the image of Lord Mahavira in the front on his birth anniversary every year. Important Jaina temples are also treated as places of pilgrimage and the Jainas visit these places of pilgrimage from all corners of India.

10. Principal sects

We have seen that in Jainism the virtue of non-possession *(Aparigraha)* and a saintly life of self-mortification have been given much importance and value. It is on the point of an extreme or a relatively moderate application and interpretation of these two that Jainism split up into two sects – the Digambara and the Svetambara. The Digambara sect takes the virtue of non-possession in rather a more extreme sense and holds that a perfect saint should possess absolutely nothing, not even a rag of cloth on his body. Consequently members of the Digambara sect prefer absolute nudity and do not wear any cloth. The Svetambaras on the other hand do not go to that extreme and in the name of purity and austerity they prefer wearing white cloth on their bodies. In certain other respects also the Digambaras are relatively more rigid and go to a greater extreme in observing austerities and principles of saintliness than the Svetambaras. A glimpse of the differences on these accounts may be marked here and there in our account of the Jaina ethics and other religious practices. But on the whole there is hardly anything very important to distinguish sharply between the beliefs and practices of the Digambaras and the Svetambaras. Both of the sects seem to be one in so far as the essential principles of their beliefs and practices are concerned.

5

Zoroastrianism

1. Introductory

Zoroastrianism is one of the oldest religions of the world, perhaps 2500 to 3000 years old. It has now very few followers and many will dispute even its claim of being a living religion at all. But still it merits our study here because of its intrinsic value as an ethical religion as well as for the immense influence it has exerted on Judaism (through the medium of Jewish exile in Babylonia) and again through Judaism on Islam and Christianity. It is the religion of the ancient Persia, and Parsees all over the world (although very few in number) even now observe this religion. Prophet Zarathustra, also known as Zoroaster in its latinised version, is regarded as the founder of this religion. There are controversies regarding the actual birth date of Zoroaster, although several Zoroastrians take it as 628 BC Since he is believed to have lived for 77 years, his period may be taken as 628 BC to 551 BC. However, despite the controversy regarding the period of Zoroaster, this much seems more or less undoubted that he was contemporary with many of the vedic sages of ancient India. *Zendavesta*, or simply *Avesta*, is the basic sacred text of the Zoroastrians. There are obvious signs of vedic influences at many places in *Zend-avesta*. It contains three main parts – the Yasna, which constitutes the liturgy, the Yashts, i.e., the sacrificial hymns addressed to specific deities or angels, and the Videvdāt or the 'Law against the Demons', which is concerned mainly with matters of ritual purification. Into the *Yasna* are incorporated a series of songs or hymns, known as *Gāthāṣ*. These *Gāthās* are written in the first person and so they are believed to be the direct works of Zoroaster himself. These Gāthās, then, are the principal, or rather the only, sources of the doctrines actually attributed to Zoroaster.

Before the advent of Zoroaster on the religious scene of ancient Persia, ritualism, ceremonialism, priesthood and all such vices were rampant in the field of religion and an unmitigated type of polytheism was prevalent everywhere. The prevalent confusion in the sphere of religion has been very well described in the very opening verse of first Gāthā of the *Avesta*. There it is related that confused and distracted humanity approaches God, the supreme creator with the complaint that evil had encumbered the entire earth and therefore he should send a saviour on it. The Supreme Lord thereupon asks the angels around him whether they could name any soul who could undertake this task. When the angels show their inability in this regard, the Lord himself names Zoroaster as the saviour of mankind and sends him on earth. Howsoever mythical this story may look, it nevertheless shows the perilous state of affairs in ancient Persia in which Prophet Zoroaster took birth. Zoroaster first began to live like an ordinary household with wife (rather three wives) and children. It was at the age of thirty that he received a revelatory message from God. By the bank of a river he had a vision of the angel Vohu Mana who appeared nine times the size of a man. The angel told Zoroaster that there was only one God,

h and that he (Zoroaster) was to serve as his prophet. During the next ten years Zoroaster had other visions too in which each of the angels of *Ahura Mazdah* appeared and revealed further truths to him. Zoroaster began to preach religious truths in accordance with his revelations at once, but at first with no success. He was rather condemned by people as spreader of evil spirits. But ultimately he succeeded in converting at least his own cousin Maidhyomah. Then he and his cousin took a travel to the court of a monarch in Bactria, named Vishtaspa. The two cousins tried much to convert the monarch, but they could not succeed until Zoroaster healed an ailing horse of the monarch who was very favourite to him. Now the monarch and his entire court and kingdom became the followers of Zoroaster and herefrom a turning point comes in the history of the spread of Zoroastrianism. In the years following, Zoroastrianism spread very rapidly by the help of the king, sometimes also through holy wars. Zoroaster was murdered at the age of seventy-seven at the hands of an enemy soldier.

The most important teaching that Zoroaster imparted to his people was his incipient ethical monotheism. Against various deities that people worshipped, Zoroaster taught that *Ahura Mazdah* was the only God to be worshipped. Zoroaster was well aware of the Aryan tradition which saw only one reality behind all the various deities that people worshipped at the Vedic age. The supreme being is one whom the wise call by various names (*Ekam Sadviprā Vahudhā Vadanti*). This was the characteristic Aryan faith and Zoroaster was well aware of it. Zoroaster characterised *Ahura Mazdah* in essentially ethical terms. He called him the Lord of supreme good and taught people a life of righteousness and good whereby they could strengthen God's power of goodness. Zoroaster's three most important ethical commandments were: good thoughts, good words and good deeds. These show how Zoroaster wanted to build up an ethically pure religion devoid of all ceremonialism and ritualism.

2. Basic features of Zoroastrianism as a religion

As every religion is known for what it is by virtue of some of its distinctive features, so is Zoroastrianism. The details of its features will come to us in due course when we will be dealing with the religion on specific points, but here to have a preliminary idea we must mention them in brief –

1. Zoroastrianism is a monotheistic religion believing in only one almighty God. Of course, the monotheism of Zoroastrianism is controversial, but the background against which Zoroaster, the prophet founder of the religion, propounds and propagates it shows that the religion must be monotheistic. For, the background is that of polytheism which Zoroaster hated strongly. Despite that some take Zoroastrianism to be a ditheistic religion admitting of two gods – one of the good and another of the evil. However, the gensal concentious seems to be that in its overall nature, Zoroastrianism is a monotheistic religion admitting of a kind of internal dualism in respect of Godhead.

2. On the whole, *Ahura Mazdah* is regarded as the one supreme God who is essentially regarded as the God of goodness although he is all powerful and all wise also. He is subtle and therefore is not given to ordinary knowledge of human beings. However, he sometimes reveals himself to men through his archangels.

3. The world, including everything in it, is the creation of *Ahura Mazdah*. He is not only the creator, but also the ruler of the world. Nothing happens in the world without his knowledge, will and power. It is said in Zoroastrianism that creation is simply "thought" by God into existence. This perhaps means that God simply thinks about the world and the world comes into being. This may be taken to mean that God has created the world out of nothing. It is simply a product of his thought.

4. The world however is perfectly real according to Zoroastrianism. It is pictured as a real battleground of two forces – the force of good as represented by *Spenta Mainyu* and the force of evil as represented by *Angra Mainyu, which is also called Ahriman*. The battle goes on and on until finally the force of good prevails over that of evil.

5. In a sense, Zoroastrianism is a revealed religion in which God reveals himself to Zoroaster, whom he chooses as his prophet. But it is not only that God chooses his prophet, rather the prophet also has the liberty to choose

his God and Zoroaster chooses *Ahura Mazdah* as his God. This shows in general the attitude of the Lord towards man. Man has been given absolute freedom in Zoroastrianism to choose between good and evil, although God wants man to choose the good and help him in his fight against the force of evil. But at last it is totally up to man himself what side he will like to choose. If man prefers to take the side of the good, he has to do nothing but to lead a life of righteousness. That will help *Ahura Mazdah* in his fight against evil.

6. Zoroastrianism, like other religions, believes in a life after death. In this life man's place is determined strictly in accordance with the law of retribution. Those whose righteous acts excel the unrighteous ones are sent to heaven, a place of rejoice, whereas those whose evil deeds balance heavily over the righteous ones are sent to hell, a place of dreaded suffering.

7. However, Zoroastrian eschatology does not end here. At the final end, Zoroastrianism promises a good and happy life to all. Thus damnation to hell is not eternal. It is only transitional. At long last, the sinners are all purged of their sins and are granted a happy and elevated life in a world in which there is only good and no evil.

8. Zoroastrianism believes in the existence of angels also, who are good spirits. They always stand by the side of God waiting for his order. Thus these angels help God in his mission of eradicating evil and establish good.

9. Besides the angels or the good spirits, there are evil spirits also, who accompany the God of evil, *Ahriman,* in his mission of spreading evil throughout the world.

10. It is a religion of perfect ethical purity and dedication devoid of petty ceremonialism. The basic ethical virtues that men are to inculcate are good thought, good word, and good deed.

11. Although some prayer or worship of *Ahura Mazdah* is prescribed in Zoroastrianism, in the main, religious life consists in the cultivation of moral virtues.

12. Fire is regarded as very pure and is treated as a symbol of Divine Purity.

3. God

As we have said earlier, Zoroaster preached a strict monotheism in place of the prevalent polytheism. According to him *Ahura Mazdah* is the only God whom people should adore and worship. 'Ahura' means 'Lord' and 'Mazdah' means 'All-wise'. Thus by etymology Ahura Mazdah is the all-wise Lord. However, many other attributes are also given to *Ahura Mazdah*. He is regarded as all-good, perfectly holy, all-strong and powerful, unconquerable, kind etc. He is further regarded as the invisible and intangible creator and ruler of the world. *Ahura Mazdah* is subtle and therefore he is not given to human senses. But then he reveals himself to mankind through six different modes, known as *Amesha Spentas* and usually translated as "Holy Immortals". These six modes can be regarded as the six aspects of the supreme God through which he so often reveals himself. Or else, they may be regarded as the six archangels through whom *Ahura Mazdah* reveals himself to men. These six aspects or archangels are named as Asha, Vohu Mano (through whom *Ahura Mazdah* is reported to have revealed himself to Zoroaster), Kshathra, Armaiti, Haurvataf and Ameretat.

We have been saying that Zoroaster preached a strictly monotheistic religion and that according to him *Ahura Mazdah* is the only supreme God. And this seems quite natural, because the very background against which Zoroaster preached his religion was that of polytheism which he hated strongly. He regarded the old religion which recognised a plurality of Gods as "evil" and against this evil he brought about the "good" which his God revealed to him – a new religion which recognised no God but *Ahura Mazdah*. As a matter of fact, at the time when Zoroaster came on the scene' the Indo-Persian people recognised two classes of deity – the *asuras* and the *devas* in the Vedic Indian tradition and the *ahuras* and *daevas* in the Persian tradition. The two classes of deity were, however, recognised differently in the two traditions. Whereas in the Indian tradition the *asuras* were the daemons and the *daevas* were the gods, in the Persian tradition the *ahuras* were the gods and the *daevas* were the demons. Zoroaster dethroned the *daevas* completely and amongst the *ahuras*, he retained only the *Ahura Mazdah*, the wise Lord, as the one true God. Thus Zoroaster seems to have preached a perfect monotheism.

But this may sound misleading to some who are very much acquainted with the apparent dualistic nature of Zoroastrian Godhead. They will like to take Zoroastrianism as ditheistic rather than monotheistic. Apparently, there seem to be two gods in Zoroastrianism – one good God or the God of good and the other evil God or the God of evil and darkness. The first is called *Spenta Mainyu* and is so often identified with *Ahura Mazdah* himself, and the second is known as the *Angra Mainyu* or *Ahriman* (also as shaitin or satan). There is as a matter of fact some amount of controversy regarding the real nature of Zoroastrian Godhead. Some take it as a clear example of ditheism, while others argue that in spite of a place in Zoroastrianism for an evil spirit called *Ahriman*, the essentially monotheistic nature of Zoroastrianism does not break down.

Zoroaster, of course, recognises two primeval spirits – The Holy Spirit and the Evil Spirit. He regards the two as twins and identifies *Ahura Mazdah* with the former. But sometimes he also speaks of Holy Spirit as being the son of *Ahura Mazdah*.[1] Now if the Holy Spirit is the son of *Ahura Mazdah* and the Holy and Evil Spirits are both twins, then naturally *Ahura Mazdah* becomes the progenitor of the Evil Spirit also, although it is never explicitly stated in the *Avesta* that the Evil Spirit directly derives from *Ahura Mazdah*. It

1. *Yasna*, 47.3

is, nevertheless, implied therein. And if so, then *Ahura Mazdah* cannot be treated as all-good. For, it is he who has produced the Evil Spirit who spreads evil all over.

Here, Zoroaster's position seems to be that the Evil Spirit is evil not by birth, but by choice. That is after taking birth the Evil Spirit opted freely for evil. God simply "generated" the two spirits and it is by own independent choice that one of them sided with the good and another with the evil. The former was called the Holy spirit and the latter the Evil Spirit. Hence, Zoroaster, perhaps, wants to maintain that *Ahura Mazdah* is the sole overall powerful God and the Evil Spirit is neither co-eternal with him nor independent of him. But again *Ahura Mazdah* cannot be held responsible for evil, because he did not create the Evil Spirit as evil. *Ahura Mazdah* as good God has granted free will to every body and the Evil Spirit by using his freedom sided with evil by his own choice. Zoroaster thus preaches monotheism and not a ditheism or dualism in Godhead, as many take his position to be.

Nevertheless, there are hints in the statements of Zoroaster himself which point towards dualism in Godhead. As Prophet Zoroaster proclaimed, "I speak out concerning the two spirits of whom, at the beginning of existence, the Holier spoke to him who is evil, 'Neither our thoughts, nor our teachings, nor our wills, nor our choices, nor our words, nor our deeds, nor our convictions, not yet our souls agree."[2] We can see that this and such other proclamations well contain the seed of ditheism or primeval dualism in Godhead. What could be said of Zoroaster then despite his overall emphasis on the supremacy of one God *Ahura Mazdah*? Here, perhaps, we have to concede with R.C. Zaehner that, "Zoroaster, however, was a prophet, not a theologian; and prophets in their direct apprehension of

2. *Yasna*, 45.2.

deity are liable to leave all manners of loose ends for the theologians to tidy up later."[3]

Theologians were indeed kept absorbed for many years with the question of the actual nature of Zoroastrian Godhead. They kept on discussing the issue even after the Mohammadan conquest of the Persian empire. Seeing the ambiguity of the whole situation, many posited a principle above both *Ahura Mazdah* and *Ahriman* and took it as the principle of Time (Zurvān i akanārak). This principle of Time was taken as the first principle out of which both *Ahura Mazdah* and *Ahriman* arose. This kind of position become able to save Zoroastrianism from lapsing into dualism on the philosophical plane, but religiously speaking, a strict dualism in Godhead was brought in which led Zoroastrianism to be characterised as a ditheistic religion. And this position prevailed until in the last century the Parsees in India, who have really kept the Zoroastrian faith somehow alive even today, questioned this rigid dualism and reverted back to the prophet's original monotheism.

What, however, seems worth mentioning to us in the context of this controversy is that, in the earlier *Avesta*, which is specially attributed to the authorship of Zoroaster, there is definitely an emphasis on strict monotheism and Zoroaster seems to have only vaguely spoken of an evil spirit as a hostile or rebel spirit there. But in the later *Avesta*, where there again arise signs of polytheism, the evil spirit is regarded as an independent God. Even the six Holy Immortals mentioned earlier are gradually taken as six different gods and many other gods such as Atar (Fire), Mithra (the Invincible Sun) etc. are also added. Also so many rituals and ceremonies are reintroduced in the religion, as is obvious by a study of the third book of the *Avesta*. The following observations of Bouquet may be of relevance here:

---

3. *The Concise Encyclopedia of Living Faiths*, p. 204.

"From the Gathas it is clear that the doctrine of Zarasthustra himself was a sublime and distinct monotheism, though below the Supreme Being are satellites or Amesha spentas, who are of the nature of archangels. ... Later Persian religion also mentions the god Mithras as possessing almost equal honour with Ahura Mazdah. But it is fair to say that Zarathustra was as much a monotheist as the second Isaiah. When in later Zoroastrianism we find reference to the evil spirit Ahriman, we are in a different atmosphere."[4]

4. World

The world is created by *Ahura Mazdah* the all-powerful, wise Lord. In fact, everything including heaven and earth is created by him. The Yasna says that his creation is 'thought' by him into existence, which perhaps means that he has created the universe out of nothing. The Prophet asks God and replies himself as follows regarding the creation of everything.

"This I ask thee, Lord, answer me truly: who is the first, the father of Righteousness through generation and birth? Who appointed their paths to the Sun and the stars? Who but thou is it through whom the moon waxes and wanes? This would I know, O wise One, and other things besides.

"This I ask thee, Lord, answer me truly: who set the earth below and the sky above so that it does not fall? Who the waters and the plants? Who yoked swift steeds to wind and clouds? Who O wise one, is the creator of the Good Mind?

"This I ask thee, Lord, answer me truly: what goodly craftsman sleep and wakefullness? Who made morning, noon and night to make this wise man mindful of his task?

"This I ask thee, Lord, answer me truly: who created Rightmindedness venerable with the Dominion? Who made the son dutiful in his soul towards his father? Recognising

4. A.C. Bouquet, *op. cit.*, pp. 99-100.

thee by these signs as the creator of all things through the Holy Spirit, I go to help thee."[5]

The above shows that everything has been created by God through the Holy Spirit. Even righteousness and such other moral virtues have been created by God. As everything in the material world is created by God through the Holy Spirit, it is all good and therefore not to be despised in any way. Matter is not to be taken as evil and physical life is to be regarded as sacred. Zoroastrians' reverence for physical things may be seen in their reverence for such material elements as fire and water.

God has not only created the world, he also sustains it and rules over it. The world is fully dependent on God. Nothing happens in it beyond his will and knowledge. Nevertheless, the world is perfectly real and is a ground for man's action.

If, however, it is asked, why, after all, God created the world, the answer (in the light of Zoroastrian faith) will perhaps be that he created it with a perfectly ethical purpose. The entire world is represented in Zoroastrianism as a stage of constant struggle between the forces of light and good on the one side and the forces of evil and darkness on the other. The fight between the two sides is to go unabated until the forces of good prevail upon those of evil and darkness. This is surely to happen one day. But when it will actually happen is not known. When this final aim of *Ahura Mazdah* will be fulfilled, he will bring the present world to an end and bring about a world which will be completely free from all evil and suffering. The present world, therefore, is a ground for the exercise of man's free moral choice.

Later, theologians, however, who interpret Zoroastrianism as a rigid dualism, have a different answer to the question, why, after all, God did create the world.

---

5. *Yasna*, 44. 3-5, 7.

They say that God created the world to protect himself from his enemy *Ahriman*. He created the world, because he had to create it. Because *Ahura Mazdah* is the wise God, so he created the world in such a manner that the force of evil could be entrapped into it and would perish due to its own stupidity and inner contradiction of nature. The force of evil would invade Ahura Mazdah's world, as it were, but once he entered into the world, he would become a prisoner into it, like a beast trapped in a cage and would thus bring his own ruin. Creation in this sense, then, is like a net in which the devil is trapped and destroyed. Man is to play a very vital role in God's exercise of trapping the devil and destroying him.

In any case, the world with all its multiplicity is, according to Zoroastrianism real and in no case one is to abandon it. Asceticism is decried in Zoroastrianism. Being a real creature of the world, one is to lead a life of perfect righteousness by following the moral virtues of truthfulness, chastity, charity, kindness etc. One will have a future life strictly in accordance with his performance in this world. So this world is very real and vital for man. He should never adopt an other-worldly attitude.

5. Man

We have seen that in the beginning Zoroaster is chosen by God as a prophet, but it is not only that: the prophet also chooses his God, "O, wise Lord," he exclaims, "Zarathustra here chooses for himself thy spirit which is the most holy." The relationship between God and his prophet is, thus, one of freedom. Zoroaster is not constrained to choose his God like the Hebrew prophets. He rather chooses his God freely by seeing his holiness. It is in this free interchange between God and his prophet that the general relationship between God and man is reflected. Unlike that in Islam or Judaism where man is regarded as a servant or slave of God, here in Zoroastrianism man is taken as a free partner of God having full freedom to choose between good and evil.

Zoroastrianism, thus, allows a big status to man by granting him the status of being a partner of God in his ultimate scheme of establishing complete good all over the world by defeating the force of evil. The world, we have seen according to Zoroastrianism, is a ground of struggle between the forces of good and evil and man has to pay his role in it. He is born pure and sinless (compare Islam which also takes man as born sinless and contrast Christianity according to which man is born with the burden of Original Sin) and is free to choose either the path of good or of evil. God wants man to take the side of good so that he (God) may be assisted in his ultimate aim of establishing the reign of good on earth. But it is up to man to choose any side according to his will. He is completely free in taking his own course and his final destiny fully depends upon the exercise of his free choice. If he opts for the good and thereby assists God in his mission, he is bound to have a place in heaven, otherwise he is to be damned to hell. Zoroaster says to men –

> "Hear with your ears the highest truths I preach,
> And with illumined minds weigh them with care,
> Before you choose which of two paths to tread –
> Deciding man by man, each one for each,
> Before the great New Age is ushered in
> Wake up, alert to spread Ahura's word."[6]

Thus in only one life one can attain perfection if one chooses the path of righteousness. A scheme of multiple life one after another as in Hinduism is neither recognised nor required, "Within the span of this one life of earth,

---

6. *Yasna*, 3012.

prefection can be reached by fervent souls, ardent in zeal, sincere in their toil."[7]

Man is taught an active ethical conduct in Zoroastrianism. It depreciates asceticism and teaches an ethical life of good thought, good words and good deed. It teaches man to lead a healthy natural life and not to resort to secluded jungle life. The world is taken as a real battle ground and man has to play his role in a righteous manner. He is not to escape from the world. He is fully responsible for whatever he does and therefore he should assert his responsibility by taking the side of the good and thereby helping the cause of *Ahura Mazdah*..

In the Zoroastrian conception of man as outlined above, we can mark certain very important points which give it a distinctive character in contrast from Hinduism, Islam and Christianity, although it is believed that it was very much allied with the former and exerted significant influence on the latter two. Unlike Islam the religion believes in perfect freedom of human beings such that they are fully responsible for all their good and bad deeds. In this the religion is nearer to Christianity, but then unlike Christianity it takes man to be born pure and sinless. Human beings, according to Christianity, being the descendents of Adam come on earth with the load of the Original Sin and they are always to look for the grace of God for forgiveness. Similarly according to Hinduism also man comes to earth pressed with his past *karmas* and he has to undergo sufferings and pains in this life in accordance with his past deeds. But the Zoroastrian conception of man is free from all such burdens of Original Sin or past *karmas.* Man in Zoroastrianism is completely free from all such burdens and he has to work in this life with full responsibility for promoting the cause of good which is really the cause of the great God, *Ahura Mazdah.*

7. *Yasna,* 51:12.

6. Evil and suffering

Of all its various features Zoroastrianism is best known for its views on evil. Asha and Druj, truth and falsehood, righteousness and unrighteousness, order and disorder, good and evil are the basic opposites which we come across again and again in the Gāthās. At the time of Zoroaster these distinctions very much referred to the gulf between Zoroaster's own religion and the traditional religion of ancient Persia. In the latter, besides many kinds of sin, which Zoroaster hated, there was a cult of offering bulls in sacrifice and eating them along with fermented Haoma juice (compare with Soma rasa of Hindu faith) which Zoroaster hated most. This is why he treated the old religion as evil and in contrast his own religion of truth and righteousness as revealed by the wise Lord as good.

But in the religion of Zoroaster himself, there is a distinction between the righteous and the unrighteous, Truth and Lie, good and evil, etc. and one has to choose between the two. God with his Holy spirit chooses the former and expects human beings also to choose the same and help him fighting the force of evil. But the question is: Whence evil? God is all-powerful and he has created everything. So, evil also must be his own creation, for, if not so, God cannot remain all-powerful. But again he is all-good also and so why should he create evil, after all? We have seen above that God has not created evil. He has created all things good and righteous. But the question again is: whence evil then? Here again, we will have to refer to what we have already said above. God generated two spirits, one of whom opted evil by choice. He created none of the spirits as good or evil. The spirits by their own choice sided with good and evil respectively. One which sided with good was called the Holy Spirit and the other which sided with evil was called the Evil Spirit. The evil all over the world is the creation of the Evil Spirit (Ahriman) and God can not be held responsible for the same. God rather invites people to come to his assistance so that he could fight the evil force and eradicate it completely from the world in this ultimate victory over it.

Thus even if the evil spirit is not co-eternal with and independent of God, the latter cannot be held responsible for evil. It is the result of the wrong use of the freedom granted to the evil spirit by God. We have seen that the Zoroastrian God grants freedom to every body including men, spirits and archangels and it is by misusing freedom that *Ahriman* sided with evil. God is not at fault in any way in this connection. Similarly God is not responsible for moral evils also, because they are the result of the misuse of freedom by men. Of course, men are seduced towards sin by the evil, *Angra Mainyu* himself along with his demons, but nonetheless *Ahura Mazdah* is free from any responsibility of evil. *Ahura Mazdah* is all-good and he cannot be a party to the evil of the world. He is always anxious for establishing the complete reign of good in the world by defeating the force of evil and for that he seeks the help of the righteous people.

Thus Zoroastrianism accounts for evil by attributing it wholly and solely to *Ahriman*, the force of evil and darkness and the supreme Lord, *Ahura Mazdah*, cannot be held responsible for that. But the question is: Is *Ahura Mazdah* really saved from the responsibility? It can be very well seen that so long as Ahura Mazdah is regarded as one and only one all-powerful and all-strong Lord, he cannot be saved from the responsibility of creating and sustaining evils. He can be saved only when a dualism in the nature of Godhead is allowed in Zoroastrianism in which case, *Ahura Mazdah* no longer remains the all-powerful supreme Lord. Ahriman becomes a parallel God, who at least for the time being is not under the control of *Ahura Mazdah*. But in that case, *Ahura Mazdah* becomes a limited God who is engaged in a constant strife with *Ahriman* to defeat whom he requires the help of human beings. And if it is said, as is sometimes actually said, that *Ahriman* is not an independent force and he is fully under Ahura Mazdah's control, then howsoever pure and ethical the purpose of *Ahura Mazdah* may be in allowing evils, he becomes directly responsible for them. The explanation for evils then in Zoroastrianism will be the same as it is later on to be found in Judaism and Christianity. *Ahura Mazdah* is fundamentally responsible for all evil, but then he has allowed them for ethical purposes. He has deliberately brought about the strife between forces of good and evil so that men may have an occasion for utilising their freedom for either of them. However, God has so ordained the course of nature that ultimately it is the good which will prevail and the force of evil will be annihilated for ever. Thus in accounting for evil by attributing it to *Ahriman* in a bid to save the all-good God *Ahura Mazdah* from the responsibility for it, Zoroastrianism either lapses into a clear dualism or does not really become able to free *Ahura Mazdah* of all responsibility for evil.

7. Life after death

Like other religions Zoroastrianism also believes that death is not the final end of man's being, there is some kind of life after death also. Zoroastrianism, in fact, has a very lively eschatology of its own. Every man has an after-life in accordance with his righteous or evil deeds during his earthly life. The righteous find a place in heaven, which is full of all sorts of pleasant experiences, and the evil-doers are damned to hell, which is a place of terrible suffering. As is said in the Yasna, the righteous rejoice in the "House of Song"; the wicked, on the other hand, meet lasting torment, feeding on foul food in the "House of Lie". The prophet himself proclaims in this connection, "Then did I realise, wise Lord, that thou wast holy when I saw that in the beginning, at the birth of existence, thou didst ordain that deeds and spoken words should meet with (just) requital – evil for evil, but good reward for whose is good....."[8]

By way of developing its eschatology in details, Zoroastrianism points out that the soul after the physical death of man remains for three days with the body and meditates upon its deeds. On the fourth day the soul parts with the body and makes a journey to the place of judgment. God's archangel keeps a complete record of every man's deeds on earth, and with reference to his account, he balances the good and bad deeds of the soul in a scale. Those whose good deeds balance over the bad ones are sent to heaven and those whose evil deeds balance over the bad ones are sent to hell. If the good and bad deeds are, more or less, equal, the soul is sent to a kind of purgatory. The soul in its way to heaven or hell has to cross a bridge (called the Chinvat bridge). For a soul destined for heaven the bridge proves to be a very easy path. Moreover, the soul is greeted by beautiful maidens who escort it to the paradise. But an evil soul has a quite different experience. The bridge for it turns upon its edge and becomes as hard to walk as on the edge of a sword. Moreover, it is tormented by an old hog. Eventually it falls off the bridge and goes deep into the hell. We will find later on that the eschatology of Islam seems directly taken from Zoroastrianism and that of Judaism or Christianity is also very much influenced by it.

However, the eschatology of Zoroastrianism does not end here. The allotment of heaven or hell to the souls is not eternal according to it. The souls in accordance with their deeds abide in heaven or hell only until the world comes to its final end. At a specified time in future the world will come to its final end. At the end-point *Ahura Mazdah* would have attained his final goal of wiping out every trace of evil

8. *Yasna* 30:11.

from earth and establishing the reign of complete good all over the earth. At that point souls from hell will be brought out and purified. After purification they will join the souls of the righteous and a new cycle of earth will begin in which there will be no evil and no misery. In this world all souls will remain for ever without growing old or facing decay. In this world there will be only good and no evil.

This later eschatology, however, seems to have developed after Zoroaster, although its hints were there in the ideas of Zoroaster himself. As we can see, there is in this later eschatology an idea of the resurrection of the dead bodies. This idea centres around the figure of what is known as 'Saoshyant'. The word is usually translated as 'saviour' or as one who will bring good fortune'. The word occurs many times in the Gāthās, but there it seems mostly to refer to Zoroaster himself. Later on it begins referring to a 'Saviour' who will bring about the establishment of the kingdom of Righteousness on earth. It is believed that at the final end of creation (perhaps after twelve thousand cosmic years), Saoshyant will be born miraculously from the "seed" of Zoroaster and will arouse the bodies of the dead. These bodies will be reunited with their souls and will be plunged into a sea of molten metal so as to purge them of all their remaining sins. Thereafter, they are taken to remain for ever in this world which will be reduced to an immortal Paradise devoid of any evil or sin whatever. This may be called the final Rehabilitation of creation (Frashkart).

8. Ultimate destiny

We have seen in Zoroastrian eschatology that in his after-life man finds a place of happiness or suffering strictly in accordance with his deeds. No power can save him from the consequences of his acts. Here Zoroastrianism seems to believe in something like the Hindu Law of Karma, without believing in its adjunct Saṃsāra. Law of retribution is strictly followed in the scheme of *Ahura Mazdah*. Thus the destiny of man clearly seems to consist in an abode either in heaven or in hell in accordance with his deeds.

But that is not all. Zoroaster sometimes speaks of the attainment of 'wholeness' and 'immortality' as the final destiny of man, specially of such a man who performs good deeds in the world. "I shall speak out the word which the Most Holy One declared to me – the best of all words for men to hear: 'who so shall hearken even unto him, my Prophet, for my sake, shall attain to wholeness and immortality by performing the works of the Good Mind'."[9] Similarly, we are told of a fuller, higher life in Yasna, 30.11.

"False brings an age-long punishment and Truth leads on to a fuller, higher life." All this seems to imply that those who perform good deeds do not simply get a life of rejoicing experiences in heaven, rather they attain to a qualitatively superior life which is a life of perfection. The exact meanings of 'fuller, higher life' or of 'wholeness' do not seem to be very clear, but they definitely indicate towards a qualitatively superior life. 'Wholeness' perhaps means completeness or perfection, which seems to be the nature of Zoroastrian God also. So a man of good deeds attains to a life similar or equivalent to God.

But again, we have seen that according to Zoroastrianism, even he who is allotted hell as a punishment of his bad deeds is not damned to hell eternally. The idea of ultimate destiny of man is full of a high optimism. Even the sinners will ultimately have the opportunity to share the membership of a world full of good, pleasure and happiness. Damnation to hell is only transitional. It may be very long, but it is not eternal. Thus Zoroastrianism promises a very happy and elevated life for all its followers in the ultimate analysis. The ultimate destiny of man is bound to be good and great, because *Ahura Mazdah* is essentially of the nature

9. *Yasna*, 45.5.

of good. But it is up to man himself whether he would like to expedite his attainment of the final destiny or he would delay it by his own acts of unrighteousness and sin. *Ahura Mazdah* is kind and great enough to grant a life of eternal blessing to every body.

9. Ethics and ways of prayer etc.

We have said that Zoroastrianism as preached by Zoroaster is a great ethical monotheism and therefore naturally ethical virtues play a dominant role in a religious man's life here. Zoroaster, as we have seen, preached good thought (*Humata*), good word (*Hukhta*) and good deed (*Harshta*) to be the essential virtues or duties for every religious man, *Ahura Mazdah,* the supreme Lord, is all-good and he requires no worship from men other than a life of goodness. Living a righteous life is all that is required in the religion of Zoroaster. Quite in consonance with his three basic virtues mentioned above, Zoroaster also wants men to inculcate the virtues of truthfulness, justice, compassion, chastity, charity, honesty, purity, care of cattle, service of human beings etc. We can thus see that all virtues of higher religious life are preached by Zoroaster for the followers of his religion to inculcate. Zoroastrianism, therefore, in its essentials is an out and out ethical religion, although like many other religions, in course of its later developments it made room within it for many kinds of rituals and ceremonies.

Zoroastrian worship mainly consists in offering prayers to *Ahura Mazdah* requesting him to offer help for living a righteous life. Thus even the Zoroastrian prayer is mainly ethical in nature. No sacrifice other than offering sandalwood to sacred flames exists in Zoroastrianism. There are fire temples in which sacred flames burn eternally. Priests tend these fires and Zoroastrian people often visit these temples with sandalwood to offer to the burning flames and to receive ashes of these sacred flames. Blood sacrifice is strictly prohibited in Zoroastrianism.

Fire is regarded as very pure by the Zoroastrians. Although fire is not the direct object of worship or devotion, it is a symbol of divine purity. The priests while tending the fire wear surgical masks on their faces so that their breath may not contaminate the sacred fire. Dead bodies are also not burnt by the Zoroastrians with the same fear of contaminating fire thereby. As a matter of fact, they do not even bury the dead bodies into graves. They have a peculiar custom in this regard. They have got a specific place, called Tower of Silence, for the funeral of the dead. At this tower of silence, dead bodies are exposed on raised platforms so that vultures may pick the flesh from the bones. The bones devoid of flesh are then thrown after a few days into a deep well dug nearby.

10. Sects

The only surviving group following Zoroastrian faith is that of the Parsees living in India. These Parsees are supposed to be descended from a group of Zoroastrians who were banished from Persia by Muslim persecutors in about 716 A.D. These Parsees brought with them their sacred fire which still burns on, perpetually tended, in their so-called fire-temples. Of course, the religion of these Parsees has been mainly Zoroastrian, but it has not been without the impact of Hinduism on it. For example, the system of hereditary priesthood has been adopted into it from Hinduism. For some time, the essential teachings of the Gathas were neglected and a host of rituals crept into the Parsee practices. But after some time, the Parsees were stimulated by Christian rivalry, and a reform movement was introduced. The chief slogan was 'Back to the Gathas' and voice was raised against unnecessary set of rituals. The rituals were purified and prayer to *Ahura Mazdah* before the sacred fire was given first importance. The ethical side was revitalised and every child initiate was asked to take the vow to perform good thoughts, good words and good deeds. This revitalised Zoroastrianism is still observed by Parsees residing in India.

Two sects of Parsees may be distinguished the Shahansahis and the Kadmis. Their chief difference lies in a simple fact of history – as to when the fall of the last Sassanian King of Persia (the Yazedegard) took place. The day of the fall in observed by the Parsees as the Day of Yazedegard, the New Year's day.

6

Judaism

1. Introductory

Judaism is the religion of the Jews, the descendents of the ancient Hebrews, "the chosen people". It is based on a revelation made to the prophet Moses on the Mount Sinai. It is thus a revealed religion and is "the classical paradigm of a God-made religion". It is an assertion of the faith that God speaks to man, giving him clues to the path he must follow. It has three main pillers – Jehovah, the God; Covenant and the Torah (the Law). Judaism is a strictly monotheistic religion believing that religiosity consists in nothing but observing the contract (the covenant) made with God and following the commandments and the laws given by him. The sacred text of Judaism is the Old Testament of the Bible. The true nature of this religion, however, cannot come to the front unless one goes into at least a brief history of its early phases. The story of the origin and early development of the religion is given in the Old Testament itself. In a sense the story is quite exciting, adventurous and interesting, and imbibes within it the reasons that made Jewish people the type of people they actually happened to be and Judaism in its essentials the type of religion it actually came to be. Judaism, although essentially bound up with the name of Moses for its origin in any definite shape and form, has really for its origin the prophet Abraham as its founder and a chain of prophets after Moses to shape and reshape it amidst various ups and downs that it experienced from time to time.

Before Moses, as we have said above, the Hebrew people had for their prophet Abraham, who lived a nomadic life moving from one place to another. While living in Haran (a place somewhere situated in the Mesopotamian valley) in course of his wandering life, he took EL Shaddai, the god of Mount Shaddai, as his deity. Therefore on the advice of his god he moved to Cannan and settled on its outskirts. But after some time he had to face a terrible famine there and his descendents moved into Egypt. But there the Egyptians began making them slaves and treated them very badly. In accordance with the beliefs prevalent in those days, the Hebrews felt that they had to suffer the subjugation of the Egyptians because the latter had more powerful gods with them to help and protect them. Naturally they were in search of a more powerful deity whom they could adopt as their God. It is during this time that Moses took birth. As he grew up he could not tolerate the plight of his people. Once when he saw an Egyptian beating a Hebrew, he was so enraged that he killed the former and himself fled eastward beyond the Red Sea. He entered the land of Midian where while tending flocks near the base of Mount Sinai he came into contact with the god of this mountain. This god known as '*Yahweh*' (Jehovah as it is called in English) impressed Moses much and it is reported that he had certain miraculous talks with the deity. He then thought to bring his people there from Egypt and convert them to a faith in Yahweh. He actually brought them across the Red Sea to the foot of Mount Sinai and himself climbed to the top to talk things out with the deity. The deity announced conditions under which he was ready to adopt the people and protect them. Moses had really a contract (Covenant) with the deity and the deity gave many other laws for the guidance of the people. According to the contract, Yahweh was to protect the Hebrews, give them their own land of Cannan and in return they had to serve him for ever. Yahweh is reported to have spoken to Moses in the following words –

"I am the Lord. I appeared to Abraham, to Isaac, to Jacob as God Almighty, but by my name of Lord I did not make Myself known to them. And I established My Covenant with them, to give them the land of Cannan, the land of their sojournings, wherein they dwelled. Moreover, I have heard the groaning of the children of Israel whom the Egyptians keep in bondage and I have remembered my Covenant. Therefore, say to children of Israel, 'I am the Lord, who will bring you out from under the burden of the Egyptians, and will deliver you from their bondage, and will deliver you with an outstretched arm and with great judgements. And I will take you to myself for a people and I will be your God; and you shall know that I am the Lord your God who brought you out from under the burdens of the Egyptians. And I will bring you into the land concerning which I lifted up my hand to give it to Abraham, Isaac and Jacob. I will give it to you for a heritage; I am the Lord.... Now, therefore, if you will obey My voice and keep my covenant, you shall be My own possession among all the people, for all the earth is Mine, and you shall be to Me a kingdom of priests and a holy nation."

Moses summoned all his people and said to them, "Hear, O Israel, the statutes and the ordinances which I speak in your hearing this day, and you shall learn them and be careful to do them. The Lord, our God, made a covenant with us in Horeb. Not with our fathers did the Lord make this covenant, but with us, who are all of us alive here this day.... You all stand this day before the Lord, your God, your princes, your tribes, your elders and your officers, all the people of Israel, your children and your wives, and the stranger that is in the midst of your camp, from those that hew wood to those that draw water; that you enter into the covenant of the Lord, your God, and into His oath, which this day the Lord, your God makes with you, that He may establish you this day as a people to Himself and that He may be your God, as He has spoken to you, and as

He swore to your fathers, Abraham, Isaac and Jacob. 'Not with you only do I make this covenant and this oath but with him that stands with us here this day before the Lord our God and also with him that is not here with us this day.

"I will betroth you to Me for ever, I will betroth you to Me in righteousness and in justice, in love and in mercy. I will betroth you to Me in faithfulness, and you shall love the Lord."

With this covenant Moses led his people in the direction of Cannan, "the promised land", which was part of the covenant as people understood it. However, the promised land was not to be a free gift. It was rather to be fought for and so in effect Yahweh promised to be a god of war.

Thus it is Moses who gave the Jews a new religion with Yahweh as God and also the promised land of Cannan (which was later on divided into Israel and Judah). But the religion after him faced many severe threats, to the extent that *Yahweh* was forgotten as the God of the race and it was by the serious efforts of the several prophets from time to time like Elijah, Amos, Hosea, Isaiah, Jeremiah etc. that the religion could survive and went on taking newer and newer forms. The greatest shock to the religion and the people came at the hands of Nebuchadnezzar who demolished Judaic temple in Jerusalem and forced the Jews for an exile to Babylonia. Yahweh-worship now seemed to go for ever, because the Babylonian gods were more powerful. But it was Cyrus, the great Zoroastrian, who conquered Babylonia after about 50 years and restored the Jews their homeland. But as a result of this exile and the later victory of Cyrus, Judaism was very much influenced by the Babylonian ideas and the Zoroastrian faith. One such effect may clearly be seen in the idea of the devil, the Satan, which came to Judaism directly from Zoroastrianism. Before exile, Judaism is said to have no devil, but the theology of the post-exilic Judaism had a devil.

In the chain of the prophets, Deutro Isaiah, a post-exilic prophet, led Judaic monotheism to its height by declaring in unequivocal terms that Yahweh was the only God and there was none other. Further, he clarified the idea of "chosen people" by pointing out that the people of Israel were the chosen people not in the sense that they alone were to receive God's favour unconditionally and in an unearned manner. Rather they were the chosen people in the sense that they were the real servants of *Yahweh* for carrying his message to the whole world. As a matter of fact, Yahweh is the God of all mankind and the entire world is his sphere of action. He needed someone to carry his message to the entire world and for that he has chosen the people of Israel. Salvation is not only for the "chosen people". It is open to all, if they obey the law of righteousness. God is long-suffering and forgiving in nature and he ever awaits the reform of the sinning man. The Jews have many times forgotten Yahweh even in spite of the clear covenant, but Yahweh has always waited for their return to the right path and has forgiven them. This speaks of the real ethical nature of the God of Judaism. Judaism is essentially an ethical religion believing its God to be essentially imbued with such ethical qualities as justice, mercy, love etc. True religion consists in nothing but establishing moral relationship with God and with one's fellow beings. It consists, in other words, in the imitation of God's moral qualities.

2. Basic features of the Judaism as a religion

(1) Judaism is a classical example of a revealed religion in which God himself has given the entire body of religion to his "chosen people." It is an example of the fact that God speaks to man giving him the clues to the road he must follow for his redemption.

(2) It is a strictly monotheistic religion, believing in one and only one God. God has a personality, of course, not in

the ordinary human sense. He is a Person in the sense that he has got consciousness and will and he listens to and answers to the peoples' prayer etc.

(3) Besides having the metaphysical attributes of omnipotence, omniscience etc., God is pre-eminently imbued with such moral qualities as justice, mercy, kindness, love, holiness etc.

(4) With its God being pre-eminently imbued with moral qualities, Judaism is primarily an ethical religion giving out moral rules of conduct and a way of life – of justice, mercy, humility, modesty, etc God, of course, requires man to serve and to pray him, but the least of service that man is required to do is in the form of the observance of the Torah (the Law) and the commandments given to people by God.

(5) The world is created by God and is dependent upon him, but then it is real. The world is not to be treated as a place of scorn and lamentation, rather it is to be taken as a working ground for righteousness, justice etc. In the form of his existence on earth, man has got an opportunity to lead a life of righteousness and serve the purpose of God.

(6) Judaism believes in many prophets of whom Moses is treated as the greatest and the most favoured messiah of God.

(7) It also believes in angels and spirits, both good and bad. Satan is taken to be the chief evil spirit, the Devil, who contributes to the spread of evil in the world. However, Satan is not taken as beyond God's control.

(8) Judaism believes in the immortality of soul and consequently in a life after death. Although the idea about the life after death does not seem to be very clear in Judaism, its chief ingredients may be taken as the resurrection of the dead, and the assignment of heaven or hell to them in accordance with their earthly deeds.

(9) In spite of its emphasis on the primary value of the moral conduct of man, Judaism abounds in ceremonies, religious festivals, ritualistic ways of prayer and worship etc.

3. God

Judaism, as we have said earlier, is strictly monotheistic, believing in one and only one God. The very opening word of the Jewish confession of faith, *Shemma*, declares,"Hear, O Israel, the Lord, our God, the Lord is one."[1] Much about the nature of this Judaic God can be learnt from the history of the origin and development of the religion itself. God according to Judaism is personal, meaning thereby not that he has got a personality like ordinary human beings, but that he has got consciousness and will such that everything is done according to his will and he speaks to men and responds to their prayer etc. With the conception of God as Lord is blended the conception of his omnipotence (all-powerfulness) . Similarly he is also taken as omniscient and omnipresent, but most of all, the Judaic God appears as a God full of such ethical attributes as justice, mercy, righteousness etc. and above all, holiness. About the essentially ethical nature of the Judaic God Prof. Bahm observes, "There is but one God, who is an essentially ethical being dealing ethically with men and expecting them to deal ethically with him."[2] God is the creator and the ruler of the world. All that exists is created by him and all that happens is his will. He is eternal, having no beginning and end. His powers are unlimited, but he limits them by his own will and grants freedom to human beings. God is both transcendent and immanent. His transcendence is emphasized in two senses – in the sense of his being not limited to this world alone and also in the sense of being incomprehensible, inscrutable and mysterious for human understanding. His nature and functions really elude human understanding. His ways prove to be inscrutable and mysterious for human beings. When Moses asked God

1. *Deuteronomy*, 6:4.
2. A.J. Bahm, *op. cit.*, p. 250.

after his talks with him as to what he would say to his people when they would ask him about the nature of their God, Jehovah replied – Tell "I am what I am" (Exodus 3:14). This shows the mysterious nature of the Judaic deity. God appears to men in many ways and is known according to his deeds.

God's 'holiness' is also much emphasized in Judaism. Holiness implies two things – spiritual eminence and moral excellence. God is thoroughly spiritual and abounds in moral qualities. His aim is moral governance of the world in which people may be elevated to the path of highest morality and goodness. God loves his people and forgives their sins. The history of Judaism shows that the Judaic God is long-suffering and patiently waits for the reformation of his people. God's love to his people and his concern for their reformation and redemption is clear from the fact that he has taught them the way to redemption, the Torah. Because the real duty of a Jew is to follow the ways of God, therefore it is said that to every Jew God commands' "Be ye holy, for I, they Lord, am Holy". Although God is long-suffering and merciful, in the end he rewards and punishes. He is simultaneously the God of love and God of retribution. Mercy and justice both are attributed to him and therefore, he is called father and king both at the same time in Judaism. Thus service to God both in terms of prayer etc. as well as in terms of ethical relationship with him is recommended in Judaism. "You shall love the Lord your God with all your heart, with all your might and with all your soul", says the Deuteronomy (6:5). Thus absolute devotion and love to God are recommended. And because God is also morally perfect, he requires a life of perfect righteousness and love from every man towards his fellow beings also.

One may mark in the nature of the Judaic God as outlined above an attempt at steering a happy balance between the nature of God as an almighty, all-powerful, magestic and just ruler king and as a merciful, loving, benevolent and forgiving father. The ethical qualities of justice and mercy are both highlighted and emphasized together. The one implies a neutral, detached, impartial attitude, while the other implies a sympathetic, kind and loving attitude. The one points to God as a ruler, the other as a loving father. Franz Resenzweig, the last great theologian of the German Jewry, speaks of this balancing nature of the Judaic God in the following words, "To his people, God the Lord is simultaneously the God of retribution and the God of love. In the same breath, they call Him as 'our God' and as 'King of the universe', or – to indicate the same contrast in a more intimate sphere – as 'our Father' and 'our King'. We want to be served with trembling and yet rejoices when His children overcome their fear at His wondrous signs. Whenever the scriptures mention His majesty, the next verses are sure to speak of His meekness. He demands the visible signs of offering and prayer brought to His name and of the 'affliction of our soul' in His sight. And almost in the same breath He scorns both and wants to be honoured only with the secret fervor of the heart, in the love of one's neighbour' and in anonymous works of justice which no one may recognise as having been done for the sake of His name. He wants every knee to bend to Him and yet He is enthroned above Israel's songs of praise. Israel intercedes with Him in behalf of the sinning peoples of the world and He afflicts Israel with disease so that those other people may be healed. Both stand before God: Israel His servant, and the kings of the peoples; and the strands of suffering and guilt of love and judgment, of sin and atonement, are so inextricably twained that human hands cannot untangle them."[3] In the same vein Rabbi Joshua says, "Wherever you find a description of the greatness of the Holy one, praised be He, you find a

---

3. F. Rosenzweig and N. Glatzer, *Frenz Rosenzweig, His Life and Thought* (Jewish Publication Society, Philadelphia, 1953), pp. 304-5.

description of His consideration for the lowly. This is written in the Torah, repeated in the prophets and stated for the third time in the Writings."[4] Explaining the cause of being both merciful and just in his relationship with the world, God himself is reported to have said – "If I create the world solely on the basis of My attribute of Mercy, its siris will become too many. If I create it by My attribute of strict Justice, how will the world be able to exist? Therefore, I will create it with both attributes, both Justice and Mercy, and would that it stand. So the Judaic God, in essence, appears both as a just ruler and as a loving father.

4. World

The world has been created by God. However, he has not created the world in the fashion of man making something out of some given material. God has created the world *ex nihilo*. He simply willed and everything came about. The story of the creation given in the Bible is well known. "In the beginning God created the heaven and the earth" (Genesis, 1:1) and everything else was created gradually by God's will. In all, creation took six days. The world has been created in time. It is not co-eternal with God. There was a time when only God was and the world was not. At a particular time God willed and the world came to be. However, it does not mean that there was time from beforehand. Time itself is the creation of God and God himself is beyond time. The world, again, is not a finished product. It ever finds care of God and is renewed day by day, God resides in the world, although he is also beyond it. He ever maintains and sustains it. So the world is ever dependent upon God. Everything in the world has been made by him and every event happens according to his will.

---

4. *Exodus Rabbah*, 3:6.

"Praised be you, O Lord, Our God, king of the universe.
You fix the cycles of light and darkness.
You ordain the order of all creation.
You cause the light to shine over the earth;
Your radient mercy is upon its inhabitants.

In your goodness the work of creation
Is continually renewed day by day
How manifold are your works, O Lord,
With wisdom you fashioned them all.
The earth abounds with your creations."

The world is absolutely dependent on God in all its aspects. Nevertheless, it is real. The world is a real working ground for man. Although Judaism believes in an after-world and an after-life, its utmost emphasis is on the reality of this world and man's active participation in it for the realisation of the good. Man has the power to do whatever he likes only when he is here in this world. He should, therefore, take maximum advantage of his present worldly life by choosing the good and forsaking the evil. So present worldly life is not to be resented. It is rather to be hallowed and treated as an opportunity for serving the cause of God.

"... a servant of God is not one who detaches himself from the world, lest be he a burden to it, and it to him; or hates life, which is one of God's bounties granted to him. ... On the contrary, he loves the world and a long life, because it affords him opportunities of deserving the world to come. The more good he does the greater is his claim to the next world. ..."[5]

The world is ruled by God, but his governance of the world is tinged with justice and mercy. The world is really the unfolding of the purpose of God and therefore

5. Quoted by Arthur Hertzberg (ed.) in his *Judaism* (George Braziller, N.Y. 1962), on p. 181 from *Judah Halevi, Kuzari*, Part III.

everywhere it is full of God's ethical purpose. The world is a moral ground, where man is to add to the purpose of God by fostering good and fighting evil.

The Jews, however, believe that although God is present everywhere in the world, Israel is his chosen land and the people of Israel are the chosen people through whom particularly he wants to champion the cause of goodness in the entire world.

5. Man

'God created man in His own image' – this is the essential Biblical doctrine of man. This implies that man is essentially spiritual in nature and God has granted special status to man in creation. Man is the goal of creation. This is the significance of his being created on the last day of creation. Thus man has a special dignity in Judaism. "Man is dear to God, for he was created in the divine image. Man is especially dear to God in that he has been made aware that he was created in the divine image...."[6] God wants man to be his partner in his aim of the ultimate establishment of good on earth. For that, man's essential duty is to imitate God. God is essentially holy. Therefore man also has to be holy. "Be ye holy, as I, thy Lord, am Holy," God's nature is essentially an ethical nature and therefore he requires from man a strictly moral conduct surcharged with justice and love. Man's essential duty is to observe the Moral Law, the Torah, given by God. "A life of habitually right conduct affectionately devoted to the observance of divinely appointed moral law and the practice of neighbourly good will towards one's fellowmen are the only sacrifice that God needs."[7] When God was about to create man, the angels asked, "What is man, that you are mindful of him? Why

6. *Mishnah Avot*, 3:14
7. A.C. Bouquet, *op. cit.*, p. 215.

do you need man?" God answered, "who, then, shall fulfil my Torah and commandments?" This shows clearly that man has been made by God essentially to play the role of a moral agent, so that God's cause of establishing the reign of righteousness and good in the world may be served and fulfilled.

God is all-powerful, but by limiting his power by his own will, he has granted freedom of will to man. Man is, therefore, responsible for his own actions. He, however, does not owe responsibility to himself. He is responsible also to the society he lives in. Judaism does not teach asceticism, rather it teaches an active social life of love, righteousness, justice etc. Because man is free and responsible for his own actions, therefore he is to be blamed for his misdeeds. God is the judge of his actions, but being merciful God does not give forth-right punishment to man for his sin. He waits and sees so that man may come to the right path. However, if sin becomes habit, God punishes. Judaism unambiguously believes in the possibility of sin, because man has been granted free will. There is no righteous man on earth whose deeds are good and who does not sin."[8] However, with sincere repentance, man is forgiven. "Return, and repent for all your transgressions by which you have transgressed, and make yourselves a new heart and a new spirit for why will you die, O house of Israel? For I desire not the death of any one, says the Lord, God; therefore, return and live."[9]

Thus, God's relation to man in Judaism is very pious. It is based on a sense of partnership and is always surcharged with love and forgiveness. Man is sometimes called the servant of God in Judaism, but that is not perhaps literally meant. Prayer and absolute devotion to God are also

---

8. Ecclesiasticus, 7:20.
9. Ezekiel, 18:30-32.

prescribed for man in Judaism but observance of the Torah and the Commandments appears to be primary. Hence man appears to be an active partner of God in his moral governance of the world.

Man due to his essentially spiritual nature can attain eternity with God. The world is not eternal, nor can it ever be so. But man can attain eternity by his good and righteous deeds.' "There are unbelievers who maintain that the world is eternal, but this view is baseless. The truth is that the world and all that it contains can exist, but it need not necessarily; only God *must* exist. . . . Man can become part of God's unity, which is eternal, only by forgetfulness of self; he must forget himself completely in order to partake of the divine unity. . . . When man attains his level, his soul becomes an existential necessity, *i.e.*, he ascends from the realm of the possible to that of the eternal."[10]

6. Evil and suffering

Like all other theistic religions, Judaism has to face the real problem of evil. It takes God as all-powerful, just and merciful and so it has to account for evil. As regards moral evil, the answer of Judaism is simple. Because God has granted free will to human beings the latter themselves are responsible for the various kinds of sins they commit. Sin is a rebellion against God. It is astraying from the path of God; it is alienation from God. It is best illustrated in the Biblical story of the Original Sin committed by Adam. And quite *a propos* with this explanation, natural evil or suffering is also indirectly attributed to the sin committed by man. Suffering is nothing but a punishment for sin. As is said in the Isaiah:

> Tell them, 'Happy is the virtuous man,
> for he will feed on the fruit of his deeds;

10. Quoted by A. Hertzberg, in his *op. cit.*, p. 182.

Woe to the wicked, evil is on him,
He will be treated as his actions deserve'.[11]

And such an explanation is implicit in the very idea of Covenant. Covenant relationship is one of promise and punishment, and therefore those breaking the promise are punished. But this explanation hardly suffices, because even the innocents suffer natural sufferings. Rather sometimes it is found that innocents suffer while the wicked prosper. This leads to another aspect of the problem of evil – the problem of distribution, which the prophet Jeremiah himself seems to raise when he asks in anguish:

"You have right on your side, Yahweh,
When I complain about you,
But I would like to debate a point of justice with you.
Why is it that the wicked live so prosperously?
Why do scoundrals enjoy peace?"[12]

One answer to this problem seems to be that one should not be restless about the prosperity of the wicked; there may be delay but ultimately they will be punished. As has been said in the Proverb:

Do not be indignant about the wicked,
do not be envious of evil man,
Since there is no morrow for the wicked man;
the lamp of the wicked will be snuffed out."[13]

But obviously this is no answer. As a matter of fact, apart from certain other hints here and there, the overall explanation of Judaism regarding natural evil seems to be that it is a mystery which cannot be unveiled by human beings. God may have his own reasons in allowing evil and

11. Isaiah, 3:10f.
12. Jaremiah, 12:1.
13. Proverb, 24:19f.

suffering in the world and it is impossible for us to decipher those reasons fully. This much is certain that evil is not meaningless and purposeless. God has some purpose, perhaps some good purpose, behind allowing evils to exist. But what that purpose actually is, is hidden from us. The ways of God are unknown and inscrutable and we cannot say why evils are there. Man is too small a fragment to understand all of God's ways:

"I know that you are all-powerful; .
What you conceive, you can perform. . .
I have been holding forth on matters I cannot
understand.

. . . .

I retract all I have said,
and in dust and ashes I repent."[14]

The Ecclesiastes points evil as a total mystery. According to it no solution of the problem is possible.

However, at certain places in Judaism evil has been characterised as a test of faith. By inflicting suffering God actually wants to measure the depth with which one has faith in him. Such a view is implicit in the very story of Jewish people's long suffering. The entire suffering that they had to undergo as a race from time to time is attributed by them to Yahweh himself, but all this he did only by way of testing their faith in him. The book of *Job* explains the innocent suffering of Job as a test of his faithfulness. Similarly, the following Hasidic prayer makes evil both a mystery which human mind is unable to unravel as well as a thing which tests the faith of the believer – "God, do not tell me why I suffer, for I am no doubt unworthy to know why, but help me to believe that I suffer for your sake."

Sometimes, evil is taken in Judaism as corrective or reformatory in character and one is advised not to be very

---

14. Job, 42:2f, 6.

much concerned about these reformatory sufferings. They are like the rebukes or punishments of a loving father whose ultimate aim is to reform and correct. "For whom the Lord loves He chastens, as a father the son in whom he delights." Or as is said in the following verses of the Proverb (3:11) –

> "My son, do not scorn correction from Yahweh,
> do not resent his rebuke;
> For Yahweh reproves the man he loves,
> as a father checks a well-loved son."

Sometimes, again, evil is made redemptive, a sign of better things to come. This is also implicit in the story of Israel itself. We have seen that everytime when Israel had to suffer, it came out with something better. So evil or suffering in Judaism is taken as a symbol of something better to come. This implies the theory that every evil is good in disguise and therefore suffering is not to be treated as unqualified evil. God has allowed evil to exist only for the ultimate good of human beings. There is no absolute evil. Evil may be taken as a lower degree of good, as Rabbi Israel Baal Shem says.

Thus, we can see that evil is accounted for in Judaism in various ways. But one thing is clear in all these explanations and that is that, although ultimately it is God who is the cause of evil, he has his own justification for allowing evils to continue. In no case evil is to be attributed to some cruel intention of the Creator. He has some good purpose behind evil, although that purpose is not always known to human beings. For the most part, evil is a mystery. However, there is a thinking according to which evil in Judaism is not at all attributable to God. Evil is due to the devil Satan. Taking clue from Zoroastrianism, some believe it to be true for Judaism also. For instance, Charles Francis Potter remarks in his work *The Story of Religion* as follows – "Evidently the Jews had been somewhat troubled by the very obvious inconsistency of having Jehovah function as both the author of evil and its punisher, and welcomed the dualism of Zoroastrian theology which relieved Jehovah of such an embarrassing inconsistency."[15] But this view does not seem acceptable in the light of all-powerfulness and absolute oneness of Jehovah as the God of the Jews. Satan may have a subsidiary role under all-powerful God to pollute people and make them inclined towards sin. This could give God an occasion to test a man's moral worth and his faith in the goodness of Jehovah. Satan cannot be regarded as a force by himself who could be the cause of all evil and suffering. This clearly goes against the strict monotheistic character of Judaism.

7. Life after death (Eschatology)

Jewish ideas about life after death do not seem to be very clear. However, Judaism has got an eschatology of its own in as much as it does not seem believing that life ends with physical death. It believes in the resurrection of the dead and a world yet to come in which the resurrected souls will have their share. But again there is a view within Judaism according to which it seems that the advantage of resurrection and after-life is to be had only to the righteous and the wicked are to perish for ever along with their physical death. As Maimonides, the great Jewish thinker, says, "The good which is stored up for the righteous is life in the world to come, life unaccompanied by death, good unaccompanied by evil. ... The punishment of the wicked is that they will not merit such life but will be utterly cut off in their death. Whoever does not merit such life is a dead being who will never live but is cut off in his wickedness and perishes like an animal."[16] In this view, the world to come in a life after death is a world only meant for the

15. Quoted by A.J. Bahm in his *op. cit.*, p. 250.
16. Maimonides, *Misnah Torah, Hilkhot Teshvah*, 8.

good and the righteous in which they will be allowed to live eternally in nearness to God and his angels with all pleasure and happiness. This is, more or less, a life of heaven. Thus no idea of hell seems to be there. The wicked perish for ever with their death. As a matter of fact, in the Bible itself there does not seem to be any clear idea either of heaven or of hell. The ideas of heaven and hell seem to be a later development. As Hertzberg says in his (ed.) book *Judaism*, "In the Bible itself the arena of man's life is this world. There is no doctrine of heaven and hell, only a growing concept of an ultimate resurrection of the dead at the end of days. The doctrine of the resurrection was debated in post-Biblical times and the normative view became that held by the Pharisees, that there would be a resurrection of the dead. Consequently, the notion of judgement of the individual in the after-life beyond the grave, his consignment to heaven or hell began to arise."[17]

The above clearly shows that the ideas of heaven and hell in Judaism are somewhat a late development. Any way, Judaism, as it now stands, seems to have a definite belief in things like the day of final judgment, resurrection of the dead and the heaven and hell. These seem to be the overall faith of all the Jews. Saadia in the 9th century concluded that the doctrine of resurrection was accepted by all the Jews, most of whom identified that event with the end of time. He writes, in his work *The Book of Beliefs and Opinions*, "The author of this book declares that, as far as the doctrine of the resurrection of the dead is concerned – which we have been informed by our Master will take place in the next world in order to make possible the execution of retribution – it is a matter upon which our nation is in complete agreement.... We consequently do not know of any Jew who would disagree with this belief."[18] Writing in

17. A. Hertzberg, *op. cit.*, p. 207.
18. Treatise V, Chap. I.

the same book at another place he further says, "God has also informed us that during our entire sojourn in this workaday world, He keeps a record of everyone's deeds. The recompense for them, however, has been reserved by Him for the second world, which is the world of compensation. This latter world will be brought into being by Him when the entire number of rational beings, the creation of which has been decided upon by His Wisdom, will have been fulfilled. There will He require all of them, according to their deeds."[19] This quotation clearly shows that Judaism believes in the last day of judgment when the good and bad deeds of all will be weighed by God and consequent retribution will follow. A clear indication of belief in heaven and hell is given in the following words of Rabbi Johanan ben Zakai, which he gave out to his visitors while he was ill. When visitors came to see the ailing Rabbi, he began to weep. The visitors then asked why a wise man like him wept. The Rabbi then answered, "If I were being led before a king of flesh and blood, I would weep, even though his anger, if he were angry with me, would not be everlasting, though his prison, if he imprisoned me, would not hold me for eternity, though he could not sentence me to eternal death and though I could appease him with words and bribe him with money. And now I am being led before the King of Kings, the Holy one, praised be He, who lives and endures to all eternity. If He is angry with me, His anger is eternal. If He imprisons me, His prison will hold me eternally. He could sentence me to eternal death. And I cannot appease Him with words nor bribe Him with money. And furthermore, *two paths lie before me, one to the garden of Eden, and one to Gehinnom*, and I know not in which I will be led. Should I then not weep? [20] But then there is a view in Judaism according to which the period of the wicked in

---

19. Treatise VII, Chap. I.
20. Berakhot, 17 a, Quoted by A. Hertzberg in his *op. cit.*, p. 209. (Italics ours.)

the hell (*Gehinnom*) lasts for only twelve months. "We have learnt that the judgment of the wicked in the *Gehinnom* lasts twelve months."[21] So what exactly is the faith of Judaism in eschatological matters is not very definite and clear. Nevertheless, from whatever we have seen so far, it may be gathered that at least in the post-Biblical period the Judaic eschatology has generally been of the faith in the last day of judgment, the resurrection of the dead, the weighing of their deeds by God and their apportionment in heaven or hell in accordance with the balance of their good or bad deeds.

But again, there seems to be yet another view in Judaism regarding life after death and that is that, after bringing all dead to life on the day of judgment, God "heals" them all expect those few "who brought injury to everyone." It is not, however, clear what this healing actually means. It may perhaps mean curing the defects, deficiencies or diseases that one had during his life time. When a man regains life after death, he does so with all the defects and diseases that he had during his life time, but immediately after resurrection, his ailments are healed by God. Only a few who have been too unrighteous do not gain this favour. "The Holy one, praised be He, said, 'Let them rise with defects they had in life, and I shall heal them.....' Later even the animals shall be healed.....However, the one that brought injury to everyone shall not be healed." But it is not clear whether this healing implies pardoning also. If it be so, then it is difficult to understand what the idea of retribution, as previously referred to, would mean under Judaic faith. And if not; then one finds oneself unable to work out the full implications of the idea of healing by God. Thus it is difficult to pinpoint the elements of Judaic eschatology in exact unambiguous terms.

---

21. Quoted by A. Hertzberg from Midrash Mishle (17:1) in his *op. cit*, p. 210.

8. Human destiny

As it may be collected from the general picture of Jewish eschatology outlined above, man's ultimate destiny is to attain the membership of heaven where he will live eternally in perfect pleasantness with God and his angels. In this ultimate life which the righteous people attain, there is neither human body nor any bodily function. Human beings reside there in their pure spiritual forms in perfect peace, serenity and calm. God is spiritual and in every human being there is a divine spark in the nature of his soul. In his eternal life of heaven man endures eternally in the form of pure spirit. Heaven consists of a society of spirits only. These spirits lie there in constant and eternal company of God. It is said about this life that "there is neither eating nor drinking nor procreation, nor business dealings nor jealousy nor hate nor competition. But righteous men sit with their crowns on their heads and enjoy the splendour of the *Shekhinah*.[22]" Endorsing the above view of Jewish eternal life and explaining some of the concepts involved in it, Maimonides says, "In the world to come there are no bodies but only the souls of the righteous alone without bodies like the angels. Since there are no bodies in the world to come, there is neither eating, nor drinking nor anything at all which the bodies of men require in this world. Nothing occurs in the world to come which would involve bodies, such at sitting and standing, sleep and death, sadness and laughter etc. Thus the early sages said: There is no eating, drinking or sexual intercourse in the world to come, but the righteous sit here with their crowns on their heads, enjoying the splendour of the *Shekhinah* (Barakhot 7a). Clearly there are no bodies there, for there is neither eating nor drinking there, and the statement of the sages that 'the righteous sit there' was stated as a parable, the righteous there neither

22. *Shekhinah* – Light emanating from Jehovah in heaven.

work nor strain. The statement that their crowns are on their heads meant to say that the knowledge they possessed, on account of which they visited life in the world to come, is there with them and this knowledge is their crown...."[23]

The above is a picture of the destiny of man as believed in and understood in the Jewish tradition. But it does not imply that every body after death shares this destiny without any distinction. From our account of the Jewish eschatology it is clear that only the righteous attain such a life and those who have been sinners in their earthly life have to suffer damnation. The life eternal or the immortal life, as the life of heaven may be called, is the destiny of those few who have followed faithfully the Jewish discipline during their life time. But those who have not observed the Torah and the Commandments are sent to hell. But again, as we have seen in course of our account of Jewish eschatology, it is not clear whether according to Jewish belief the damnation in hell is eternal or only temporary. Sometimes it seems that, like Zoroastrianism, Judaism also believes in an ultimate happy life granted to all. This view finds support in the Jewish belief that some day or other a Messiah will come on earth to redeem everybody. "When that time is here, none will go hungry, there will be no war, no zealousness and no conflict, for goodness will flow abundantly, and all delights will be plentiful as the numberless mates of dust, and the whole world will be solely intent on the knowledge of the Lord." Thus it seems that according to the Jewish belief a time will come when the world will be reduced to one in which there will be only righteousness and good and all will remain in that world in perfect pleasure and happiness. The Christians take Jesus to be the redeemer Messiah, but the Jews do not believe like that, and this is a great point of difference between the Jews and the Christians. The Jews still await the arrival of that redeemer

23. Maimonides, *op. cit.*

Messiah who will redeem Israel from all its limitations, problems and sufferings.

9. Judaic discipline (Ethics, prayer etc.)

The basic principle of conduct in Judaism is *imitatio Dei, i.e.,* the imitation of God. But what does this imitation of God mean? It means imbibing in oneself the attributes of God. "Be ye holy, as I, thy Lord, am Holy." We have seen that the Judaic God is imbued with essentially such ethical qualities as justice, mercy, righteousness and holiness. The basic ethical virtue therefore consists in the cultivation of these qualities. To be more specific, Judaism counsels its followers to do such acts as clothing the naked, visiting the sick, comforting mourners, burying the dead and so on. In essence, it teaches acts of love and kindness. The Torah begins with an act of love and kindness and ends with an act of love and kindness. Besides, the qualities of modesty, humility etc. are also much emphasized "Let all your words be gentle and let your head be bowed; let your eyes be directed to the ground and your heart on high..." Speaking in praise of humility, the Proverb declares. "The reward of humility is the fear of the Lord." Judaism counsels men to think at all times that they are standing before God, that all things are being done in the presence of God. It asks men to avoid the following because God hates them – pride or arrogance, lying, shedding innocent blood, devising wicked plots, creating mischief, presenting false witness and sowing the seed of misunderstanding amongst brethren. As is well said in the Proverb –

> "There are six things which the Lord hates,
> Seven which are an abomination to Him :
> Haughty eyes, a lying tongue,
> Hands that shed innocent blood,
> A heart that devises wicked plots,
> Feet that are swift to run to mischief,

A false witness that utters lies,
And one that sows discord among brethren."[24]

Similarly, Judaism disapproves of the following three also – Speaking one thing from the mouth and entertaining something else in the heart; knowing of evidence in favour of someone, but keeping silent over it and testifying alone against someone for some disgraceful thing in him (since, according to the Judaic thinking, a minimum of two witnesses is required to prove someone guilty; only one witness merely gives the defendant a bad reputation). Judaism is very much against charging interest for money from someone. (Perhaps Islam has adopted it from Judaism that charging interest is bad). The sin of taking interest, is so great that whosoever commits it, is considered as one who denies the God of Israel." "If he lends at interest, and takes increase, shall he live? He shall not live."[25] In commenting upon this the Judaic sages have said that 'He shall not live' means that such a man will not be entitled for resurrection. Judaism also seems very keen in prescribing something like Hindu *Aparigraha*. Excessive attachment to worldly objects and accumulation of wealth by foul means and beyond one's genuine requirements are decried. Profit making is a big vice. One should cultivate a sense of detachment from the world and be inclined towards God. "If a man is attracted by things of this world and is estranged from his Creator, he is corrupted and he can corrupt the entire world along with him. However, if he controls himself, cleaves to his Creator and makes use of the world only to the degree that it helps him in serving his Creator, he raises himself to a higher level of existence and the world rises with him."[26]

---

24. Proverb, 6:16-19.
25. Ezekial, 18:13.
26. Quoted by A. Hertzberg in his *op. cit.*, p. 194, from Moses Luzatto's *Mesitlat Yasharim*, Chap. I.

A clearcut mandate has been given for the Jewish way of life in the form of the ten moral precepts, known as the Ten Commandments. These commandments are considered as given by Jehovah to Moses for the guidance of the children of Israel. These ten precepts are – (1) Thou shalt have no other gods before me (*i.e.*, before Jehovah), (2) Thou shalt not make any graven image, (3) Thou shalt not take the name of the Lord thy God in vain, (4) Remember the Sabbath day (the seventh day of the week, *i.e.*, Saturday, on which all Jews are required to refrain from all kinds of work and join the Divine worship) to keep it holy, (5) Honour thy father and thy mother, (6) Thou shalt not kill, (7) Thou shalt not commit adultery, (8) Thou shalt not steal, (9) Thou shalt not bear false witness against thy neighbour, and (10) Thou shalt not covet thy neighbour's house wife, man-servant, maid-servant, ox, ass, etc. We can see that the last five moral precepts are very much like the Hindu (or Jaina or Bauddha) moral virtues of *Ahiṃsā*, *Brahmacharya*, *Asteya*, *Satya* and *Aparigraha* respectively.

Although Judaism is very much an ethical religion and a way of life, it lays no less stress on service and prayer of God. It is said that the purpose of the creation of man is the service of God. And this service essentially consists in praying God with inner heart without any outside thought or preoccupation. God hears our prayers and answers to them. This does not mean that he always gives the answer that a man wants. God's ways are not very obvious. Judaism does not leave prayer very much to human option, rather it makes it a spiritual necessity. A man must pray with true inwardness regularly at stated times and occasions. A man is obliged to pray three times a day – in the morning, in the noon and in the evening. "Evening and morning and at noon I utter my complaint and moan, and He will hear my voice."[27] Jewish prayer is petitionary and devotional. It is

27. Psalm, 55:18.

both individual and collective. Certain specific provisions regarding the ways of prayer are laid down in Judaism. They are as follows –

(a) One who prays must be conscious of the meaning of the words he utters.

(b) One must utter the words carefully.

(c) One should place his feet close together, as though they were one, to be likened to the angels. One should lower his head slightly, and close his eyes so that he will not look at anything. If one prays from a prayer book, he should not take his eyes off it. One should place his hands over his heart, his right hand over his left, and pray wholeheartedly in reverence, awe and submission like a poor beggar standing at a door.

(d) When one is praying from outside the Land of Israel, he must face in the direction of the Land, when one is praying in the Land of Israel itself he should face Jerusalem and if one is praying in a place where he cannot specify the direction, so that he is unable to know the proper direction, he should direct his heart to God.

(e) There are certain definite rules regarding various postures of bowing etc. which we are leaving aside.

Congregational prayers are generally done in Jewish synagogues.[28] There is a little difference in the ways of an individual and a congregational prayer. Act of congregational worship or prayer is more often performed in the form of hearing the study of passages from the Torah. Specially on the Sabbath day and on festivals, people assemble in the synagogues to listen to such reading of the passages from the Torah.

Judaism started as a religion of spiritual purity but, as it has happened with almost all world religions, gradually it

---

28. Synagogue is a "building in which the Jews meet for common prayer, divine worship and public instruction."

lapsed into a net of various ceremonies and rituals. The ceremonial law expects each Jew to do the following besides praying thrice every day (the prayer beginning with the opening lines of the *Shema*) – to recite a blessing before and after each meal; to thank God for any special pleasure, such as a curious sight, the receipt of good news, etc., to wear fringed garment about one's body, to recite passages from scriptures, to take the Torah in a procession etc. etc. A host of other rituals also gradually crept in and apparently Judaism remained nothing more than a network of rituals. This paved the way for reformation which took shape in the advent of Jesus Christ and his message.

10. Principal sects

Th e two main divisions in Judaism are between the Orthodox and the Progressive. The orthodox are those who insist on the strict observance of the Mosaic Law and the Talmud (a compendium of 63 volumes consisting of the Jewish civil and canonical laws, which were traditionally formed and compiled by the Rabbis), whereas the Progressives do not give much weight to these. They admit the value of these to a limited degree only and give much freedom to the individual in the observance of true moral and religious Jewish principles. The Orthodox are much more engaged with the festivals, ritual practices and priestly dictates, whereas the Progressives are little interested in these things and give greater value to the truly moral and spiritual aspects of their religion.

Amongst the Progressives also, there are two groups – the Reformists and the Liberals. But this division seems true mainly of Britain. In America the Jews seem to be divided between the Orthodox and the Reformists and in between the two, there seems to be a third group also of the Conservatives. The Reformists of Britain, although little devoted to tradition, still give it some value in the service of the synagogue, but the Liberals have departed very much from the traditional forms and ways. In America, the Reformists seem very near to the British Liberals, taking little of tradition with seriousness and devotion. They recognise unlimited development and change in the Jewish religion and they are not ready to stick very much literally to the tradition. The Conservatives in America lie in between the Reformists and the Orthodox. They see much value in the traditional religious practices and at the same time try to mould themselves in the light of continuing reforms.

Broadly speaking, therefore, we can say that there are two groups amongst the Jews – one group of those who stick strictly to the tradition and the other of those who believe in reform and purification.

7

Christianity

1. Introductory

Of all the Semitic religions, Christianity has proved to be the most influential and has dominated a large population of the world, specially the western world. As is well known, it has its origin in the teachings of Jesus, a Jew by birth and reported to be born of a virgin mother, Mary. The religion seems to be essentially monotheistic, although the idea of Trinity found in it sometimes raises doubts whether it is really and strictly to be regarded as a monotheism. Although the Christians claim that their religion has come directly out of the revelations and insights of Jesus, it can hardly be disputed that Christianity owes much for its origin to Judaism. As we have said, Jesus himself was a Jew and he never thought of founding a new religion while he was preaching his own religious ideas. He was only trying to cleanse Judaism of the rubbish which clustered around it in course of time. We have seen that Moses gave the Jews a very pure ethical religion, but later on, as is the case with almost every religion, the Jews brought in many kinds of superstitious ideas, rituals and ceremonies to their religion. Jesus wanted to play only the role of a reformer, but it is the accident of time that his teachings, which sometimes differed importantly from the traditional Jewish beliefs and practices, gave birth to a new religion of which he was begun to be treated as the founder and the prophet. He himself repeatedly asserted that he had come not to destroy (the old faith), but to fulfil the Law and the prophets. He ever regarded him a Jew and wanted to teach people the true Jewish way of life. The Ten Commandments of Moses were respected by him and he kept them in tact only by restating them in the light of his own conception of God as Love. He accepted a kind of Messianic role to restore Jewish faith in God in its true nature. The Old Testament of the Bible is as much as sacred text for the Christians as for the Jews. Only the Christians have also a New Testament incorporating specially the teachings of Jesus. Thus in no case, the Jewish heritage of Christianity can be ignored. Christianity can well be regarded as an extension of Judaism in a more elevated direction. The following two-sentence summary of the commandments as rendered by Jesus is nothing but a more or less repetition of the Jewish Torah – (1) "Thou shalt love the Lord, thy God, with all thy heart, and with all thy soul, and with all thy mind." And (2) "Thou shalt love thy neighbour as thyself."

Jesus is treated variously in Christianity. He is so often regarded by the Christians as the "Son of God". They believe that in Jesus God's word became flesh. (In Judaism and Islam God's word became the Book, but in Christianity God's word became the flesh in the form of Jesus). Then again Jesus is regarded as the true image of God, as his representative, his messiah carrying his (God's) true image to men. Sometimes he is regarded as God and some times as man. He is in a sense taken as God-man. He forms the second person of the Christian Trinity (which comprises the true Christian, at least the true Catholic Divinity). Sometimes he is also taken as the incarnation of God to give people the true divine message. His teachings, therefore, are regarded as the true divine message imparted to man.

By now, it goes without saying that Christianity originated in the teachings of Jesus, but it is to be clearly taken in mind that what at present constitutes the body of

Christian beliefs and practices is not in its entirety the gift of Jesus alone. There have been a host of other saints, mystics and thinkers who have added much to it. At least the impact of St. Paul, who immediately followed Jesus, cannot be ignored. According to many it is Paul, and not Jesus, who should be regarded as the real founder of Christianity. Although Christianity, without doubt, originated in the teachings of Jesus, it took definite shape as a religion at the hands of St. Paul. St. Paul not only propagated the teachings of Jesus with full sense of devotion and honesty, but also added important ideas from his own side. And thus Christianity as it spread may be taken as Christianity of Jesus's teachings combined with Paul's. We shall, however, base our treatment of the religion here mainly on the teachings of Jesus himself, although we will not totally ignore the beliefs and ideas of the important Christian saints who followed Jesus and made Christianity what really it is today by adding much from their own side by way of interpretation, explanation and ramification.

2. Basic features of Christianity as a religion

Despite having its roots in the essential Judaic teachings and also being influenced to some extent by Zoroastrian faith, Christianity has some of its own distinctive features. We are mentioning below some of these important features in bare outlines. The elucidations of the points will come up in due course while we will be dealing with the specific beliefs and practices of the religion in somewhat greater details:

(1) It is a monotheistic religion believing in one and only one God.

(2) God is of the nature of a Person, although not in the ordinary sense of the term 'Personality'. He has consciousness and will and is of the nature of Pure Spirit.

(3) Although God is one, he is an internal trinity, the trinity being – God the father, God the son, and the Holy Spirit. He is three in one.

(4) Jesus, regarded as the son or sometimes the messiah of God, is the founder of the religion. He represents the true image of God on earth.

(5) God has many metaphysical and ethical attributes, but essentially he is of the nature of a loving father.

(6) God is the creator, sustainer and destroyer of the world. He has created the world out of nothing and may destroy it any time according to his sweet will.

(7) Man is created by God in the latter's own image and so potentially man is great. But he has degenerated into sin by misusing the free will granted to him by God. Committing Original Sin by the first man Adam is the root cause of man's suffering. Sin is nothing but disobedience to God.

(8) Nevertheless, God being essentially kind and loving wants man's redemption and it is for this purpose that he sent Jesus on earth to educate people on proper lines. Thus Jesus is the redeemer of man.

(9) True religion consists in nothing but loving God as well as one's fellow beings in utmost sincerity and humility.

(10) Although a sincere moral life of love is sufficient for man's redemption, simple prayer to God without any rituals and sacrifices is also taught in Christianity. Redemption or liberation is ultimately the fruit of God's grace.

(11) Christianity believes in the immortality of soul and therefore it believes in a life after death also. The final day of Judgment, resurrection of the dead on the final day and also allotment of heaven and hell in accordance with the earthly deeds of men are the chief ingredients of Christian eschatology.

(12) Hell is eternal damnation and heaven is the symbol of eternal immortal life in constant followship with God.

(13) Christianity also believes in heavenly angels, both good and bad. Satan is the chief evil angel, the devil, who contributes to the spread of evil by instigating people to sin. Adam's disobedience is also attributed to his instigation.

However, he is not beyond God's control. Satan is also deemed to be the master of hell.

3. God

Christianity believes in the reality of only one supreme God. This God is of the nature of a pure spirit and has got will and consciousness. Thus although Christian God is regarded as having a personality, it is not implied thereby that he is of the nature of an ordinary person. God is unlimited, infinite, omnipotent, omnipresent and omniscient. He is eternal and his existence is necessary. No body can conceive his non-existence. He is without beginning and end. God is the creator and sustainer of this world . He has created the world out of nothing. He lives within it and is also beyond it. In other words, he is both immanent and transcendent. He can also destroy the world at his own will. His nature is mysterious and therefore although he sometimes reveals himself to men in mystic experiences, no body is able to know him fully. God is unlimited and supreme but yet he has limited his power by his own will to grant freedom to human beings. God is all-perfect and all-good, but above all he is infinitely kind and loving. As a matter of fact, Christianity lays utmost emphasis upon God's attribute of kindness and love. In a way, God is identified with love here. It is really this emphasis upon God as Love that distinguishes Christian God from the Judaic one. The idea of God as loving, forgiving and long-suffering was present in Judaism itself and in a way it is nothing new for Christianity. Still it is this identification of God with Love which Jesus so often emphasized that gives the Christian God somewhat a distinctive character. Jewish conception depicted God essentially as powerful and just. He was also sometimes characterised as wrathful and revengeful. Further Jewish God had a contract that he would save the Jews only if they served him. But the Christian God loves his people unconditionally. He is like a loving father who loves his children without any precondition, contract or sense of return: God is now no cause for fear. He is absolutely benevolent and kind and forgives even the worst of sinners if they sincerely repent for their sins. Jesus is regarded as the concrete and living paradigm of God's love. God is the redeemer of his children and it is for this purpose of redemption that he occasionally sends messengers to earth. He finally sent Jesus as his Messiah. Through him God wanted to teach people the right lesson so that they could attain the life eternal and be saved from damnation.

We have said above that St. Paul exerted a great influence on Christian beliefs and ideas. Of course, his teachings were very much the same as those of Jesus, but he sometimes added important ideas from his own side also. Here in connection with the nature of God he seemed reintroducing some of the Jewish traits. Jesus had laid exclusive emphasis upon God's loving nature. But Paul again painted God as just, wrathful, mysterious etc. besides being kind and loving. However, the characteristic fatherly nature of Christian God did not mark any substantive change. it was pointed out that just as sometimes a father is angry with his children and sometimes he also inflicts some amount of pain and suffering for the good of the child, similarly God is also sometimes wrathful and he is just in his dealings with all. Thus in spite of some of the characteristic Jewish traits reintroduced, the essentially fatherly nature of Christian God did not change and it remained his distinguishing character.

Although Christianity is essentially monotheistic believing in only one God, yet sometimes, specially in Catholicism, God is painted as three persons into one. This idea of God as three persons into one is known as the idea of Trinity. The three Persons in one are: God the father, God the son and the Holy Spirit. Jesus is the second person, the son incarnate and the third person is the Holy Spirit, the spirit of Love. The Holy spirit is taken to proceed from the Father and the Son. The Trinity is a mystery, but yet it is for the Catholics a firmly revealed truth and absolutely necessary belief for the membership of the church.

The idea of Trinity, however, sometimes raises doubts in the minds of some about the monotheistic character of Christianity. Prophet Mohammad of Islam criticised Christianity much for its Trinity doctrine. According to him this Trinity really vitiates the unitary character of God and Christianity no longer remains a monotheism. But the Christians forcefully maintain that despite Trinity, God remains, on the whole, a unity and the monotheistic character of Christianity is not in the least disturbed. The Athanasian creed very emphatically maintains. ". . . the Catholic faith is thus : We worship one God in Trinity, and Trinity in unity, neither confounding the persons for dividing the substance. For there is one Person of the Father, another of the Son, another of the Holy Ghost. But the Godhead of the Father, of the Son and of the Holy Ghost is all one : the Glory co-equal, the Majesty co-eternal. Such as the Father is, such is the Son, and such is the Holy Ghost. The Father uncreated, the Son uncreated and the Holy Ghost uncreated. The Father incomprehensible, the Son incomprehensible and the Holy Ghost incomprehensible. The Father eternal, the Son eternal and the Holy Ghost eternal. And yet they are not three eternals, but one Eternal. . . . So the Father is God, the Son is God and the Holy Ghost is God; and yet they are not three gods, but one God. . . .

And in this Trinity, none is before or after the other; none is greater or less than another; but the three persons are co-eternal together, and co-equal; so that in all things the Unity in Trinity, and the Trinity in Unity is to be worshipped. He, therefore that will be saved must thus think of the Trinity."

4. World

The world is quite definitely and unequivocally God's creation. God created the world *ex nihilo*, out of nothing.

As to the mode of creation, Christianity believes in the story of Genesis as related in the Old Testament of the Bible. Every thing was created by God in six days. God willed that something be created and it was created. God willed that there be light and there was light. In the beginning God created the heavens and the earth. Everything else was gradually created in six days and on the seventh day he signalised the end of the process of creation and resorted to rest. Towards the end of creation, that is, on the sixth day, God created man. The world is not only created by God but is also sustained and maintained by Him. The world is absolutely dependent upon God for its maintenance. If the sustaining power of God could be withheld, the world with all its creatures would have simply ceased to be. Nevertheless, the world is real. It is a real effect made out of nothingness. Because the world has been created by God, who is all good and loving, it is full of intrinsic goodness. "And God saw the things that he had made, and they were very good."[1] The world is, however, not eternal. It is contingent. It is created in time and it may end at any time according to God's will. Thus the world cannot be regarded as co-eternal with God. However, the world as a real contingent effect is a real acting ground for people. It is neither to be given up nor despised.

We have seen above that the world according to Christianity is a real creation of God rendered at a definite point of time out of nothingness. But here two main difficulties arise: (1) How could the world be made *ex nihilo?* Nothing can come out of nothingness. (2) If the world did not exist co-eternally with God and He created it at a particular point of time, it means that time pre-existed creation. If not, then how could the world be said to have been created in time? Christian saint philosophers like

1. Genesis, 1:31.

Augustine, Aquinas etc. have really taken up these questions and have tried to answer them in the light of the Christian faith. God is omnipotent and mysterious. He can do any and everything and his ways are not fully open to human knowledge and scrutiny. Hence although creating something out of nothing may look impossible or obscure from the ordinary point of view, it is neither impossible nor absurd in the case of God. God is not bound by the laws of ordinary logic. The limit of our thought is not the limit of God's way of working. As to the problem regarding the creation of the world in time, it is pointed out by Christian saints that time did not pre-exist creation, rather both were created by God simultaneously. We can best explain this point here by quoting St. Augustine himself from his *The City of God*: "And if the sacred and infallible scriptures say that in the beginning God created the heavens and the earth, in order that it may be understood that He had made nothing previously – for if He had made anything before the rest, this thing would rather be said to have been made in the beginning – then assuredly the world was made, not in time, but simultaneously with time. For that which is made in time is made both after and before sometime – after that which is past, before that which is future. But none could then be past, for there was no creature by whose movements its duration could be measured. But simultaneously with time the world was made, if in the world's creation change and motion were created, as seems evident from the order of the first six or seven days. For in these days the morning and evening are counted, until, on the sixth day, all things which God then made were finished, and on the seventh the rest of God was mysteriously and sublimely signalised."[2]

2. St. Augustine, *The City of God*, XI, 4-6.

5. Man

According to the Genesis, God created man in his own image on the final day of creation. Both these points – God creating man on the *final* day and God creating man in his *own* image – are significant in so far as the status of man is concerned. Man's creation on the final day makes him the final fruit of creation. In other words, he is to be taken as the greatest of all the creatures on earth. Then God creating man in his own image signifies God's special preference for man. God chooses man to be his fellow partner in the fulfilment of his final purpose of the establishment of the kingdom of good all over the world. God gave everything to man – insight, intelligence, sensitivity and all other such qualities. But above all he chose man to stand in a special relationship with himself to be his fellow partner in the creation of values on earth. God made man essentially a spiritual being as himself. Besides the perishable body that man outwardly has as his being, he has got a soul which is immortal. Death of the body is not the death of the soul. It is immortal. However, human soul is finite and in no case it is able to attain the Divine infinitude. By nature man is capable of every thing, but he can never attain God's perfection. Moreover, man being everything that he is, is nevertheless God's creature and is fully dependent upon him. Both these aspects of man's nature – his potential greatness and at the same time his utter dependence upon God – have been well highlighted by A.C. Bouquet in his following lines: "Christians are committed officially to a very high belief in the potential greatness of man. He is a little lower than God (Ps. viii). He is made in the image of God (Gen.i). The spirit of man is the candle of the Lord (Proverb 27). Yet Christians are equally committed to the belief in man's utter need of God. Man needs God. Man cannot be all that he ought to be, or fulfil his grand possibilities, if he tries, as he so often does, to be the artist of his own social and individual life – 'on his own', so to speak – apart from the life of God."[3]

He has to follow God's path of love and kindness, otherwise he will be astraying from the path of God and will be regarded as a sinner. God as a benevolent father has granted free will to man – both the freedom to choose and freedom to act – and it is upto man to utilise his freedom either for the cause of good or for that of evil. Obeying the will of God is working for the good and disobeying him is committing sin. Adam, the first man or the original forefather or man, committed Original Sin by disobeying God. He, therefore, lost the grace of God and made his entire descendancy victim of his Original Sin. Adam's sin, the Original Sin, is sin for every man and that sin is the main cause of human suffering. It is due to this sin that man was sent to the world to suffer. However, God as the loving father promised man his redemption from suffering and it is to fulfil this promise that he sent Jesus on earth to teach people the right path. By following the teachings of Jesus, therefore, man can get rid of suffering. Even by Adam's fall man has not lost his intrinsic nature completely. He has simply weakened it and he is fully capable of regaining his high position by God's grace. For that what is necessary is that, man should love God with all his heart and with all his mind and he should also love his fellow beings. Love is the basic lesson that Christianity teaches men. It is by love and love alone that man can attain his redemption, *i.e.*, his original nature.

6. Evil and suffering

Christian God being essentially kind and loving, no less than a loving father, the existence of suffering in the world poses a very serious challenge to Christianity. When God loves

---

3. A.C. Bouquet, *op. cit.* p. 257. (1961 edition).

his creatures as a father loves his children and he is also all-powerful, why so much of evil and suffering in the world? Christianity first seems trying to meet the challenge by holding Satan, the Devil, to be responsible for evil. But obviously, this plea cannot hold very sound, because the natural question will be, whether Satan is well under God's control or independent. If the second alternative is taken to be the answer, God certainly is saved from the responsibility of evil, but he no longer remains all-powerful. In the Old Testament, Satan appears not as an independent embodiment of evil, but as a member of the heavenly court whose job is to provoke people towards evil and inflict suffering on them so as to test the sincerity and depth of their faith in God. We have thus found that in Judaism evil and suffering are taken as tests employed from the side of God for measuring the sincerity of faith. But later on Satan seems playing a different role, the role of a rebel, and he enters the garden of Eden to mislead Adam to the disobedience of God which proves to be the cause of all human suffering. Here two factors in a combined fashion become responsible for evil – the devilish provocation of Satan and the utter misuse of the free will granted to Adam. But here again the situation is well under God's control. Accounting for evil through Satan and human free will does not imply that God has no control over the situation. Hence so far Christianity tries to cut both ways – shirks from making God directly responsible for evil and is yet concerned about maintaining his all-powerfulness. Thus at this stage it takes another plea to explain evil. Although Satan's devilish nature is at the root of man's suffering it is not beyond God's control. This means that God himself allows evil to exist as a mark and means of discipline. "You must endure it as a discipline: God is treating you as sons. Can anyone be a son, who is not disciplined by his father?"[4]

4. Hebrews, 12:3.

Thus at this stage Christianity seems to adopt an instrumental view of suffering. Suffering, therefore, is not to be complained against, rather it is to be silently endured as a mark of God's stick of discipline. In this solution of the problem of evil, there is obviously both a theoretical and a practical appeal. Theoretically, suffering has some good purpose behind it and on the practical level it is to be patiently endured. Christ himself suffered on the Cross. A Christian should learn from this suffering of Jesus on the Cross. Jesus had to suffer but ultimately he was triumphant. The triumph is well symbolised in the resurrection of Christ. As crucification was an event, so was resurrection. And so a Christian's practical response to suffering must be based on an outlook towards these two events. The imitation of Christ involves enduring suffering for the sake of good.

The practical value of suffering has been understood in Christianity in a different manner also. Evil has proved a boon in disguise in as much as it rendered God make a promise of the redemption of his children through Christ. It was because human beings had to suffer due to the Original Sin of Adam, that God felt the need of sending his messiah to earth to teach people the right lesson so as to achieve redemption. Thus it is due to the presence of suffering that Christ had to come amongst the people. Evil has, therefore, proved to be an occasion for the good. It has proved to be good in disguise. This has been the characteristic Augustinian approach to evil in Christianity. John Hick in his book *Evil and God of Love* has outlined two different but related approaches to the problem of evil as found in Christianity. The one he calls the Irenaen approach (It is so called because first of all it was formulated by Irenaeus) and the other Augustenian approach. According to the first, evil is taken as an instrument of moral development or moral discipline. According to the second, evil is not opposed to good, it is simply the privation of good. In other words, it is good in disguise. It has appeared due to the human misuse of free will as symbolised in the Original Sin of Adam. God was aware of the misuse of free will, but he allowed it, because it was still under his control and because it was better in his thinking to bring good out of evil than to exclude evil outright from existence. This path had a greater moral value and this is why God adopted it. That the situation is well under God's control is demonstrated in the work of Christ which effectively met and redeemed the situation.

Thus in a nutshell, the Christian approach to suffering makes Satan on the one hand and man himself on the other to be directly responsible for evil, but God has allowed it without interference with a moral purpose of the ultimate good of man.

7. Life after death

As the soul in man is immortal, death is not the total and final end of man. There is an after-life too, the main ingredients of which are – the Day of Judgment, Resurrection of the Dead and the assignment of Heaven or Hell to people in accordance with their good or bad deeds on earth. Thus the after-life account of Christianity is not basically different from that of Judaism or Islam or even of Zoroastrianism to a great extent. However, the details are not identical. As is already said above, when the body of man is destroyed with death, the soul endures. When the world comes to its final end, there is resurrection of the dead. In this resurrection, souls of all men are reunited with their bodies and men again come in the fullness of their nature. When exactly this end of the world and the consequential resurrection will take place is known to God and God alone. It depends upon his will. But the Scripture indicates that the final end will be preceded by Christ's rearrival as the judge of all men, the universal preaching of the Gospel by him, the total conversion of the Jews and the extra-ordinary disturbances in nature. The end of the world will mark the arrival of the final day of judgment. On this day of judgment all souls united with their bodies will be brought before God for the final assessment of the value of their deeds done by them during their earthly lives. Those whose deeds have been in accordance with the teachings of Jesus are sent to heaven and those who have been unrighteous and sinful are sent to hell. Hell is a place or state of eternal punishment and eternal separation from God, while heaven is a state or place of eternal happiness through communion with God. It is a state of perfect and unceasing joy. Describing the joy of heaven, it has been said, "Eye hath not seen, nor ear heard, neither hath it entered into the heart of men, what things God has prepared for them that love Him."

Christianity seems alive regarding a question that may naturally arise in the wake of the eschatology outlined above: what happens to the individual soul in the intermediary period, *i.e.*, during the period between the death of an individual and the final day of judgment? Where does the soul lie during this period? To answer this question, Christianity seems to believe in two kinds of judgment – the particular judgment and the universal judgment. The universal judgment is the final judgment made at the end of the world which is applicable to all. But before this final or universal judgment, there is a particular judgment, i.e., judgment in case of a particular individual immediately after his physical death. There is the idea that if a person dies in the love of God and his fellow-beings, he is taken as unstained and is "straightway received into heaven." And again the soul of a man who has lived a sinful life quite in disobedience of God's will straightway goes down to hell. Those souls which although have been stained by sins, but have shown sincere repentence and have undergone penance etc. are first sent to the Purgatory for purification and thence to heaven. Purgatory is deemed in Christianity as a place (or a state) in which the souls of those who have been stained by sin but have died in repentence are detained for purging or cleansing, so that they may be rendered fit for the company of God. After this act of purging they are sent to heaven.

8. Human destiny

'Salvation", 'Immortality', 'Life Eternal', and 'Redemption' are the words so often used in Christianity to denote the nature of man's ultimate destiny. To understand, therefore, what man's ultimate destiny is, we have to understand what any or all of these words actually mean. The two words 'Salvation' and 'Redemption' have got a more negative overtone about them than an affirmative one. They carry with them a sense of getting rid of something or 'being free from' something. The two remaining words 'Life Eternal' and 'Immortality' speak more of the attainment of a positive status than getting rid of something. But the Christian idea of ultimate destiny is to be understood by a combination of both the negative and positive overtones of the words referred to above. Man's ultimate destiny consists in getting rid of his present status and attaining to a status which may be called a status of life eternal or that of immortality. Our present status is one of suffering. This mainly consists in our alienation from God and falling on to earth in a state of punishment from God for disobedience. This is all symbolised in Christianity in the Fall of Adam, the first man. Our redemption or salvation, therefore, lies in getting rid of the suffering. For that, man will have to follow the path of Christ, because he was sent by the loving God to earth for teaching people the right ways to redemption. Christ has been the real redeemer of people. But does redemption consist in merely getting rid of suffering or does it require redemption from this world too? In a sense redemption from suffering implies redemption from world because it was as a mark of punishment that Adam was sent by God to the world. And it is because of this that he and his descendants had to suffer. Release from suffering, therefore, naturally consists in release from the world. Man's real salvation consists in the revival of his original status, his spiritual abode in the Eden Garden in nearness to God. Eternal life or immortality actually means in Christianity eternal fellowship or communion with God. In other words, it consists in achieving the membership of the kingdom of God. But what does this 'Kingdom of God' mean? Where is it situated? Is it to be here in this world itself or in a world beyond it? Christian belief in the reality of heaven and hell leads one to believe that the kingdom of God really lies in heaven, a realm beyond this world. And, therefore, salvation or eternal life really consists in attaining the membership of heaven. It is only in heaven that one is to attain eternal nearness to God.

But, nevertheless, this point regarding the real nature of redemption and eternal life seems a bit confused and controversial in Christianity. In early Christianity, it seems undoubted that redemption and release meant not only getting rid of suffering but of world itself. Jesus himself and some of his followers repeatedly maintained that the end of the world was very near and that after the end of this world kingdom of God would arise. Even many modern scholars take redemption as an escape from this world and an attainment of the life of heaven. As A.G. Hogg very clearly puts the matter in his work *Redemption from this World*, "Too commonly redemption means for us only redemption from sin, or even only redemption from punishment, whereas by those who first experienced redemption through Christ it was conceived of as redemption from the many sided tyranny of an evil world-order, of which guilt and moral importance were only factors, although doubtless the most outstanding and momentous factors."[5] Or again as Sydney Cave puts it in

5. A.G. Hogg, *Redemption from the World*, Edinburgh 1922, p. 13.

his book *Redemption, Hindu* and *Christian*, "The consummation of the kingdom would not come by the gradual education of the race, nor even by the progressive influence of the Church. It would come by the power of God. The kingdom was the heavenly realm in which men might share already the life which is eternal and triumphant. To be a member of the kingdom is thus already to be redeemed from the world."[6] But again the Protestant Christian theology does not take redemption from the world as a necessary ingredient of Eternal Life. Kingdom of God or Heaven will dawn upon this world itself and one need not escape from this world. The only need is to follow the path of Christ and Life Eternal will dawn upon the earth itself. Even Jesus said, they point out, that "the Kingdom of Heaven lies within you." It is not far off. It is here in this world itself. The only way to bring it about here in this world is to open the doors of love that lies closed within every man's heart. In any case, in Life Eternal man is to attain a permanent communion with God by being free from all kinds of sins and sufferings. The soul is to stand immortal in this sate of fellowship with God.

Again, by attaining eternal life, man attains to his original spiritual perfection. Nevertheless, man ever remains finite and in no case becomes infinite like God. He neither becomes one with God nor does he attain a likeness with God. Man is always man in comparison with God. But then he is free from all sin and suffering and enjoys perfect peace and joy in fellowship with God. This is called eternal or immortal life.

We have said earlier that man's soul is immortal. Therefore, to some it may sound odd that attaining immortality is the destiny of man's life. When the soul is immortal by its nature, what can attaining immortality then

---

6. Sydney Cave, *Redemption, Hindu and Christian*, Oxford, 1919, p. 231.

mean? Here it should be understood clearly that man's soul is immortal in the sense that it does not perish with the body. But it is a gift equally shared by every body – the virtuous and the sinner alike. But the immortality to attain is not a talismanic gift, as Pringle-Pattison would say, equally shared by everybody; it is a prize to be won by one's own moral efforts. This immortality is eternal life spent in constant communion with God. And this is achieved by the virtuous alone. However, life eternal is ultimately achieved only by the grace of God. It is true that understood from the human side, eternal life is to be achieved by anyone only if he lives a life of sincere love for God as well as for his fellow beings, but in the ultimate analysis it is a fruit of God's grace. Without the grace of God, salvation is never possible. This grace, of course, has to be won by one's efforts, it is not automatic. Nevertheless, it is necessary for salvation.

9. Ethics and prayer etc.

Christianity, as we must have seen by now, is a religion of redemption from a life of sin and suffering. Jesus Christ, the founder of the religion is regarded as the redeemer of man and therefore the true religious path is nothing but to imitate his ways. *Imitatio Christi* is, therefore, the basic Christian principle of religious or moral life. What does, after all, imitation of Christ consist in? It certainly consists in cultivating all the virtues that Christ demonstrated throughout his life. And Christ's life is certainly the paradigm of a life of deep love, humility and suffering. Thus love, humility and suffering for the sake of others as well as for the sake of soul instead of flesh are the basic moral virtues that Christianity teaches to its followers. The suffering of Christ on the Cross is really a symbol of suffering for the sake of spirit. The cross symbolises the crucification of the flesh for the sake of the spirit. The senses are to be controlled and the spirit or soul within is to be adored. Further, the life of Jesus is a burning example of a life of extreme love and humility. Thus Christianity essentially teaches a life of love and humility. This is really the core of its ethical teaching. 'Love thy neighbour as thyself' and 'Turn to him your right cheek who slaps on your left one' are the two Christian ethical teachings which speak for its most earnest concern with the virtues of love and humility. Even hatred is to be met not with hatred but with love. Love is the essential nature of God himself and therefore it is the greatest virtue to be followed by every Christian in his relationship to both God and man.

When, however, we enter into somewhat greater details of Christian ethical teaching, we find a host of other allied virtues and duties prescribed in it. First of all, it adopts the famous Ten Commandments of the Jewish tradition in somewhat a modified or 'Christianised' form, as it is called, as the basis of its ethical discipline. The first four, as we have seen in connection with Judaism, refer to one's duties towards God and the rest towards members of the family or society. The last five are negative in nature being really prohibitions from murder, adultery, stealing, false witness and covetousness. They are very much like the Hindu virtues of *Ahimsā*, *Brahamcharya*, *Asteya*, *Satya* and *Aparigraha*. These negative injunctions have been understood in Christianity in somewhat positive terms as virtues of respect for life, honour and property, veracity and contentment. Besides, being influenced by Greek sources, virtues such as justice, charity, temperance, wisdom, fortitude etc. are also emphasised in Christianity. St. Paul has listed the following nine virtues to be followed by a Christian as a mark of his duties towards God, other men of the society and to himself: Love, Joy, and peace in relation to God; patience, kindness and goodness in relation to others; and faithfulness, gentleness, and self-control in relation to oneself. Of course, the classification does not seem to be very scientific and virtues listed under one head might more reasonably be put under another head. For example, the virtue of faithfulness might well fit more in relation to God than in relation to oneself. However, we are not at present concerned much with such comments of logical propriety of classification etc. We are mainly concerned with the moral virtues and duties more often and essentially prescribed in Christianity. And we can well see that the most emphasized virtues are those of love, kindness, humility and self-control.

Besides a primarily ethical life of love that is essentially required of every Christian, Christianity also prescribes and believes in the efficacy of prayers to God in so far as man's redemption is concerned. God's grace is essential in Christianity for salvation of man and for winning the grace of the Almighty, prayers are important. Prayers may be individual or congregational. They are more often observed in Churches. Congregational prayers are mostly observed on Sunday. Christian Churches are devoid of any images or idols. They are simply taken as sacred places where people congregate for prayers to God. Christian prayers are petitionery as well as of other natures, such as those of adoration, confession, meditation, acts of will and surrender etc. Even such prayers which may be regarded as petitionary are not for asking petty things of material nature. They are petitions asking for strength so as to lead a righteous life. As an example of such a petitionary prayer, we may cite the following –

> Father, hear the prayer we offer:
> Not for ease that prayer shall be,
> But for strength that we may ever
> Live our lives courageously.

10. Principal sects

Broadly speaking, Christians are divided into two sects – Catholics and the Protestants. In a general way it can be said that the former represent the traditionalists and the latter reformists. The two are divided mainly on the question of the authority of the Church. The former believe that the Church is the representive of God on earth, that God reveals his truth through it. The sacraments of the Church, therefore, are a must for the redemption of men and the Pope (as well as the clergies) possesses a divine authority. The latter hold that man can directly establish his relation to God, that man is directly responsible to God and the mediation of Church is not needed for him. Bible is the only sure source of Christian faith and practice and only the authority of the Bible is to be accepted. Jesus can be regarded as the sole representative and messiah of God on earth and his power is not vested in the Pope and the priests. The clergies have assumed an unauthorised domination over people. It must be wiped out. The latter is thus a reform movement, a protest against the false domination of the Church and its priests over people. The "priesthood of all believers" is to be accepted within the Church and only a few selected are not to be regarded as divinely empowered masters. Man is not to be subordinated to the power of any human institution. He has to depend upon the Bible alone to guide and direct him as the mediating agency of God's authority and that he has to put his faith in Jesus Christ whom God sent to earth for saving people. There is no third authority. Thus the protestants speak of two things as the guiding principles of a Christian – Justification by faith and the Infallibility of the Scriptures as giving the rules of life. Man is to renounce trust in any external authority and he is to trust Christ alone.

In a wider sense, any one who is validly baptized and is a member of the Holy Catholic Church is known as a Catholic. But Catholic Church is divided into Roman Catholic and Eastern Orthodoxy. Sometimes the word 'Catholic' is claimed to be exclusively used for a member of the Roman Catholic Church. However, the schism between the two Churches is there and both are Catholic, of course, with certain differences in their faiths and practices. Some of the important points in which the Eastern Churches differ from the Roman Catholic ones are that the former in opposition to the latter do not accept such doctrines as the bodily ascent of Mary, the purgatory, the celibacy of all priests, the infallibility of the Roman Pope and so on. There is an interesting controversy between the two churches on the question whether the Holy spirit proceeded from the 'Father and the Son' or from the 'Father through the Son'. The Eastern Orthodox Church seems to accept the former. The following seven sacraments are recognised and observed by both the groups – Baptism (by triple immersion in infancy), Confirmation, Penance or Confession, the Eucharist (A sacrament of eating the body and the blood of Christ transubstantiated in bread and wine by priestly blessing), Marriage, Holy orders and Anointing the sick. In the last point there is some amount of difference between the two groups. While the Roman Catholics observe it only as the extreme function (*i.e.*, anointing the sick at the point of death), the Eastern Catholics take it as their religious duty to anoint the sick even at the stage of mere sickness prior to death.

Amongst the Protestants also, there are various groups or sects: there are Lutherians, Calvinists, Presbytarians, Anglicans, Congregationalists and so on. Of these, the first two are associated with the names of the two great Protestant Reformists – Luther and Calvin. As a matter of fact, it is Luther who gave the Protestant Reformation a serious and explicit orientation, although it cannot be denied that protests against the Roman Church had started even before him. Luther's protests against the Church and its priesthood can very well be seen in his following lines – "It has been devised that the Pope, Bishops, priests and monks are called the Spiritual Estate: princes, lords, artificers and peasants, are the Temporal Estate; which is a very fine, hypocritical device. But let no one be made afraid by it;

and that for this reason; that all Christians are truly of the Spiritual Estate, and there is no difference among them, save of office alone."[7] Instead of the supremacy of the church and its priests, Luther preached the supremacy of the Bible and raised a kind of "Back to the Bible" slogan. He called on each individual to read the Word of God for himself and make his path of redemption self-guided. He proclaimed a "universal priesthood of all believers, instead of the clergies as a special class."

Calvin, although protesting against the mediacy of the Church between man and God laid greater emphasis upon the grace and gift of God, instead of individual freedom to choose one's own path in the light of Biblical teachings. In consequence, Calvinism seemed lapsing into a kind of predestination theory in which everything including the individual faith, his chances of being saved etc. was a matter of God's grace. It is held by Calvinism that God from the very beginning has chosen a certain number of his creatures out of his grace and love to be redeemed, while others are destined to damnation. As a matter of fact, mankind due to the Original Sin are totally debased and do not deserve redemption. But for some there is hope. God out of his grace has been pleased to elect some for eternal life. Those who do good works do not do so out of their own independent will so that they may be saved, rather they do good works because they are already saved by God's grace. The supremacy that the church claims with all its priests is a gross mistake of human imperfection and this claim must be regarded as sinful. Only the supremacy of God is to be granted and it is his grace which can save man. In bestowing this saving grace God does not make any distinction between those whom he chooses. We can thus see that Calvinism is protestant in its own peculiar way. In

---

7. Martin Luther, *First Principles of the Reformation* (London: 1883), p. 21.

one sense, it is worse than Roman Catholicism, because unlike the latter it takes away the freedom of man totally. This is why many Calvinists now tend to stress the need for personal effort in shaping human destiny.

Presbyterianism is a branch of Calvinism. Calvin really propounded a theocracy in which God was everything and man was simply to obey his dictates. Yet decisions in many matters had to be taken by men and this job was given to elders (presbyters) who were supposed to be maturer. Those who believed in a system of governing and teaching functions by the presbyters were known as Presbyterians. However, there is no hierarchy like that of Roman Catholic Church in Presbyterianism. All presbyters are taken to be of equal rank and they are not seen as having divine authority or powers.

Anglicanism represents the form of Protestantism that flourishes specifically in England. It seems to provide a middle course between Roman Catholicism and extremer sorts of Protestantism. It claims to be Catholic and Reformed both at the same time. The Holy Scripture together with the Book of Common Prayer is the final authority in Anglicanism. The form of Christianity that is found in the Church of England since Reformation is taken as representative of Anglicanism, although it is claimed by the Catholics that the Church of England has ever represented the type of Christianity that has existed in England from the early times. But if one remembers the fact that Reformation came in England in its outstanding form with Henry VIII who in protest against the Roman Catholic Church declared that the Bishop of Rome had no jurisdiction over the Church of England and that the Church of England would have its own Thirty-nine Articles of religion and faith, one may see that the Church of England since Reformation is a representative of protestant movement, of course, not of its extremer form.

Congregationalism is taken to have been founded by Robert Browne between 1578 and 1586. He developed the view that religion was a matter of individual conscience and was not to be enforced by political action. In this he was opposed to both the Presbyterians and the Church of England, who, whatever, their differences, were agreed on the matter that it was the duty of the state to enforce religion. Congregationalists were therefore primarily and preeminently independents. They were really called Independents at an earlier stage and it was only later on that they were begun to be called Congregationalists. Their fundamental principle is that, each Church or Congregation stands directly under the authority of Jesus Christ and there is no human master of the Church to whom it may be responsible. Every Church is self-governing and entirely voluntary religious community which has to make its own rules in all religious matters. They, therefore, are the favourites of Free Churches in which the Bible is the only rule of faith.

Besides the above there are many more groupings and regroupings within modern Christianity such as those of the Methodists, of the Unitarians and so on, but we will not take up a description of all of them here.

8

Islam

1. Introductory

Islam is a prophetic religion of a comparatively late origin. It has its origin in the teachings of prophet Mohammad, who is taken by its followers as the messenger (*Rasul*) of God (Allah). Islam does not disbelieve in the reality and authenticity of other prophets such as Abraham, Moses and Jesus, but Mohammad is taken as the last and the mightiest. His teachings are regarded as final and they are to be observed and followed by all. Although Islam claims to be an independent religion coming directly out of the revelatory experiences of prophet Mohammad, traces of Zoroastrian, Judaic and Christian influences are obvious on it. Many say that Islam is nothing but Judaism added with a missionary zeal. Its ethics is treated as a practical application of the Sermon on the Mount. We do not think that these observations are to be taken as literally true, but this much seems obviously certain that the impact of Judaism on Islam is tremendous. And this is not strange, because Islam shares a common Semitic origin with Judaism and Christianity. We will see that it has striking similarities with these religions in matters of the conception of God, eschatology and the ideas of heaven and hell. Nevertheless, it puts on a distinctive character of its own by virtue of the distinctive way of life that it teaches to its followers in the form of a rigorous discipline of daily life.

Mohammad was born in Arabia in the year 570 AD. At that time Arabia was a land of polytheism and many kinds of ritualism and idolatory were present there. Against these, Mohammad preached a religion of strict monotheism and a life of rigorous discipline devoid of any ritualism or idolatory. Thus the religion of Mohammad came to Arabia in the form of a reformation of prevalent religious beliefs and practices. In this its role may be compared to that of some other religions such as Buddhism and Christianity. For some time after birth, Mohammad used to live like an ordinary man. He had a wife named Khadijah and also children. But at the age of forty he was called on to a divine revelation made to him through God's angel Gabriel. As a matter of fact, it was even from before this revelation that signs of abnormal spiritual genius were visible in Mohammad. It was so often that he retired to caves and mountain for prayer and meditation. He had become fond of solitude. In the revelation through Gabriel, Mohammad got a call from God for prophecy. The voice that Mohammad heard in this revelation is reported to be the following – 'O Mohammad, Thou art the Apostle of God and I am Gabriel.' Then Gabriel asked Mohammad to recite the following:

"Recite: In the Name of thy Lord who created,
Created man from clots of bloods,
Recite! Thy Lord is the most beneficent,
Who taught by the Pen,
Taught that which they knew not unto men."

Mohammad recited it and Gabriel departed. But after this vision, Mohammad was filled with terror. It is when Khadijah consoled him and Gabriel again appeared to remind him that he was the Prophet of God that Mohammad came to senses. In the first instance when Mohammad began propagating his message, there were very few as his followers. Perhaps the first to believe in his message was his wife Khadijah herself. But later on when

Abu Bakr, the first Caliph, joined the movement started by Mohammad, it was greatly strengthened. Then it spread swiftly by political patronage and military conquests. After making zealous personal efforts to propagate his message through political assistance and military conquests, Mohammad died in 632 AD.

Islam is said to be the religion of the Book. All the basic principles of Islam as a religion are contained in one book called 'Quran' or sometimes' Koran'. Quran is said to be the word of God revealed to Mohammad through Gabriel. The word 'Quran' comes from a root which means 'Recite'. It is thus a recital given by the prophet Mohammad to his followers who wrote it. Officially, Quran in Islam is regarded as eternal, the uncreated eternal word of Allah. Mohammad got it through Gabriel and recited to his followers. Thus Quran is the sacred revelatory text of Islam which, being divided in 114 chapters (Surahs), contains in verses all the basic principles of the religion. Quran is supplemented by another less important Islamic text, the *Hadith*, which is comprised of the sayings *(Ahadis)* and practices *(Sunna)* of prophet Mohammad and his companions.

2. Basic features of Islam as a religion

In spite of its being influenced by Judaism, Islam has got certain distinctive features of its own. We are giving below some of the important features of this religion in bare outlines. Details will follow at appropriate places.

(1) Islam believes in one and only one God, called 'Allah'. It is, therefore, out and out a monotheistic religion.

(2) It believes in the reality and authenticity of prophets who are regarded as carrying the message of God to people. It admits that there have been prophets like Noah, Abraham, Moses and Jesus even before Mohammad, but Mohammad is the last, the greatest and the mightiest amongst prophets and his message is to be respected by all.

(3) It believes in the sacredness and authoritativeness of

many scriptures such as the Torah of the Jews, the Gospel of Jesus, etc., but it takes Quran as the greatest and the most sacred. As we have said above, it is the Book on which the entire structure of Islam in its fundamentals is based.

(4) It believes in the existence of angels and spirits, both of good and evil dispositions. Angels of good disposition always stand at God's call in heaven to carry out his orders. There is no distinction of sex amongst the angels, as they are all spiritual. They maintain a record of man's conduct for the last judgment. On the Day of Judgment the angels bring people from their graves to God for final judgment. Besides good angels, Islam also believes in one fallen angel Iblis and his companions. Iblis is the ruler of the hell. Besides angels, Islam also believes in good and bad jins.

(5) Islam believes in a life after death comprising of the resurrection of the dead on the Day of Judgment and retribution of reward and punishment by God in the form of membership of heaven and hell. Its eschatology is very well-defined and graphically described.

(6) Heaven and hell are regarded by it as permanent abodes of the righteous and the evil doers respectively after their physical death.

(7) It is out and out a legalistic religion providing its followers with definite codes of ethical, religious and other individual and social conduct.

(8) It is totally opposed to polytheism, ritualism, idolatory and priesthood. As a matter of fact, it came to be preached against these vices which were prevalent at the time of Mohammad in Arabia.

(9) It believes in the absolute decree of God and therefore fatalism and predestination seem to be the primary overtones of Islamic faith. Nevertheless, free will and human responsibility are not absolutely denied.

(10) It teaches an ethics of perfect purity, service of humanity and brotherhood of man.

(11) It also seems to preach a holy war *(Jihad)* against all those who are unbelievers. *Jihad* is also interpreted as exerting for the cause of religion.

(12) Amongst many ethical and religious duties as prescribed by Islam, absolute submission *(Islam)* to God in perfect piety is regarded as man's primary duty.

3. God

As we have said above, Islam is strictly a monotheistic religion. It believes in one and only God having no place for any other. It is so much conscious of and emphatic about its monotheistic character that the Quran reminds us surah after surah that there is no God except one called' Allah'. It is to keep this basic truth always in the mind of every Muslim that Islam makes it a basic duty for every Muslim to repeat the following words before every prayer, "There is no God but Allah, and Mohammad is His Prophet *(La ilaha ila' llahu, Muhammad resulu' llah)* ". Also the Imam or the Mullah with a view to remind every Muslim of the basic monotheistic character of his religion cries every morning and evening from the top of the mosque, " *Allahu Akbar, La ilaha illa' llahu, Muhammad rasulu' llah* (God is great, there is no God but Allah, Mohammad is the Prophet of God)." Again to emphasize the strict unity or oneness of God Christian Trinity is forcefully rejected by Islam and the various Arabic gods and goddesses are treated ridiculously. It is said in the Quran that Allah alone is the creator of everything. The false gods have created nothing, but are themselves created. (Surah 25) .They "will not create even a fly, even if they join together to do it." (Surah 22).

It is clear from the above that God, as the supreme reality, is the lone creator of everything. Again, he is not only the creator but also the sustainer and destroyer of everything. He sustains and maintains everything and also destroys the entire world whenever he so likes. The world is entirely dependent on God. He is all-powerful, omnipotent. As a matter of fact, the all-powerfulness or almightiness of God is very much emphasized in Islam and this is taken as an example of Judaic influence on it. The very name 'Allah', which is a short form of 'Al llah', means' 'The strong', 'The mighty', 'The powerful'. Thus it is clear from the very name given to God that his all-powerfulness is much emphasized in Islam. Divine will is regarded as absolute and perfectly arbitrary. It is bound by no law and can change in any way. His ways are totally inscrutable and mysterious. In this sense God is absolutely transcendent. In all, God appears in Islam as an all-powerful master and ruler to whom man is simply to submit with a sense of absolute devotion and service. The very word 'Islam' means 'submission'. As A.C. Bouquet remarks in this connection, "Allah is separated from his creatures by an impassable chasm, and the whole duty of man is Islam (submission)"[1] In the words of Kraemer "Allah in Islam becomes white-hot Majesty, white-hot Omnipotence, white-hot uniqueness." The ideal believer is the *'abd'* ('slave'). Thus God in Islam is painted as an absolute Master maintaining a distance from men and requiring from them unqualified service. God is however omnipresent too, in the sense that it is his glory that is manifest everywhere and everything gets sustenence from him. God is so often characterised in Quran as all-hearing, all-knowing, all-glorious, all-subtle, all-aware, all-powerful and so on. All sorts of personal qualities are thus given to God in Islam, but no Muslim would ever perhaps refer to him as personal. He is regarded as having will and power, but he has no form or shape. Thus he cannot be regarded as personal in any ordinary sense. He is eternal and unchanging, but yet he is dynamic. This is why he ever brings changes in the world.

Besides having the various metaphysical attributes as mentioned above, God is also regarded as having various

1. A.C. Bouquet, *op. cit.*, p. 272.

ethical attributes such as compassion, mercy, justice etc. These are all influences from Judaism. The very opening surah of Quran characterises. God as compassionate and merciful. He is also described there as the King, the Lord and the Guide. The opening surah runs as follows –

"Praise be to God, Lord of the worlds,
The compassionate, the merciful,
King on the Day of Judgment.
Thee only do we worship, and to thee do we cry for help.

Guide thou us on the straight path,
The path of those to whom thou hast been gracious
With whom thou art not angry, and who go not astray."

In an ethical perspective, God is so often characterised in Quran as all-forgiving, all-compassionate, all-merciful and so on.

Although God is regarded in Islam as absolutely transcendent and mysterious, it is believed therein that God sometimes reveals himself to men through his messengers, speaks to them through his messiahs. God is also regarded as the final judge of all the good and bad deeds of human beings. On the final day of judgment, God performs his role as retributor by rewarding and punishing people for their good and bad deeds.

4. World

The world is the creation of God. Everything in it – the rivers, the mountains, the trees, the animals, the birds and every other thing – has been created by God. The Quran repeatedly reminds man that he is surrounded everywhere by things created by God. Everything in the world speaks of God's glory and power. However, Islam does not seem to accept the Genesis story of creation although like many other Biblical stories the Genesis story of creation is narrated in the Quran. According to it, no one can say how God has created all that we find in the world. We simply know that the heaven and earth are all his creation and it is by him and him alone that all are sustained and maintained. Creation on the whole is a mystery. Islam does not expressly maintain like Judaism and Christianity that the world has been made by God *ex nihilo.* It also does not expressly maintain that God has made the world out of material lying beyond or outside him. It simply says that everything has been made by God. The question of 'how?' is left unanswered, perhaps implying thereby that it is all a mystery.

The world is finite and temporal. It is not co-eternal with God. It has been created in time. But again time did not pre-exist. Both space and time have been created by God himself. The world exists at God's sweet will. Whenever he will like he will destroy it. The world absolutely depends upon God and nothing can happen in it without God's will and knowledge. The world will not stay even for a moment without God's support. His presence can be felt everywhere in the world.

However, the world, according to Islam, is perfectly real and not illusory. It is absolutely dependent upon God, no doubt, but then it is real. Men's future depends upon their action in this world. The world is a place for full moral activity and an attitude of escape from this world seems absolutely absent from Islam. The attitude of Islam may thus be called this-worldly or world-affirming. The world is imperfect and finite, but not evil. In other words, imperfection of the world is not evil, rather it is an occasion for making effort so as to make it perfect. The world is a place of enjoyment also, but, of course, with certain moral bindings. Everything that God has made in this world is for man's enjoyment and benefit, but such an enjoyment must be devoid of indecencies, sin and wrongful activity. Quran declares in this connection, "who dared to forbid man the enjoyment of his things of beauty, of the delicacies of food, of raiment and other good things of God's bounty?" (Surah, 7:31) Again, emphasizing on the rightful and decent enjoyment of the worldly objects, Quran commands the Prophet to teach the following: "Teach that things all belong to this earth to those who are faithful...., Teach that God forbids only indecencies, such of them as are apparent and such as are hidden. He forbids sin and wrongful oppression." (Surah, 7:32-33) Thus Islam teaches moral worldly enjoyment, which may be compared with Hindu teaching of pursuing *Kāma* and *Artha* within the boundaries delimited by *Dharma*.

5. Man

Clearly, man, with everything else in the world, has been created by God. It is said in the Quran that man has been created by God from "Clots of blood". In the very first revelation that Mohammad is reported to have had through Gabriel, it is mentioned that man was created by God from clots of blood.

> "Recite: In the name of thy Lord who created,
> created man from clots of blood."
>
> (Surah, 96:1)

However, man has been given the status of the deputy of God on earth. In other words, God has created man as his vicegerent so that he may carry out God's purpose of establishing final good on earth. If someone backs out from serving this moral purpose of God, he is punished. If one serves the cause of God, he is loved and rewarded. It is said in the Quran, "It is God who established you as his vicegerents on earth and raised some of you higher than others and of different ranks...... O men who believe, if you turn back from your religion...... if you will not go forth to fight in God's cause, to obey His command, to realise the divine pattern, He will inflict upon you a painful punishment and will choose in your stead a people other than you, who will love Him and whom He will love." (Surah 6:166, 5:55) Thus God wants man to become his partner in his pious mission of eradicating evil from earth. Man, therefore, although absolutely dependent upon God, has still a status of his own. However, one thing that becomes clear from the above quotation is that it is God himself who has granted man his higher or lower status in the society.

The above account shows that in a sense God has granted a special status to man. He is his (God's) co-partner. Not only this, Quran gives man the highest status of all creatures by maintaining that God endowed man with his own spirit, his own light (*noor*). "Blessed is God, the best Creator...... who well-formed man and breathed into him of His own spirit......" (Surah 23:12-14). In creating man with all this, God did not heed even to an objection raised by the angels, who asked him (God),"will you plant therein a being who sheds blood and works for evil, while we perennially worship you and praise you?" God answered to this by saying: "I know better and you do not." (Surah 2:30)

But despite all the above, man is nothing more than a servant of God. His only job is to serve God in humble submission. "Teach and remind men, O Mohammad, – for teaching does benefit the believers – that I have not created man and *jinn* (spiritual beings between angels and men) except to serve Me." (Surah 51:55-56). Man is possessed of no right against God; he has only duties. His duty is only to pray and serve God. Even during prayer he is not to ask for anything from God except his grace and guidance. It is in this sense that Bouquet remarks about Islamic prayer that it is simply reverential and not petitionary. And as an explanation to this he adds, "This is easy of explanation, since the practice of submission to an inscrutable and arbitrary Divine will leave no room for petitionary prayer."[2] Every man's course of action and final

2. A.C. Bouquet, *op.cit.*, p. 281.

destiny are absolutely predetermined by God. The prophet has said, "There is not one amongst you whose place is not written by God whether in Fire or in Paradise." This shows that there is nothing like human free will in Islam. Man proves simply an obedient servant of God whose conscience is suppressed. There is no scope for moral ought in Islam. It is also expressly said in the Quran, "Allah leads astray whom He pleases and guides whom He pleases, and no one knows the hosts of the Lord save Himself." But this position of strict determinism is not accepted by many Islamic scholars. They argue that there is ample scope in Islam for human freedom and refer to Quran itself for the substantiation of their view. The Shias seem to take a middle position regarding the issue. According to them, human will is neither completely free nor completely determined.

Amidst all such controversies we feel that a sympathetic reader of Islam as a religion (and not as a system of philosophy) would not conclude in any unqualified manner that freedom and responsibility are completely derecognised in it. It is, of course, a fact that in practice fatalism has been the dominant note of Muslim piety. But that is perhaps an inevitable result of its overemphasis on God's all-powerfulness. Had the elements of human freedom and responsibility been totally neglected in Islam, there could have been no talk in it of good and bad deeds and of God's rewards and punishments. When the followers asked the Prophet Mohammad, 'O Prophet! since God has appointed our places, may we confide in this and abandon our moral and religious duties?', the Prophet replied, "No, because the righteous will do good works and the wicked will do bad works". This shows that freedom and responsibility are not completely denied. The doctrine of predestination so often emphasised in the Quran must not prevent man from asking God in prayer to lead him on the right path. If he does not do so he will be surely held responsible for his evil inclinations and deeds. However, man is very insignificant before God and will for ever remain so. Even when man will attain nearness to and companionship with God in heaven, he will remain finite and very much limited in comparison with God. He will never be as perfect as God is. Thus it may be seen that in Islam man has got in relation to God a status which is much inferior to that got by man in Hinduism and to a great extent, in Christianity too.

But again, howsoever insignificant man may be in relation to God, he is, according to Islam, a real unit of existence. Although he is absolutely dependent upon God, still he exists as a separate reality. He has his own real existence. Furthermore, man in Islam has got one more significant point in his favour, and that is that he is born innocent, pure, guiltless and sinless. This is an important point which distinguishes Islam from Christianity, in which man is born with a sense of sin or guilt. It also distinguishes Islam from Hinduism in which every man is born with ignorance. In Islam man begins his career as a clean slate, as it were. Of course, man here may be a victim of predestination, as we have seen above, but that is a different matter. Even being born with a predetermined career on earth, at least morally man is stainless at birth. In this connection, Ismail Ragi al Faruqi perhaps rightly remarks, "Morally speaking, against the Augustinian anthropology of sin, guilt and damnation at birth, Islam declares man essentially wholesome and innocent, and judges him only with regard to his deliberate, conscious, free-willed and mature deeds. In contrast to Christianity and Indian religions, both man and this world receive from Islam credentials of innocence."[3]

---

3. *The Great Asian Religions* (Macmillan, London, 1969) p. 313.

6. Evil and suffering

As Islam is strictly monotheistic and repeatedly emphasizes the absoluteness and all-powerfulness of God, it is quite easy to see that whatever is there in the world is God's creation and everything lies within his control and power. "Truly God has power over every single thing", says the Quran. And if so, God is directly responsible for the existence of evil and suffering in the world. How can then he be called all-compassionate and all-merciful? Such questions really do not seem to be raised and answered in Islam. Quran takes suffering in simple and direct terms as it occurs, and not as a theoretical problem. The idea seems to be that man's sole duty towards God is unconditional submission and no doubts are to be raised against his plan of work. His ways are inscrutable, and therefore instead of scrutinising his ways, one is simply to bear them in absolute piety. God is in full control of the world and therefore suffering must be a part of his plan or purpose. It would be simply irreligious and impious to question the merit of God's plan.

However, the Quran seems to decipher at places God's purpose behind allowing the existence of evils in the following two ways, which on the whole present, like Judaism, an instrumental view of suffering – (1) Suffering is a punishment for sin and (2) Suffering is a trial or test for faithfulness in God. The first one, however, raises the problem of distribution and therefore the second one is to be regarded as more important. It asserts that by inflicting pain and suffering on the people, God actually wants to test their endurance and the depth of their faith in him. There are people who seem to believe in God only half-heartedly on a kind of experimental basis. If as a consequence of their faith and prayer, they are rewarded by God, they continue to have faith in him, otherwise they turn unbelievers. Such people are not regarded by God as real believers, and it is to distinguish such fencesitters from real believers that God has allowed evils to exist. As the Quran says in this connection –

"There are some among men who serve God on an edge.
if good befalls them they are well-content,
if a trial befalls them they turn completely rand.
They have lost this world and the next;
that is an unmistakeable loss "

(*Surah*, 22.11)

Thus evil, according to Quran, seems to be a necessary part of God's purpose. It discriminates between the sincere and the insincere and, in effect, not only forms character, but also exposes that.

The Quran also narrates the Judaeo-Christian myth that at the time of creation, one of the angels, Iblis, resented Adam's prominent position and refused to acknowledge it. At this God wanted to destroy Iblis but he was prevailed upon by other angels and Iblis was allowed to exist. Since then Iblis with his other evil companions worked as a rebel and provokes people to commit evil. This story may tempt some people to attribute all evil to Iblis so that a kind of dualism may creep into Islamic Godhood. But it will be wrong to understand Islam in this light. The important point is that whatever may be the working of Iblis, he is still well under God's control and there is no question of treating Iblis as an independent source of evil. At most he may be regarded as instigating people to create moral evil, but such instigations also are to be treated as Allah's test of the moral strength of a man. Hence evil in Islam in all its forms is to be taken as existing fully under God's control and it may be accounted for as serving a useful moral purpose.

7. Life after death

The Islamic eschatology seems to be a combination of Zoroastrian and Judaic ideas in this respect. It is very clear, vivid and picturesque. It mainly consists in the ideas of the day of final judgment, the rising of the dead from their graves and God's assigning to the souls their shares either in heaven or in hell according to their deeds in their earthly lives. Islam believes that man's life does not come to a final end with his physical death. Though his physical body is consumed by the earth in the grave, yet one aspect of his being, the spiritual aspect, remains uncorrupted till the last day when the world comes to its final end. In the intermediary period, the soul rests in a place called Al-Berzahk. When exactly this final day of world's doom will come is known to nobody except God, but whenever it actually comes it will be announced by the blow of a trumphet. This day is called the Day of Judgment. On this day, all the dead rise from their graves. Their souls reunite with their bodies and are brought before the Allah by his angels for the final scrutiny of their deeds in the world. Those whose good deeds balance over the bad ones are rewarded by God by having a place near him in the heaven and those whose evil deeds over-balance the good ones are eternally damned to hell.

Heaven and hell are really very graphically described in the Quran. Heaven is painted as a rose-bed of pleasure and hell as an unending abyss of terrible pain and suffering. Briefly speaking, heaven is described as a place of green meadows, beautiful gardens, running waters, orchards filled with ripe fruits, and so on. Moreover, there is plenty of wine to be taken and beautiful black eyed girls move here and there. Seven heavens are mentioned in the Koran which really represent seven stages of celestial bliss. Similarly seven hells are also described. Hell is pictured as a place of fearful torments. Scorching fires are burning everywhere along with boily waters, burning winds, thorns, smokes, scorpions etc. When after God's final judgment, one has to go to heaven or hell, he has to pass over a bridge called 'Alsirat'. For those who are awarded hell, the passage of the bridge becomes like a sword's edge, so that being unable to cross it, they fall below in the abyss of hell. But for those who have to be enjoyers of heavenly pleasure, the bridge proves sufficiently wide so that they easily cross over to the heavenly side. Thus heaven and hell in Islam are the places of eternal pleasure or eternal damnation meant for good and bad people respectively.

The above gives us an idea of the simple and straightforward eschatological beliefs that the Muslims have. They are clearly based on the simple idea of retribution. God is finally painted in the light of these ideas as an impartial ruler and judge.

8. Human destiny

It is clear from the simple and straightforward eschatology of Islam outlined above that the destiny of man lies in assuming the eternal membership either of heaven or of hell in accordance with one's good or bad deeds on earth. However, if by 'destiny' is meant the goal to be aspired after, it is decidedly the attainment of heaven, where man has the occasion to live in eternal pleasure in the company of God and his angels. This destination can be attained by man by the performance of good deeds in accordance with the Islamic discipline as well as by paying loyal service to God with a sense of full submission. God expects man to assist him in his mission of establishing perfect good on earth and therefore one who proves up to God's expectation is granted the eternal pleasure of heaven, while one who disappoints him in the fulfilment of his mission is damned to the sufferings of hell.

Man lives in heaven in pure spiritual form like God and his angels. He does not possess any physical body there. He, therefore, is free there from all limitations of body and bodily behaviours. Nevertheless, he is not freed from his finiteness even during his abode in heaven. He remains always finite in relation to the infinite God, although he no longer suffers from the limitations of finiteness. He freely enjoys all sorts of heavenly pleasures, but never attains a status equal to that of God. God is always superior to man. In all these, Islam does not sound any peculiar or unique note. Even in Christianity or in the theistic branch of Hinduism as represented by Ramanuja, it is accepted that even after attaining nearness to God in his final destiny, man remains finite and never attains a status equal to that of God. But Islam seems overconscious in emphasizing this point, because in no condition it is ready to accept that in attaining eternal nearness to God in heaven man in any way attains a status equal to that of God. Although Ramanuja never accepts that in the shape of liberation, man becomes God, but he shows no reluctance in accepting that during this state man attains a kind of likeness with God. Perhaps, Islam would never be ready to accept even this. Man has always remained inferior to God and he will ever remain inferior to him. There is no question of attaining any kind of likeness with him. Indian systems like Jainism and a branch of Hinduism too believe that in the state of liberation, man attains infinitude, but Islam would never be ready to accept this. Infinitude is the character of God and God alone. Man could never attain it. Perhaps it is due to this emphasis on man's finiteness and inferiority in relation to God even in heaven that Islam speaks of man's nearness to God, in heaven, but hardly speaks of man's constant communion with God, as religions like Christianity and the theistic branch of Hinduism openly speak of. It seems that according to Islam, man remains in a state of utter subservience and submission to God even in heaven.

Moreover, although Islam believes in disembodied existence of man in heaven, it presents such a graphic description of heaven and heavenly pleasure and also speaks of enjoyment of pleasure in heaven in such a vivid manner, that the heavenly pleasure seems to carry with it an overtone of sensuous pleasure. This kind of pleasure seems definitely different from the bliss of Hindu conception which is supposed to be achieved by anyone who attains his final destiny, *Moksha*. Again, although in a sense the Islamic conception of ultimate destiny seems very much similar to that of Christianity (because both of them take the attainment of heaven to be the final destiny of man), still there are elements in Christian conception which tend to make it much different from the Islamic one. Without speaking about the enjoyment of pleasure in heaven in vivid terms, Christianity takes it as a participation in, or, as assuming the membership of, the Kingdom of God. In this conception spirituality seems to prevail over pleasurable enjoyment. Furthermore, when later Christianity speaks of the dawning upon of the Kingdom of God in this world itself by man's opening up the storehouse of love present in his inner heart itself, the conception of heavenly life changes completely and this changed conception hardly bears any comparison with the Islamic conception of heaven. Despite all these differences and comparative advantages and disadvantages, there is no doubt that by presenting a straightforwardly graphic description of heaven and heavenly pleasure, Islam presents an attractive motivation for a Muslim to lead a moral life and a life of total submission to God.

9. Islamic discipline

We have said earlier that the most important factor in giving Islam its distinctive character is the rigorous discipline of daily life that it prescribes for its followers. In this sense Islam may be regarded as an out and out legalistic religion, although such an observation need not and should not imply that it lacks in inner spiritual piety. The religion, we have seen, takes God as the supreme Lord and man's duty towards him is an unconditional and absolute submission. Consequently, much of Islamic discipline consists of teaching its people definite ways of sincere devotion and prayer to God. However, it also consists within itself elements of self-purification and liberality. Thus the Islamic discipline may be taken both as a religious and ethical discipline simultaneously. It consists in the following five duties known as the 'Five Pillars' of Islam –

(1) *Repetition of faith in the absolute oneness of Allah* – As a strict monotheistic religion, Islam prescribes it to be the basic duty of every Muslim that before every prayer he should repeat the following words – *"La ilaha illa' llahu, Muhammad resulu 'llah."* (There is no God but Allah and Mohammad is His prophet.) This repetition is intended not merely as a recital of words quite unmindfully but as a reaffirmation of the wholehearted conviction that Allah is the only supreme God and that this important message has been brought to the people of the world by the revered Mohammad.

(2) *Daily Prayer* – The observance of set prayers five times a day – at daybreak, at noon, at mid-afternoon, at sunset and at early night – is another important pillar of Islam. Every Muslim is expected to take as his basic duty praying to God unfailingly five times a day at the appointed hours. These prayers follow a set of formula of devotional postures. According to A.C. Bouquet, the innate psychological skill with which these devotional postures are planned is "remarkable, and the nearest parallel is to be found in the system of *Yoga* postures in India."[4]

In prayer, a Muslim has to face towards Mecca. Each complete set of prayer is called a *rakah* and consists of eight separate acts of devotion. It starts with the proclamation *"Allahu Akbar"* (God is great) and then the opening surah of Quran (praise be to God, Lord of worlds, the compassionate, the Merciful...etc.) is recited. Recitation of some other surah of Quran, mostly the following, then follows –

> "Say, He is God alone
> God the eternal.
> He begetteth not, and is not begotten,

---

4. A.C. Bouquet, *op. cit.*, p. 281.

And there is none like unto him."

(*Surah* 112)

Then after various devotional postures, the prayer is completed by uttering once again the basic creed : 'There is no God but Allah, and Mohammad is His prophet.

A Muslim is advised to pray wherever he happens to be at the time of prayer, but it is meritorious to observe prayer in a mosque. Mosques are arranged in such a way that while praying one will face towards Mecca. Both individual and congregational prayers are recognised in Islam. However, Friday is specially recognised as a holy day for congregational prayer in a mosque. Mosques are holy places of prayer, but they are devoid of any image or Idol. Islam does not recognise priesthood but a leader selected locally and called *Imam* directs the rituals of the prayer in the mosque by doing them himself.

Daily prayers have great importance in Islam. They are regarded as "Keys to Paradise". It is said, "God has promised to take into Paradise him who keeps the five prayers and omits none...."

(3) *Alms-giving* – Giving alms to the poor and the needy is another essential duty of all the Muslims. It was recommended by Mohammad from the very beginning as a mark of piety and liberality towards the poor, but later on it took the form of a regular religious tax, called *Zakat*, for the support of the poor and other state purposes. Various formula for the giving of gifts have been worked out in Islam. Sometimes, one-tenth and sometimes one-twentieth of one's land income is required to be gifted. Additional gifts by the able are regarded as signs of greater religious merit. As regards the merit of the gifts, it has been related in the Quran, that a man served God for seventy years and then committed a sin which cancelled the merit of his entire service. Afterwards he gave a loaf of bread to a poor man and God pardoned his sin and gave him back the merit of his entire service.

(4) *Fasting* – Another important religious rite to be observed by a Muslim is fasting during the whole month of Ramazan, i.e. the ninth month of every lunar year. This consists in refraining from any kind of food or drink between sunrise and sunset. Eating is allowed at night. But taking wine and practising such other impurities are forbidden for all times during the month. This fast of Ramazan is strictly to be observed by every Muslim. However, children, the sick and the travellers are made exceptions. It is believed that this fasting remits all kinds of sin committed during the whole year.

(5) *Pilgrimage (Hajj)* – For every able bodied Muslim who can take journey, pilgrimage to Mecca at least once during life-time is regarded in Islam as an essential religious duty. No religious rite does more to unite the Muslims than this pilgrimage, which is taken by thousands from all corners of the world at the same time, during the sacred month of Dhul-Hijja. The pilgrim to Mecca is required to put on a definite prescribed dress at a proper post on the route and has to perform definite rituals at Mecca. The pilgrim's prescribed dress is: two seemless white garments, a waist-wrapper from navel to knee and a shawl covering the left shoulder, and tied under the right. Sandals may be used, but not the shoes. Rituals, amongst others, consist in walking or running seven times round the *Kabba,* kissing the Black Stone each time; casting stones at three pillars at Mina, sacrifice of a sheep, goat or camel, meat being given to the poor, etc. Ten days are occupied with various such performances and prayers, and when all are done, the pilgrim puts off his sacred robe *(Ihram)* and wears his normal dress. The reward for taking the pilgrimage is a secured place in Paradise.

Sometimes a sixth pillar is also added to the above five in the name of Holy war *(Jihad).* Islam advises a war against the unbelievers. Quran itself seems to provide sanction to such holy wars when it says, "Fight those who believe not in God and in the last day, and who forbid not what God and His Apostle have forbidden, and who do not practise the religion of truth. ..." (Surah 9:29). Immediate award of Paradise is promised to those who die in holy wars. However, modern Islam does not seem to subscribe to such a view of *Jihad*. A more spiritual meaning is now given to the term and that is that, it refers to a war against sin and the sinner. It is also taken as referring to exerting for the cause of religion.

Although the observance of the above essential duties in utmost sincerity seems to be a sufficient guarantee in Islam for the attainment of heaven (the highest destiny of man), it does not nevertheless lack in ethical teaching. Quran lays down many ethical virtues and duties for the observance of every Muslim in his dealings with others. Muslim ethics, therefore, is mainly social. Hospitality is one of the greatest virtues that Islam teaches. It also preaches the ethics of the brotherhood of man and service of humanity. Furthermore, virtues like obedience to parents; avoidance of adultery, cheating and lying; refraining from stealing, murder etc. are also emphasized. Islam forbids fighting except for the cause of religion or for self-defence. It also teaches certain virtues for individual guidance. Use of perfumed oil and various sorts of intoxicating drinks are forbidden in it. The virtues of renunciation and non-attachment towards wordly objects are taught to be cultivated by the individual.

As a matter of fact, hardly any aspect of individual or social life is there for which specific rules are not prescribed in Islam. It is a thoroughly legalistic religion which codifies regulations for marriage, divorce, dowry, inheritance, funeral ceremonies and everything. Its straightforwardness and detailed prescription of rules in unambiguous terms for every sphere of life are perhaps important reasons for its being so popular and widespread.

The basic faiths and duties as prescribed in Islam can

very well be seen as summed up in the following verses of the Quran:

> "It is not piety, that you turn your faces to the East
> and to the West.
> True piety is this:
> to believe in God, and the Last Day,
> the angels, the Book, and the Prophets,
> to give of one's substance, however cherished,
> to kinsmen, and orphans,
> the needy, the travellers, the beggars,
> to perform the prayer, to pay the alms.
> ....
> O believers, prescribed for you is
> the Fast, ...
> Fulfil the Pilgrimage and the visitation
> unto God, ...
> And fear God, and know that God is
> terrible in retribution."
>
> (*Surah* 2:174-196).

10. Principal sects

Mohammad himself is said to have predicted that his followers would divide into 72 different sects, but time showed that the actual number far exceeded his prophecy. However, the most important division of Muslims has been between the Shiahs and the Sunnis. The ground of this division seems more to be political rather than doctrinal. The followers, or rather the partymen, of Ali, the son-in-law of Mohammad, are known as Shiahs. According to the Shiahs, it is Ali who should have been elected caliph as the immediate successor of Mohammad. But what really happened was that three caliphs intervened between Mohammad and Ali and they were Abu Bekr, Omar and Othman. The Sunnis, on the other hand, take this succession as legitimate. Moreover, when Ali became caliph in 655, he was assassinated only after 6 years and after him his legitimate heir, his son, Hasan became the caliph. But he resigned his caliphate in favour of Moawiya on the condition that after Moawiya he would again attain to his caliphate. But Hasan died before Moawiya and thus after Moawiya, Hasan's brother Hussain should have been the legitimate heir. But after Moawiya, his son became caliph instead of Hussain. Moreover, Hussain was slain at a place called Karbala and he was regarded as a martyr. It was from this time that the division in Islam took place. The followers of Ali and his sons took them as real descendents of Mohammad and considered the three intervening caliphs as usurpers. Twelve such descendents are named ending with Mohammad-al-Muntazar, better known as al-Mahdi (the guided one). The Shiahs believe that Mahdi did not die, rather he disappeared in 878 and he will reappear just before the day of Judgment. These descendents are all known by the Shiahs as Imams (religious leaders) and some of them even believe that these Imams were the incarnations of Godhead.

The Sunnis, as indicated above, are opposed to the Shiahs on the point of the rightful lineage of caliphate and believe that the order in which the caliphs actually held on to their positions was rightful. Moreover, there is a doctrinal difference too. The Sunnis are the followers of what is called the *Sunna* (Custom of the community). '*Sunna*' is the Islamic term for the traditional record of the sayings and doings of Mohammad. The Sunnis take these traditional sayings and doings of Mohammad to be as authentic as Quran itself, which the Shiahs deny. The latter believe in the Supreme authority of Quran only. The Sunnis are therefore regarded as traditionalists and are in majority in the Islamic world. The Muslims of Arabian and African countries as well those of Turkey are mainly Sunnis, while only those of Persia, Mesopotamia and Pakistan are Shiahs.

The Shiahs soon divided into different sects of which one called the Ismailiya sect is well known. The Ismailis take one named Ismail as the seventh Imam and they take themselves to be his followers. The Ismailis believe that the world is never without an Imam. They hold that after the sixth Imam, there has been a succession of concealed Imams. Thus there is always an Imam, although concealed. As believers in concealed Imams the Ismailis became members of somewhat a secret society. These Ismailis have also got a philosophy of their own regarding the creation and maintenance of the world. They believe that God created the world through the mediacy of a subordinate deity called Universal Reason. This Universal Reason in its turn produced universal soul. Sometimes, this Universal soul becomes incarnate in man, and the Imams have been such incarnations. The Ismailis also believe in the return of Mahdi who will establish kingdom of righteousness on earth and take vengeance upon the enemies of Ali.

One other sect shooting out of those of the Shiahs is that of the Zaidis, who are dominant in Yemen. These differ from the main stock of the Shiahs in the fact that according to them the Imams are not endowed with supernatural powers.

Some other important sects of Islam are those of the Wahhabis, Ahmediyyas and the Sufis. The Wahhabi sect was founded by Ali-Wahhab who aimed at making Islam more puritan in its appeal and outlook. He decried the ritualistic practices prevalent in Islam and also too much appeal and veneration to prophets and angels. Quran was given the utmost importance and was interpreted more literally. He also forbade the luxurious practices of using gold and ornaments, of listening to music and playing chess, of taking tobacco and other intoxicants and so on. The Wahhabi sect, in short, is a symbol of puritan movement in Islam.

The sect of the Ahmadiyyas found its origin in Mirza Gulam Ahmad of the undivided Punjab in India. Mirza Ahmad claimed himself to be endowed with divine revelation who was sent to earth with a divine mission.

Thus the Ahmadiyya sect of Islam is of Indian origin and is much influenced by Indian religions. I t is said that later on Ahmad also claimed himself to be a manifestation of Lord Krishna. The sect has established missionaries in Africa and Europe and is mainly engaged in converting people to its fold.

The Sufis represent the mystical trend in Islam. The word 'Sufi' comes from the Arabic *'Suf'* which means wool. The name Sufi was originally given to such Mohammadan saints who wore uncoloured, coarse woollen cloth as a symbol of renunciation of the worldly comforts. Later on, the name has been specifically associated with the Muslim mystics. The essential characteristic of Sufi mysticism is not different from the usual characteristic of any mysticism. It is a kind of pantheistic monism. The Sufis take the union of soul with God or rather the merger of the former into the latter, to be man's ultimate end. And thus Sufism in a sense comes very near to Hindu Vedantism. This theme of union or merger with God may look very unusual in Islam in the face of its conception of God as a distant, omnipotent, master God with whom man can have no equality or oneness. But Sufi mystics like Rabia and Hallaj lived and died for such a faith and they much emphasized the fact of love to God and union with him. Rabia, the great female mystic, who remained celibate all along her life, so often spoke in a spirit of her blind love for God. "My Beloved is with me always, and for his love I can find no substitute". These lines sound very much the same as Mira's words directed towards Krishna in the expression of her mad love for him. The general spirit of Sufism, of course, did not fit in with the spirit of Islam, but thanks to the great Persian theologian and philosopher Al-Ghazali, who worked out a reconciliation of Sufism with Islam and made the former compatible with the latter. Since his times, it has been conceivable how a good Sufi can be a good Muslim too.

9

Sikhism

1. Introductory

Sikhism is one of the latest religions of the world. It has originated on the Indian soil and flourishes for the most part on this soil itself, although Sikh people are now spread all over the world both as permanent settlers and as temporary earning members. The rise of Sikhism is seen by many as a protest against both Hinduism and Islam. Nanak, a great poet of the Sant tradition and the founder *Guru* (teacher) of Sikhism is reported to have said, "Neither the Veda nor the Kateb (the Quran) know the mystery". This statement shows Nanak's dissatisfaction with both Hinduism and Islam and this explains why he thought it necessary to impart new message to people. Sikhism, to some extent, may also be seen as a product of an attempt at reconciling Hinduism with Islam. Similar attempts may also be seen in many other poets like Kabir etc. of the Sant tradition. However, there are persons who believe that although there is an attempt in Sikhism at reconciling Hinduism with Islam, there is hardly anything of much significance taken from Islam. As Mcleod says, "It is accordingly incorrect to interpret the religion of Guru Nanak as a synthesis of Hindu beliefs and Islam. It is indeed a synthesis, but one in which Islamic elements are relatively unimportant."[1] Nanak was by birth a Hindu, but his faith was definitely influenced by Islam. It is, however, difficult to say definitely about the degree or intensity of this influence. Mcleod is of opinion that, "Islamic influence evidently operated upon the thought of Guru Nanak, but in no case can we accord this influence a fundamental significance.[2] If such observations are correct, it may be said that although Sikhism is influenced by both Hindu and Islamic ideas and beliefs, it is still nearer to Hinduism than to Islmam.

Although, as we have said above, Guru Nanak is regarded as the founder of Sikh religion, the whole of Sikhism can in no way be taken as entirely his contribution. Guru Nanak was followed by a chain of nine Gurus, the last of whom was Guru Govind Singh. Sikhism as a religion took shape under the influence and teachings of all these Gurus. However, some of the Gurus proved more influential than others in giving Sikhism a definite shape. Besides Guru Nanak, Guru Arjun and Guru Govind Singh played epoch-making roles in shaping Sikhism in its present form, the former by compiling the canonical scripture known as *Adi Granth* or *Guru Granth Sahib* (which is regarded as the basic sacred book of Sikhism) and the latter by founding the *Khālsā.* (The military brotherhood of the Sikhs) as well as by instituting explicit rules of everyday life for the Sikh community. It was Guru Govind Singh who initiated in Sikhism the custom of wearing or carrying the following five as the distinguishing mark of every Sikh – *Kesh* (Long uncut hair), *Kanghā* (A comb), *Karā* (Iron Bracelet), *Kirpān* (Sword) and *Kuchchā* (Shorts), the five K's as they are called. With the death of this tenth Guru, i.e., Guru Govind Singh

1. W.H. McLeod, *Guru Nanak and the Sikh Religion*, (Oxford University Press, 1968), p. 167.
2. *Ibid.*, p. 160.

(in 1708) the line of the personal Gurus in Sikhism terminates. And this occurs due to a declaration of Guru Govind Singh himself that there would be no Guru after him. Since then, the function of the Guru is vested in the *Adi Granth*, a copy of which is kept at a desk in every sikh Gurudwarā (Sikh Temple). However, loyalty to Guru is very important in Sikhism. Without it nobody can attain salvation.

The distinctive feature of Sikhism as a religion consists in its strict monotheism. This monotheistic faith might have got strength from the Islamic insistence on divine unity, but it is first and foremost a product of Nanak's own personal experience. In this connection, Nanak himself said, "I relate as the divine word comes to me." As a matter of fact, his and other Gurus' hymns all are born of their own inner illuminations. Some of the other chief features of Sikhism are its belief in God as the omnipotent creator, preserver and destroyer of the world, belief in *karma* and transmigration, belief in the possibility of salvation by God's grace and by the help of the Guru, belief in the efficacy of *nāma simaran* (the repeating of God's name by heart), life of meditation and good ethical conduct as means to salvation, etc. etc.

2. Basic features of Sikhism as a religion

As we have seen, although Sikhism makes an attempt to reconcile Hinduism with Islam, for the most part it is a reaction against both. Consequently, it has developed some faiths and practices which are distinctively its own and which, therefore, give it a distinctive character as a separate religion. We shall try to count here some important ones of such basic features in brief, because details will automatically come in due course.

(1) Sikhism is strictly a monotheistic religion. Its monotheism might have been strengthened by the Islamic influence upon it, but it is primarily an outcome of the personal experiences of the Sikh Gurus themselves. The oneness of God is emphasised by all of them with one voice.

(2) The one and only one supreme God is regarded as creator, sustainer and destroyer of the world. Reference to Brahmā, Vishnu and Śiva are there in Sikhism, but these all are regarded as creations of God himself and they have got no independent status of their own.

(3) Creation is neither *ex nihilo* nor from materials lying outside God; it is the result of divine self-revelation. God has revealed or manifested himself in the form of the world. But his being is not exhausted in this world alone. He goes beyond it.

(4) God is thus both immanent and transcendent. As the inner dweller of the world, he is immanent, but as eternally existing from before creation and as creator of the world, he is also transcendent to it. He is also transcendent in the sense of being incomprehensible.

(5) Creation is fully real. Because God is real and the world is the expression of God, so it is also fully real. Moreover, Sikhism does not take this world as a place from where one should always try to escape. On the other hand, according to it, it is a place where one should actively engage in righteous actions. Sikhism decries asceticism and takes a pure and disciplined worldly life as the life one should lead. The worldly life gives us an opportunity to perform righteous actions. Worldly existence, therefore, is not to be despised, rather it should be fully availed of and utilised in improving one's lot.

(6) Sikhism believes in the greatness of man in his true nature. He has a divine element in him in the form of his *mana* or *ātman*. But man, as he actually stands in the world, is a degenerate man involved in various evil passions. He has perverted his true nature by being engrossed in what is known as *"Haumai"* (Self-centredness or egoism).

(7) The *ātman* or self is, therefore, to be purged of the evil passions, the *haumai*, so that it can be purified. Without it man cannot attain his real nature.

(8) Like Hinduism, Sikhism has a firm belief in *karma* and transmigration. 'As one sows, so he reaps' – is the firm faith equally of Hinduism and Sikhism both. Those who perform bad actions under the spell of the evil passions have to undergo a fresh birth after the end of the present life, while those who perform good actions and are engaged in sincere devotion to God become free from the chain of birth, death and rebirth and attain salvation.

(9) Thus Sikhism also believes in the possibility of salvation. Negatively, salvation means freedom from the cycle of birth and death and positively, it means reunion with God.

(10) Amongst other things, performance of righteous actions, *Nāma Simaran* (Repeating the name of God), *Bhajan* and *Kirtan* (Corporate singing of the praise of God), etc. are taken as means to liberation.

(11) But again, in spite of all efforts, liberation is not possible without God's grace and the helping hand of a Guru. The importance of Guru as a spiritual guide is much emphasized in Sikhism.

(12) As a religious discipline, Sikhism much emphasizes the inner purity of mind and heart and denounces all sorts of externalism. It is totally opposed to pilgrimage, sacred baths, idolatory and such other external practices which are mere mechanical in nature having no sanction of the inner heart. Hypocrisy of all sorts is decried by Sikhism and only those practices are treated as religious which have their root in heart. *Nāma Simaran* and *Kirtan* etc. are also of no consequence if they are mere mechanical repetitions. They have religious value only if the words come from the core of one's heart.

(13) Sikhism is also opposed to casteism. It strongly denounces the Hindu caste system.

3. God

A precise idea about the God of Sikhism may be had from the very opening hymn of the *Adi Granth* which is known as the *Mūla Mantra* of Sikhism. It runs as follows:

"1 *oṅkār satnām karatā purukh nirabhaw niravair akāl mūrat ajūni saibhang gur prasād.*"

The mantra may be paraphrased as follows –

"This being is one. He is eternal. He is immanent in all things and is the sustainer of all things. He is the creator of all things. He is immanent in His creation. He is without fear and without enmity. This being is not subject to time. He is beyond birth and death. He is Himself responsible for His own manifestation (He is known) by the grace of the *Guru.*"

We can see the figure '1' at the very beginning of the above *Mūla Mantra*. This signifies the strong Sikh belief in the unity of God. The interpretation seems to be quite reasonable in the light of the strong emphasis given by Nanak and the entire Sikh tradition on the unity of God. At one place Nanak says in this regard, "The Lord is manifest in the three worlds. He is the eternal Giver and there is no other." He, of course, refers to Brahmā, Vishnu and Śiva, but he seems to take them simply as God's creatures. They have got no independent status. God is himself the creator, the sustainer and the destroyer and his direct exercise of these functions reduces all deities to shadows. "He, the one, is Himself Brahmā, Vishnu and Śiva, and He Himself performs all."[3]

The oneness of God in Sikhism however does not refer to monism. It rather refers to monotheism. Nanak clearly believed in a personal God whom he spoke of as creator, sustainer and destroyer. However , there are references in Nanak as well as in other Gurus, such as in Guru Arjan, which characterise God as both *Nirguna* and *Saguna*. As Guru Arjan clearly says, *"Nirguna āpi Saraguna bhi ohi"*. But the point must be clearly understood. In his absolute

---

3. *Adi Granth*, p. 908.

aspect, when God is not related to world through creation, he is *nirguna* in the sense that he is unconditioned, devoid of ordinary attributes and completely beyond the range of human comprehension. He, then, by his own will becomes *saguna* by revealing himself in the form of the world. As is said, "From this absolute condition, He, the Pure One, became manifest, from nirguna He became saguna."[4] Again although God has expressed himself in the form of the world, he has not done so exhaustively. He is immanent in the world, but is also transcendent to it. God was there even before creation and he is different from his creation. He goes beyond his creation and is therefore transcendent. He is also transcendent in the sense of incomprehensibility. He is not comprehensible by human mind. He can be described only in negative terms, such as, *Agam* (unfathomable), *Agochar* (inscrutable), *Anant* (infinite), *Apār* (boundless), *Alakh* (imperceptible), *Akath* (ineffable) and so on. God is eternal and beyond time. He has existed for ever and will exist for ever. As the *Adi Granth* says, "Beyond human grasp, boundless, infinite, the all-powerful, Supreme God! He who existed before time began, who has existed throughout all ages and who shall eternally exist. He alone is true. Spurn all else as false."[5] At the same time God is immanent too. He is the inner director of the world. He is present everywhere and everything shines by his light. "Thou dost pervade the waters, the land, and all that is between the heavens and the earth, indwelling in all."[6] About God's both immanent and transcendent character, the *Adi Granth* clearly says, "Having created the world, He stands in the midst of it and is separate too."[7] Again, "He is in the midst of all and is yet distinct."[8]

---

4. *Adi Granth*, p. 940.
5. *Ibid.*, p. 437.
6. *Ibid.*, p. 596.
7. *Ibid.*, p. 4.
8. *Ibid.*, p. 939.

Like all other theistic religions, Sikhism takes God as omnipotent, omniscient, omnipresent etc., but sometimes very much emphasises the omnipotence of God in the vein of Islam. As omnipotent, God's will is taken as sovereign. "Thou art absolute and whatever is in Thy will comes to pass." Again, "whatever pleases Thee, that Thou doest, and none can gainsay it."[9] Sometimes, God is also addressed as Master. "Wondrous, my Master, are Thy ways."[10] Besides, God has been described in Sikhism as father, mother, friend, brother, enlightener, protector, shelter of the shelterness, helper of the poor, etc. etc. He is kind, benevolent, loving, etc. He is really the ocean of all virtues.

Sikhism, however, does not believe in God's incarnation. And here it is nearer to Islam than to Hinduism.

4. World

The world, according to Sikh religion, is the creation of God. God has neither created the world *ex nihilo* nor out of material lying besides him. The entire world is the product of the divine will or divine order (*Hukam*). All forms and colours of the world are from God and from no where. "By Thy *Hukam* Thy didst create all forms."[11] The world is the revelation or manifestation of God. It is also called the light of God. Hence, God may be regarded in Sikhism as both the efficient and the material cause of the world. However, there seems a difference amongst Sikh thinkers on the point whether God is to be regarded as the material cause of the world and if at all He may be so regarded, in what exact sense? Some believe that God has, of course, not created the world *ex nihilo,* nor has he created it out of materials lying over and above him, but then, according to them, God cannot be said to have created the world out of the

9. *Ibid.*, p. 504.
10. *Ibid.*, p. 596.
11. *Adi Granth,* p. 150.

material of his own being. They emphasize that the world has come out simply out of divine order, that it is the product of *Hukam,* and it cannot be said that the material of the world has come out of God's being. Others believe that God has really manifested or expressed his own being in the form of the world, although he is not totally exhausted in it. He is both immanent in the world as well as transcendent to it. Although God reveals his own being in the form of freedom of the world as creator he also lies beyond it.

The cosmogeny of Sikhism is set out in Mārū Solahā 15, which begins as follows – "For countless aeons there was undivided darkness. There was neither heavens nor earth but only the infinite order of God (*Hukam*)"[12] (This has some affinity with the Ṛg Vedic creation myth set out in Ṛg Veda X.129)." When God was so pleased, He created the world. He did create everything including Brahmā, Vishnu and Śiva[13]". Thus the world was created in time, but no body knows at what time it was created. Sikhism, therefore, does not subscribe to the Hindu belief that the world has no definite beginning in time. It, however, holds like Hinduism that the process of creation and destruction has been repeated many times. Guru Arjan likens the whole process of creation and destruction to the show of a juggler. He says, "when a juggler gives a show, he appears in various forms. When he takes off the disguise, he alone is left. One space fills all the vessels, when the vessels break the space resumes its unity."

Creation, however, is a continuing process according to Sikhism. It is not that God creates the world once for all and sits apart from it. God is continually working in this world, and the act of creation perpetually goes on. Change and newness, therefore, are taken as perfectly real. Moreover, God's act of continued creation shows his

12. *Ibid.,* p. 1035.
13. *Ibid.,* p. 1036.

perpetual interest in it. The world is not, therefore, to be hated or despised. It is like God's garden where man finds an opportunity to act righteously. "Earth is the true abode of righteousness." So asceticism or the life of a recluse is denounced by Sikhism in the strongest term. The Hindu scheme of life recognises four *aśramas*, but Sikhism seems to reject the latter two, *i.e.*, the *vāna-prastha* and the *sannyāsa*, because these two teach renouncing worldly activities. Till the last day of one's life, every man is to work in a righteous manner in this world. Ascetic and monkish practices do not give salvation. Man is to seek his salvation by doing righteous actions in this world. The world is God's creation and God continually nurtures it in a benevolent manner. So seeking escape from this world is like defying God's will. The world is a place worth living and acting. Thus Sikhism presents a very positive and optimistic picture of the world, which has an echo of poet Tagore's ideas about the nature of the world.

The above gives us a clear idea of the fact that the world, according to Sikhism, is perfectly real. "True is He, true is His creation."[14] Because god is real and the world is God's manifestation, therefore, the world is perfectly real. However, sometimes the world is described as *māyā* by the Sikh Gurus. This gives an impression that Sikhism takes this world as unreal. But this is not true. *Māyā* denotes here nothing more than the phenomenon of constant change. It does not say that the world is unreal, but simply that the world is constantly changing.

Creation, according to Sikhism, has a purpose. The world is not moving blindly; it has a definite purpose. But the purpose is not revealed to man. It will be revealed to him only when he will destroy his ego (*Haumai)* and attain his real nature. However, creation having a purpose does

14. *Adi Granth*, p. 294.

not imply that by creating the world, God has any need to fulfil. God is all-perfect and he has no need of his own.

5. Man

Man in his true nature is given a very high position in Sikhism. He is rather the highest being in creation. Life and consciousness are found in various degrees in the various living beings of the world, but they are found in the most developed form in man. "Man is blessed with the light of reason and discrimination[15]". He seems to be the most privileged creature of God. "You have been given a human body: this is your opportunity to meet God[16]". Outwardly, man seems simply to be a body, but in his inner essence, he has a *mana (manas* or *ātman*). This *mana* or *ātman* in man is the divine element in him. It is just like a bubble in the ocean of divine consciousness. The separate selves are all the separate bubbles of the same ocean. In accordance with the different surroundings the different selves develop different natures. But at bottom they are all one.

The above is the true nature of man. But man as he stands in the world in his present state is in a degenerate condition, separated from his original divine source through the veil of delusion, pride, egoism, etc. which are briefly included under what is called *Haumai* in Sikhism. The pure *ātman* has become impure by the attachment of five evil passions – *Kāma* (Lust), *Krodha* (Anger), *Lobha* (Covetousness), *Moha* (Attachment to the worldly objects) and *Ahankāra* (Pride). Due to these evils man has become degenerate and lost his true nature. Being attached to these he performs *karmas* and consequently falls in bondage, *i.e.*, in the chain of birth, death and rebirth. Thus man's present state is the state of his imperfection or degeneration. This imperfection is mainly

15. *Adi Granth*, p. 913.
16. *Ibid.*, p. 12.

due to egoism or selfishness. Therefore, a man who is slave to the above passions is known as '*Manmukha*' (Self-centred) in Sikhism. The opposite of *Manmukha* is taken as *Gurumukha* (Centred to or inclined towards the Guru). One who obeys the Guru and acts under his guidance, is released from the present state of imperfection. Thus transcendence of the present position is possible. Man has got the capacity of self-transcendence. He can go beyond his present degenerate position. Man's separation from God shows that he is free and he can use his freedom to improve his present state. For this what is necessary is the purging of the *ātman* of the *Haumai* with which it is encumbered. Nanak says, "*Mana jītai jag jītai.*"[17] (To conquer the *mana* is to conquer the world). This means that one who purges his *mana* of the five evils mentioned above and makes it pure becomes released. "*Mana* which has been turned into dross can change into gold again if a man meets the Guru who has himself undergone the transformation." So being *Gurumukha* instead of *Manmukha* is necessary for release from the present degenerate position.

In the above paragraph, we have taken the word 'Gurumukha' in the sense of being inclined towards the Guru, but sometimes it is taken in Sikhism in the sense of God-centredness or God-orientedness. In this sense, a person who is Gurumukha is an ideal person, a sage. The Gurus have praised such God-centred persons like anything. It is said about such a person that he is the ocean of virtues, pure and truthful. The aim of man should be to get rid of *Haumai* and elevate himself to the position of a *Gurumukha* in the above sense. When a man becomes *Gurumukha,* he is released from the imperfections he has been subject to due to *Haumai* and attains a sort of perfection. Such a man is the servant of both God and man. He is like the Buddhist *Bodhisattva*.

---

17. *Adi Granth,* p. 6.

6. Evil and suffering

The problem of suffering is dealt with in Sikhism in the characteristic Hindu way. Suffering is all due to ignorance. It is not a constituent feature of the world. It is all due to the wrong way of looking at the world. The world is fleeting and changing, but we generally take it as something permanent and cling to it. Attachment to the world is an illusion and it is this which is the cause of all suffering. Under the spell of ignorance, we are attached with the various passions and cling to worldly objects. Attached *karmas* and rebirth are the real symbols of suffering. All human suffering is due to egoism or self-centredness (*Haumai*). The moment it is given up, suffering ends. So everything depends upon man's response to creation. The creation is a revelation of God and one who looks to it as such does not suffer. But if someone takes it otherwise and makes it a means of involving in *Haumai,* he is ruined. So the world can be a beautiful garden or a place of suffering in accordance with one's outlook towards it.

However, there is a trend in Sikhism to understand evil as a gift of God in order to correct human beings. It is said that ignorance is given to men by God. It is he who has created people and therefore ultimately it is he who is responsible for dragging people in ignorance. Here Sikhism seems to concede evil as a gift of God. "Many are endlessly afflicted by pain and hunger, but even these, O Beneficent One, are Thy gifts."[18] This gift is meant for correcting people. Dr. Vir Singh points out in this connection that due to suffering man develops fear and consequently abandons sin and attains to a higher moral life. Thus the function of evil is corrective. But we can see that this plea renders Sikhism subject to all such difficulties to which theistic religions like Christianity are subject in taking God as truly

18. *Adi Granth,* p. 5.

benevolent and omnipotent and at the same time creating and allowing evil as a corrective measure. It may be pious forbearance to take evil as God's gift, but this does not form an explanation of the point. However, the important point in Sikhism seems to be that evil is a product of wrong perspective. God is not directly responsible for it.

7. Life after death

The eschatology of Sikhism is very close to that of Hinduism. Like Hinduism, it firmly believes in the doctrine of *karma* and rebirth. The *mana* or the *ātman* of man is immortal and after the death of the body it assumes another fresh body in accordance with its past *karmas*. Although it is not mentioned in Sikhism in a very precise manner as to what sort of *karma* corresponds to what sort of birth, but this is clear that birth in various forms is sequal to the variety of corresponding *karmas*. "*Karma* determines the nature of our birth. .....[19]" That Sikhism believes in births of various forms is clear from the following: "O my Lord who can comprehend Thy excellence? None can recount my sinfulness. Many times was I born as tree, many times as an animal, many times I came in the form of snake and many times I flew as a bird.....[20]" However, rebirth in some form or other is a sequel only to bad and immoral actions. If one performs righteous actions in his life, he is released from the cycle of birth and death by having a reunion with God.

Sometimes, Sikhism seems to believe, somewhat in the fashion of Puranic Hinduism or semitic faiths, in God's taking final account of man's good or bad actions after his death and ordering either for his release or rebirth. "In (God's) presence, Dharmaraj scrutinises our record of good

19. *Adi Granth*,p. 2.
20. *Ibid.*, p.156.

and evil and in accordance with our deeds we dwell near Him or far off."[21] Living far off means going to the chains of rebirth and dwelling near God signifies release. Sometimes references to hell and the city of Yama are also found in Sikhism. "He who forgets the Name must endure the suffering. When the Divine order bids him depart, how can he remain? He is submerged in the well of Hell as a fish without water."[22] Again, "A man who is without the name collapses like a wall of sand. How can one be saved without the name? (Such a person) must ultimately fall into Hell."[23] However, it is not clear whether hell means a fixed abode somewhere for the sinners or it simply refers to the abyss of suffering that one has to undergo after rebirth. Because Sikhism believes in rebirth, the second interpretation seems to be more reasonable. But because references to hell and the city of Yama are made several times, it is possible that according to Sikh belief sinners have to spend some time in a hell before taking rebirth. In any case, men who are engaged in good deeds and in the devotion to God find release from the cycle of birth and death. Such persons are reunited with God and attain total bliss.

8. Ultimate destiny

Clearly, the ultimate destiny of man according to Sikhism is to be free from the chain of birth and death and be reunited with God. Thus, it has both a negative and a positive aspect. Negatively, it is freedom from the cycle of birth and rebirth and positively, it is union with God. But what this 'union with God' exactly means, is not very clear. It is said that it is a status which transcends all human expression and can only be experienced personally. Nevertheless, attempts at describing the status have been

21. *Ibid.*, p. 146
22. *Ibid.*, p.1028
23. *Ibid.*, p. 934.

made by the Sikh Gurus and they go both ways – sometimes it is understood simply in the sense of likeness with God and sometimes in the sense of merger with God. The trouble over the real meaning of the word 'union' or 'unity' with God may very well be exemplified by the following passage from Nanak himself, in which likeness with God and blending with God are both taken as the final destiny of man –

> "He who is immersed in His love day and night knows Him immanent in the three worlds and throughout all time. He becomes *like* Him whom he knows. He becomes wholly pure, his body is sanctified and God dwells in his heart as his only love. Within him is the word; he is *blended in* the True one."[24]

However, the frequent use of the word *'Samānā'* or *'Samaunā'* by Nanak, which means blending or 'entering into', for characterising the nature of ultimate union, testifies to his belief in the complete merger of individual soul into God, of *ātmā* into *Parmātmā,* to be the ultimate destiny of man. He is further reported to have said in this connection. "If God shows favour, one meditates on Him. The *ātmā is* dissolved and is absorbed (in God). The individual's ātmā becomes one with the Parmātmā and the inner duality dies within."[25] In any case, what is definite is that with the attainment of release, transmigration and all consequent suffering cease for all time to come. Though partial union is attained in this life also when the soul is cleansed of all passions, real union is attained only after death.

As ways to final release. Sikhism recommends the following – performing virtuous deeds, efforts at cleansing the self of all the evil passions, *Nāma Simaran, i.e.,* repeating

---

24. *Adi Granth,* pp. 7-8 (Italics ours).
25. *Ibid.,* p. 661.

by heart the name of God, taking shelter in a Guru, etc. But despite all efforts, salvation is not possible without the grace of God. God's grace is necessary even in moulding one towards making sincere efforts for salvation. "All we receive is by the grace of the Beneficent One."[26] Again "He, the one, dwells within all, but He is revealed to him who receives grace."[27] Or again, "Karma determines the nature of our birth, but it is through grace that the door of salvation is found."[28] Here Sikhism seems very much influenced by the ideas contained in the *Bhagavad Gītā* as well as by the views of Ramanuja. Christian influence also may not be ruled out in this respect. But here a question arises: How is it or why is it that God bestows his grace on some one and not upon others? How is his grace to be achieved? The answer is that it is to a great extent a mystery. Man is not given to a complete understanding of the ways of God. Nevertheless, it is pointed out as a general guide that human effort in terms of devotion and love to God elicits such grace. "The grace of the Master is on those who have meditated on Him with single mind and they have found favour in His heart."[29]

The role of Guru also seems to be very important in Sikhism in so far as the question of the attainment of release is concerned. Without the help of a Guru, release is not thought possible in Sikhism. Thus allegience to a Guru is necessary for release. Release is of course possible by winning the grace of God through devotion to God and through *Nāma Simaran*, but these latter are themselves not possible without the guiding and helping hand of a Guru. "Without the Guru, there can be no bhakti, no love; without the Guru, there is no access to the company of the sant (saint); without

---

26. *Adi Granth*, p 5.
27. *Ibid.*, p. 931.
28. *Ibid.*, p. 2.
29. *Ibid.*, p. 24

the Guru one blindly engages in futile endeavour. But with the Guru, one's *mana* is purified. ....[30]"

But the main problem is, who is a Guru. Generally speaking, a spiritual teacher is a Guru. But who can be taken as a spiritual teacher? Perhaps he who has attained exemplary spiritual purification by disowning all evil passions and who has realised the true nature of the world, self and God. Such a person imparts true lesson of spirituality, by following which one can attain release. Such a Guru is necessary in Sikhism to help attaining liberation. It is in this sense of the term 'Guru' that there have been ten Gurus in Sikhism from Guru Nanak to Guru Gobind Singh. But who was the Guru of Guru Nanak and who is the Guru after Guru Gobind Singh? To the second question, the generally recognised answer in Sikhism is that the *Adi Granth* is the Guru now. But as an answer to the first question, it is said that God himself was the Guru of Nanak. As a matter of fact Nanak himself as well as some other Sikh Gurus like Guru Arjan and Guru Gobind Singh take God himself to be the real Guru. Guru Arjan makes the point explicit when he says "The true Guru is Niranjan (God). Do not believe that he is in the form of man."[31] Thus in Sikhism, the word 'Guru' is sometimes used in the sense of a human Guru and sometimes in the sense of God himself.

9. The Sikh discipline (ethics, prayer, etc.)

We have seen that the principal vice according to Sikhism is self-centredness or egoism and this consists in being attached to the five evil passions. Hence the Sikh discipline mainly consists in cleansing the *mana* or the *ātman* of these evil passions so that one may get rid of egoism and self-centredness (*Haumai*) and become God-centred. For this

30. *Ibid.*, p. 1170.
31. *Ibid.*, p. 895.

Nanak has propounded a path of *Sādhanā*. This *Sādhanā* consists firstly in recognising that God is present in all creation, particularly in human *ātman*, and that he is the only reality to be adored. When one fully recognises this fact and becomes fully conscious of its truth, the next step is to meditate on divine qualities with sincere devotion and love towards God. Through such a meditation, the *mana* is gradually cleansed of the evil passions and man becomes free from the *Haumai*.

Nāma Simaran, i.e., repeating of God's name, is also given a very important place in Sikh religion. But mere mechanical repeating of name is decried by Sikh Gurus. As a matter of fact, Sikhism denies the efficacy and value of all that is external and mechanical. It also denounces pilgrimage, holy bath etc., if these are done without a pure and loving heart. Thus *Nāma Simaran* is of value only when one repeats God's name with full love and devotion. The name must come from the heart and not merely from the lips. Besides *nāma simaran*, Sikhism also prescribes *bhajan* and *kirtan, i.e.,* corporate singing of the praise of God, as the ways to salvation. But in every such devotional act inwardness of heart and purity of *mana* are emphasized. Sikhism is opposed to anything that is mere external ritualism. "If the *mana* is unclean, how can it be purified by worshipping stones, visiting places of pilgrimage,[32] living in jungles, wandering around as an ascetic?" Thus idolatory, asceticism, pilgrimage etc. are all ridiculed by Sikhism. It is a religion of inward discipline, and not of external, hypocritical practices. It is strictly opposed to hypocricy. There is no use of visiting places of pilgrimage. The true *tīrath* (place of pilgrimage) is within. True religion is inward and finds shape in loving devotion. All else is mere hypocrisy which has no place in religion.

---

32. *Adi Granth*, p. 886.

Besides *nāma simaran* and devotional singing of songs in praise of God, a dedicated moral and virtuous life, a life of the selfless service of the people, company of God-centred men, etc. are also emphasised in Sikhism as ways leading to final release. As ethical virtues, the most emphasised ones are humility and love. Besides, the virtues of contentment, truth, righteousness, mercy, compassion, purity etc. are all given due importance. Sikhism is vehemently opposed to casteism and it preaches love of all without any distinction of caste or creed.

At last, however, it must be added that although Sikhism in its essence is opposed to externalism and rituals, it has itself given place to certain rituals in course of time. And this is not something unusual. We have seen that this has occurred with almost all the religions of the world. A kind of baptism is prevalent in Sikhism to initiate boys and girls into the Sikh community. The daily rituals, as mostly laid down by Guru Gobind Singh himself, consist in the following – early rising, taking bath in the cold water, recitation of certain prayers morning and evening, meditation on God's Name etc. Then again, although pilgrimage is decried and discouraged in Sikhism, many Sikhs take it as their sacred duty to travel to the birth place of Guru Gobind Singh on his birth anniversary to pay their homage to him.

10. Sects

Sikhism is a relatively new religion and it has not given rise to so many sects which differ from one another on certain basic religious points. But still certain groups have distinguished themselves from the common stock on certain points, basic or otherwise. There are, for example, Namadharis, Akalis, Nirankaris and Nanak-panthis. The Namadharis are the puritans amongst the Sikhs. They basically observe the same religious principles of Sikhism, but they are puritans in their approach. They emphasize utmost purity and cleanliness and strictly observe such practices as abstaining from smoking, drinking etc. and definitely taking perfect bath in the morning and observing other sacred rituals. Further, they abstain from meat also, although meat eating was allowed in Sikhism by Guru Gobind Singh. The Akalis are basically the militant group within Sikhism. There is hardly any religious difference between them and the common stock. They are in a sense fanatics among the Sikhs who fight for the cause of their faith and religion. In modern India Akalis are mainly recognised as forming a political group of Sikhs. The Nirankaris are a special group formed around one Gurbachan Singh who declared himself to be a Guru and the carrier of God's message. He was popularly known as *Nirankāri Bāba*. It will be remembered that the tenth Sikh Guru, Guru Gobind Singh, declared himself to be the last Guru and ordered that after him only the *Adi Granth* or the *Guru Granth Sahib* will play the role of the Guru. There will be no human Guru after him. And the Sikhs solemnly accept his declaration and order. But the above mentioned Nirankāri Bāba revolted against it and called himself a Guru. It is all such who flock around him and accept his claim are called Nirankāris. The common stock of Sikhs is very much opposed to this group. Nanak-Panthis are those who do not take being a member of the *Khālsā* or carrying the Five K's as essential Sikh duties. They rather take treading sincerely on the path shown by the original Guru Nanak to be the essential Sikh duty and nothing else is necessarily required. Many Sikhs, therefore, do not recognise the Nanak-Panthis as Sikhs and consequently they have shown a tendency to melt away in Hinduism.

10

Comparison and Appraisal

We have so far outlined the contents of different religions on specific points. In so doing, we have been able to decipher some of their important beliefs and practices. Let us now try to see them in a comparative perspective, so that essential points of similarity and difference amongst religions may be brought forth. Different religions have come out of different traditions and against different backgrounds. Therefore, differences are bound to be present in them. But because religion as a whole arises in human consciousness due to certain common problems that human beings have to face in the world and because people of different traditions share certain common feelings, ideas and sentiments, therefore, there are bound to be certain similarities too amongst different religions. Thus it will be equally wrong to speak of similarities alone and leave out differences as it will be to speak of differences alone and leave out similarities. A scientific study of religions, which a comparative study of them aims at, must highlight both these similarities and differences in a balanced manner. Such balanced comparisons are not totally missing from our consideration of religions so far. We have referred to the important and glaring comparisons between religions wherever context and occasion have demanded them. But they are not sufficient. We want to see them in a more manifest manner in our present chapter. In doing this, we will have occasions to make modest critical appraisals also, but such appraisals will go only to the extent which will not adversely affect the sentiments of the followers of any particular religion. We shall take up the comparisons also in the same topic-wise manner in which we have dealt with the different religions separately.

1. God

From our elucidation of the concept of God as present in different religious traditions, we may very well form an impression that except Buddhism and Jainism, which virtually do not believe in any God at all, and also a part of Hinduism, which is either atheistic or non-theistic, all the religions of the world are monotheistic in character. Some of them (e.g. Islam, Sikhism and also Judaism) rather emphasize their monotheistic character too much. There may be a doubt regarding the monotheistic nature of Zoroastrianism, because apparently it seems to be ditheistic. Again, one may have such doubt about Christianity also in so far as it believes in Trinity. But we have seen that these religions have grounds to claim themselves monotheistic and the grounds are not merely lame excuses. The duality or trinity in Godhood in these religions is only outward and secondary. What is basic and essential is their monotheism. Similarly, there may be a doubt regarding the monotheistic nature of Hinduism, specially in its earlier phases. But we have seen that even beneath the apparent polytheism of the Vedas, there was always an undercurrent of monotheism and even now when the average Hindu worships a lot of gods and goddesses, in so doing he is fully aware that the gods or goddesses he is worshipping are all the manifestations or expressions or aspects of the same supreme, all-powerful God. Hence it seems to be a general point of unity amongst religions that most (almost all) of them either very strictly or in somewhat a lenient form believe in only one supreme, all-powerful, all-knowing creator God, although this God may have his various manifestations or aspects. However, this point cannot be ignored that there are religions in the world which either do not believe in God at all (early Buddhism and Jainism and also some aspects of Hinduism), or do not believe in any creator God (as Buddhism and Jainism in their somewhat later forms) or do not believe in a personal God, *i.e.* God having a personality (as the Advaitic or Absolutistic aspect of Hinduism).

Besides this general point of unity, religions of the world unite together in attributing to God some of the metaphysical qualities like infinity, all-powerfulness, all-knowingness and all-pervasiveness as well as some of the ethical qualities like mercy, benevolence, justice etc. Furthermore, God is also regarded by all religions as the creator, sustainer and destroyer of the world and he is taken as both transcendent from and immanent into this world. However, there are differences too. The nature of God as conceived in the Indian tradition sometimes sharply differs from that conceived in the Semitic tradition and again religions of the latter tradition too sometimes differ amongst themselves regarding the nature of God. Of course, the difference amongst the Semitic religions is mostly one of greater or less emphasis on one or another quality of God. Although, in the Semitic religions also, God has been taken as immanent and all-present in the world, but the conception of God as *Antaryāmi* (inner dweller) and as the inner soul of the world is distinctive of the Indian tradition only. Ramanuja has clearly taken God as such and also Nanak, the original propounder of Sikh religion. Moreover, some of the ethical and other qualities like truthfulness, bliss, etc. that Ramanuja gives to God seem specific of Indian tradition. Moreover, God is conceived here (both in Hinduism and Sikhism) in two forms – as *nirākāra* (attributeless) and *Sākāra* (full of attributes). In himself he is attributeless, but in human relationship he becomes *sākāra*. The element of mystery is emphasised in some of the Semitic religions also like Judaism and Islam, but religions of Indian tradition emphasise it in their own distinctive manner. They point out that God's nature is so mysterious and so beyond human comprehension that it can be conceived only in negative terms, such as *Apār*, *Agochar* etc. Judaism and Christianity take God as personal but in Hinduism God is neither taken as personal nor impersonal; he is called super-personal. The most important distinction seems to be regarding God's relation to the world which he creates. In the religions of the Semitic tradition, God is only the efficient cause of the world, and not the material cause. He has, according to them, created the world *ex nihilo*. But according to Hinduism, God is both the efficient and the material cause of the world. He has created the world not out of nothing, but out of the material of his own being. Hinduism has a firm belief that out of non-existence, existence cannot come (*Nāsato Vidyate Bhāvo*) and here its standpoint seems to be more logical than that of the Semitic faith. The world is like a body of which God is the inner soul according to Hinduism. Sikhism also does not subscribe to the view that God creates the world out of nothing. It takes the world as God's revelation, which, more or less, amounts to the view that God creates the world out of the material of his own being. Of course, some of the Sikh believers may object to any such clear statement that God has created the world out of the some material taken from his own being. They will prefer saying that the world is the product of mere God's will. But it is not clear what exactly it means. Sikhism clearly denies the view that the world has been created *ex nihilo*, and therefore any viable alternative that remains seems to be that the world has been created out of materials forming God's being.

There seems to be a striking similarity between Hinduism and Christianity in point of taking God as three into one or as one in three (Trinity). In Hinduism, the trinity is formed by Brahmā, Vishnu and Mahesh and in Christianity it is formed by God the Father, God the Son and the Holy Spirit. But then we can very well mark that there is a difference in the nature of the trinity. In the Hindu trinity Brāhmā represents the creative aspect, Vishnu the maintaining and sustaining aspect and Mahesh (or Shiva) the destructive aspect of the supreme God, but in Christianity there is no such functional distinction in the nature of Godhead.

There is also a difference between Indian religions and the religions of the Semitic tradition regarding the nature of God's concern with the affairs of the world. Hinduism believes that whenever there is a marked regression in virtuous life and evil reigns supreme in the world, God himself incarnates on earth and annihilates evil. There have been several such incarnations in the past and they are expected in future also. Religions of Semitic tradition do not seem to believe in any incarnation of this type. According to them, at times God sends messengers to instruct people about the true lessons of religion and morality. Some of them believe that such messengers may come in future also, but according to Islam, Mohammad was the last prophet and there is none to come after him.

Amongst the Semitic religions, Judaism seems to be the primary source of almost all the important beliefs and conceptions of the later two. There are striking similarities between Judaism and Islam regarding their conceptions of God. Both are strictly monotheistic religions and their strict monotheistic character is depicted in their very basic creeds which every Jew or Muslim is required to remember and repeat. The Jewish creed is depicted in the very opening line of the *Shema* as follows – "Hear, O Israel, the Lord, our God, the Lord is one" and the Muslim creed, as is well known, runs as follows – "There is no God but Allah, and Mohammad is His Prophet." Again, both these religions much emphasise the all-powerful and masterly character of God. However, Islam's emphasis on this aspect is even greater. We have seen that the very word 'Allah' means

'The mighty' and, 'The powerful' and the word 'Islam' means. 'Submission'. As contrasted to this, Judaism lays greater emphasis on the ethical attributes such as mercy, justice, holiness etc. Of course, Islam also takes mercy and justice as two very important attributes of God and that is obviously due to the Judaic influence on it. One the whole, therefore, the Jewish God impresses one as a just and merciful ruler of the world, whereas the Islamic God impresses as an absolute master having absolute decree. It does not, however, mean that the Islamic God is not imbued with such soft ethical qualities as mercy, compassion etc. The very opening Surah of the Quran runs as follows –

> "Praise be to God, Lord of the Worlds,
> The Compassionate, the Merciful."

Further, both Islam and Judaism emphasise the mysterious and transcendent character of God, although each of them takes God as also immanent. Islam adds one more character to God, his dynamism, which if not completely absent from Judaism and Christianity are surely not explicitly mentioned in them. Iqbal, the famous Islamic poet, much emphasises this character of dynamism, as attributed to God, in his writings on Islam. Althogh God is eternal, his nature is dynamic and that is why we find changes in the world. Again, in the Judaeo-Christian tradition, God is regarded as personal (as contrasted from impersonal), although it is always emphasised that he is not to be treated as a person in any ordinary sense, because he is of the nature of a spirit. But in Islam, perhaps none will ever like to refer to God as personal, because he is treated here as having no shăpe or form. Of course, God is taken as having will and power and it is in this respect that establishing personal relationships with him through prayer etc. can be justified as having any significance.

Between the Judaic and Christian conceptions of God, there is hardly any difference of such a kind which may attract the attention of a general reader. The two are essentially one, although there are certain points of difference also. Both Judaism and Christianity take God as all-powerful, all-knowing, all-present, merciful, kind, just etc., but whereas Judaism emphasises the all-powerfulness of God and lays equal emphasis upon God's attribute of mercy and justice, Christianity lays utmost emphasis upon God's character of love – so much so that God is identified with Love and the overall picture of God appears before man as a loving father and as none else. There is no cause of any fear from God now; he is completely kind and loving and loves even the worst of sinners. Judaic God is sometimes characterised as wrathful and revengeful also (although these do not represent his essential character), but there is no such thing in the Christian conception of God. We remember that the Jewish God had a contract with his people that he would save them only if and in so far as they would serve him, but in Christianity, God's love for men (his children) is not based on any precondition; it is absolute and unconditional. However, it must be noted that the idea of God as a loving father is not completely absent from Judaism; it is only that it does not lay that exclusive emphasis upon this character of God as Christianity does.

One very marked difference between Judaism and Christianity, which takes the former nearer to Islam than to the latter, is regarding the number of Godhead. Both Judaism and Christianity claim to be monotheistic, but the latter due to its doctrine of Trinity does not remain as strictly monotheistic in character as the former. It is due to this doctrine that Islam openly criticises the Christian conception of God. It is felt that the doctrine of Trinity breaks the strictly unitary character of Godhead and thus jeopardises Christian claim for monotheism. Judaic monotheism is unstained and absolute, but the Christian monotheism becomes controversial.

It does not look at all necessary now to go into the details of comparison between the Islamic and Christian conceptions of God. From our occasional remarks made above, it is clear by now that in spite of having almost all those attributes which the Judaic or Christian God has, Islamic God on the whole appears as an absolute master, whereas the Christian God appears as a loving father. However, the distinction must not be over-emphasised, because the Islamic God also does not lack absolutely in qualities like mercy, compassion etc.

So far, we have made little reference to the Zoroastrian God. We have seen that original Zoroastrianism is monotheistic, but later on there are obvious signs in it of ditheism or even of polytheism. Various gods including Fire, Sun etc. arise on the scene and one is very well reminded here of the Vedic polytheism. The dualism of Ahura Mazdah and Ahriman seems to be the dominant note of Zoroastrianism. But as we have noted earlier, the overall tone of Zoroastrianism is ever taken to be monotheistic in which Ahura Mazdah is recognised as the only supreme, all-powerful, all-wise and all-good God. In any case, Zoroastrianism seems to have exerted definite influence on Judaism and consequently upon Islam and Chrisrianity. The Satan present in all these Semitic religions is definitely a replica of the Zoroastrian Ahriman. Moreover, the characters of holiness, justice, righteousness, etc. as forming the essential attributes of Judaic God seem to be taken from Zoroastrianism itself. The quality of all-powerfulness of God also which is so much emphasised in Judaism and Islam perhaps finds its origin in the Zoroastrian emphasis on the quality as forming the essential nature of God. But the most emphasised quality of God in Zoroastrianism is that of his all-goodness. God is supremely and absolutely good and he is engaged in establishing the reign of complete good on earth. In this holy task he also expects the co-operation of men. Here in all these, Zoroastrianism seems to have influenced both Judaism and Christianity. But if the essential nature of Zoroastrian Godhead is taken as ditheistic – (the two gods Ahura Mazdah and Ahriman standing on independent footing as two contenders of supremacy and dominance), then Zoroastrianism has a distinct place amongst religions and its God or gods cannot be compared to the God of any other religion.

2. World

Religions of the world, except Buddhism and Jainism, believe that the world is the creation of God and it is also dependent upon him. They also generally believe that God brings the world to an end at his own sweet will. But they differ in details regarding the actual process of creation and the exact nature and status of the world. Although Hinduism believes in creation (at least the dominant part of it believes so), it does not seem to believe that the world was created at a definite moment of time. In it, it differs from the Semitic religions and agrees in a sense with Buddhism and Jainism which hold that the world is somehow coming down from all eternity. Of course, Hinduism (and also Sikhism) believes in a cyclic process of creation and destruction of the world and this cycle is going on alternately from all eternity. Again, because Hinduism, in general, believes that the world has been created out of the materials constituting God's being, and not *ex nihilo*, therefore, creation, according to it, means unfolding of a portion of God's being and dissolution or destruction means the return or reentry of the unfolded material into God in a contracted form. Both creation and destruction, however, occur at God's sweet will. According to the Semitic religions, creation means creation out of nothing and it has been accomplished by God at a definite period of time. (Sikhism also believes that the world has been created at a definite period of time, although no body knows when). Moreover, creation and destruction do not go on according to these religions in a cyclic order, rather the world has once been created by God and is subject to destruction by him at any time in future. Zoroastrian view also regarding the creation and destruction of the world seems to be closer to the views of Semitic religions, although it is not clear whether Zoroastrianism takes the world as created out of nothing. This seems to be the case with Islam also, which forms part of the Semitic faith itself. Moreover, while both Judaism and Christianity have similar creation myths, Zoroastrianism and Islam do not seem to have any such mythical stories regarding the exact process of creation. Islam seems to regard the fact of world's creation a mystery and points out that it is difficult to say how exactly or through what exact process the world was created. Nevertheless, according to both these religions, as according to others also, the world is definitely a creation of God and is fully dependent upon him for its sustenance.

As to the nature and status of the world, it may generally be said that almost all the religions take it as real. Of course, some religions lay greater emphasis on the reality of the world as compared to others, but no religion, perhaps, takes the world as wholly unreal. Judaism, Zoroastrianism and Sikhism seem to lay specifically explicit emphasis upon the reality and significance of the present world, while from the overall attitude and tone of Hinduism and Buddhism it appears that they do not want to emphasise the significance and reality of the world too much. But undoubtedly they do not regard the world as unreal. There is so often a criticism against Hinduism that its attitude is other-worldly and that it regards the present world as unreal. Dr. Radhakrishnan has considered such criticisms against Hinduism at length in his book *Eastern Religions and Western Thought* and has very competently come to the conclusion that they are totally mistaken and misconceived. First of all, it is only against Advaita Vedānta, which represents only one aspect of Hinduism and not the whole of it, that such criticisms may have any relevance. This system of Hindu thought, of course, takes the world as *māyā*, which apparently implies that the world is unreal. But there are parallel systems, not less influential, like those of Ramanuja and others which explicitly maintain that though the world is dependent upon God, it is fully real. Critics of Hindu thought and religion totally miss these trends present in it. Secondly, even Advaita Vedānta, properly interpreted, does not regard this world as wholly unreal. From the practical standpoint it takes the world as fully real. The doctrine of *Māyā* only indicates that the world has got a deeper significance than what on the face of it appears to us. It is spiritual out and out and unitary in its inner character. The world is, therefore, not negated here; it is only seen in its deeper, more real perspective.

Thus no religion takes this world as unreal in the sense that it is a non-entity or that moral and other activities performed here have got no real value. But then every religion in one way or other takes excessive attachment to the world as undesirable and therefore does not take this world as something which is ultimately real. Of course, religions of Indian origin – Hinduism, Buddhism and Jainism – lay much emphasis upon this aspect of the matter and therefore it seems that they possess a negative attitude towards the world. Religions like Judaism and Zoroastrianism much emphasise the role of man in this world in so far as his entire future according to these religions depends upon what he does here. If he adopts good and shuns evil, he has a bright future, otherwise he has to take the doom. Zoroastrianism explicitly paints the world as a ground of constant strife between the forces of good and evil in which man has to take active part. Those who take the side of the former really take the side of God and therefore thay are sure to be rewarded by God. But those who take the side of the latter go against God's will and they are sure to be punished. But such ideas are not absent from the eastern religions. They also clearly maintain that only our actions in this world determine our future.

The law of *Karma* actually stands for such ideas and beliefs. What these religions teach is not the unreality of the world, but a lower reality of it as compared to the higher and the ultimate one. And such a distinction between the higher and the lower, between the spiritual and the profane, is necessary for religion. As a matter of fact, all the religions of the world are based on such a distinction. It is not a fact that religions like Zoroastrianism, Judaism and Christianity take attachment to this world as desirable. On the other hand, they also teach non-attachment as a virtue. Hence, all religions with greater or less emphasis take this world as real, although all of them take excessive attachment to it as undesirable.

3. Man

Man has been given a very high status in almost all the religions. Buddhism and Jainism do not believe in God. Naturally, therefore, man becomes the highest being in them. He is potentially capable of attaining Godhood by himself. It is only due to the cloud of ignorance that his real great nature is temporarily hidden. In Hinduism and Sikhism also, man is regarded as the highest creature. The soul within him is really the divine spark and thus of all the creatures he is specially privileged. It is due to ignorance that man fails to recognise the greatness of his being and suffers within various limitations. The moment he realises his real nature, he becomes infinite and free from all limitations. Judaism and Christianity also in their own ways make man the greatest of all creatures. According to them, God made man in his own image on the final day of creation to be its final fruit. Moreover, man has been made to act as the fellow partner of God in his scheme of establishing the complete reign of good on earth by eradicating evil. Zoroastrianism also gives the same status to man. According to it, in the constant strife between the forces of good and evil on earth, man is to play the role of the fellow partner of

Ahura Mazdah so that he can be able to dislodge the forces of evil completely and establish the reign of perfect good on earth. It is only in Islam that man seems to be very small and insignificant in relation to God. Man seems to have no status here. He appears to be more or less a slave whose only job is to serve God with a sense of unqualified submission to him.

Of all the religions, however, Zoroastrianism seems to give the greatest dignity to man and at the same time inflicts the greatest responsibility upon him. According to it man is completely free and unstained in his original nature. He can do whatever he likes. Ahura Mazdah has made him completely free to choose between good and evil and act accordingly. Of course, God wants man to choose the path of good, but it is upto him what path he chooses. According to Christianity man comes to earth being stained by Original Sin and according to Hinduism, Buddhism and Jainism he takes birth with the blurring cloud of ignorance and the burden of the past karmas. But according to Zoroastrianism man is born completely pure and spotless with perfect freedom of will. Thus for every act of him, man himself is fully responsible. This is not the case in the context of other religions. In Hinduism, Buddhism and Jainism man comes to earth with certain limitations and therefore in one sense neither he can be taken as completely free nor he can assume the full responsibility for his work. In Islam, the case seems to be even worse. Islam's belief in absolute decree of God and predestination of everything tends to make man an insignificant plaything in the hands of God and thus he seems to have been denied freedom of will completely. Of course, certain lines of Quran seem to make some room for man's freedom, but the overall tone comes out to be deterministic. Hinduism, Buddhism etc. cannot be called deterministic, but obviously they do not grant man that amount of freedom which Zoroastrianism seems to grant. Law of *karma* is a symbol both of determinism and freedom.

Judaism and Christianity also grant freedom to man in their own ways. They point out that although God is omnipotent, he has willingly imposed a limitation upon his all-powerfulness and has granted freedom of will to man. Man can use his freedom in any way he likes. In the end it can be said that every religion, including Islam, grants some amount of freedom to man because of their talks of a bright future of man by virtue of his own good deeds on earth. If freedom does not mean anything, man cannot be held responsible for his good or bad destiny.

As to the nature of man, religions of Indian origin are very clear in saying that man is essentially spiritual in nature. Man has got a soul within him which constitutes his essential nature. This soul is immortal and therefore man in his essential nature is immortal. Even Buddhism which apparently seems to deny this soul virtually accepts it in its own special manner. Judaism and Christianity also maintain this essentially spiritual character of man by maintaining that God has created man in his own image. Because God is spiritual in nature, so man is also spiritual. However, we do not find in these two religions that much of emphasis upon the spiritual and immortal nature of man as we find in Hinduism, Jainism etc. Soul in man is not given that important and distinct status by these religions which is given to it by Hinduism, Jainism and Sikhism. Islam hardly gives any such clear indication which may show that according to it man's nature is essentially spiritual. Like all other religions it also believes in a life of man after death and from that, of course, one can very well guess that according to it also, there is some spiritual element in man which is immortal. But there is no clear statement about the presence of an immortal soul in man which constitutes his real and essential nature. On the other hand, the Quran explicitly maintains that God has created man from clots of blood. This gives an impression that man's essential nature is physical or physiological and there is hardly anything spiritual in his constitution. Zoroastrianism also does not seem to be so very explicit about the presence of an immortal soul within man, although it cannot be said that it denies it.

4. Evil and suffering

Because suffering is a burning fact of life, every religion takes care of it and considers it as a problem. But the reactions are not always the same. Religions of Indian origin generally take the problem of suffering in a practical perspective and take it as their chief burden to point out ways and means for getting rid of suffering. Of course, in this connection they also point out the cause of suffering. Religions of Semitic origin, on the other hand, react to it in, more or less, a theoretical perspective. They want to advance an explanation, a reason of, suffering. Why is suffering there at all? Or what can be its justification, when the world is taken as created and maintained by an omnipotent and benevolent God? – is the kind of problem which these religions somehow seek to answer. Zoroastrianism also seems to adopt this very perspective. Now, although in the details of such explanation, these religions differ, in essence, they all accept that evil and suffering have been allowed by God for some good inherent purpose. The ways of God are mysterious and we human beings are not able to know his entire plan. Apparently, suffering seems to be an evil, but really or ultimately that is not evil. God must have some good purpose behind that.

As cause of evil, Zoroastrianism and all the Semitic religions tend to hold a devil with all his evil spirits responsible. In Zoroastrianism, the devil is named Ahriman, in Judaism and Christianity Satan, and in Islam Iblis. But then no religion seems disposed to take the devil as an independent force falling out of God's control. So ultimately, it is omnipotent and benevolent God himself who becomes responsible for all evil and suffering. So the occasion for justification remains and all the religions advance some such justification in their owm ways. Zoroastrianism seems to hold that the Ahura Mazdah has allowed the forces of evil to work only with a moral purpose. Judaism and Christianity also seem to share in this explanation, although they have other explanations also. Islam shares in its explanation mainly with Judaism. Amidst many other explanations, Judaism holds that evil is a mystery, the real secret of which is known to God alone. In the main, exactly this explanation is given by Islam also. Further, both Judaism and Islam hold that God has allowed evil and suffering to test the intensity and sincerity of faith that man possess towards him. God rewards those who amidst all suffering do not disbelieve in him, and bear the pinch in utmost piety. Thus evil is a test of moral and religious strength of man. A more or less similar view is expressed by Sikhism also when it asks its followers to take suffering as God's gift and bear it with a sense of piety. However Sikhism extends this explanation further to point out that God has bestowed this gift upon man with a view to correct him. So the value of suffering is corrective. When man will suffer, he will give up the wrong course and adopt the right path. This reformatory or corrective character of suffering is sometimes emphasised in Judaism and Christianity also. The father-God of Christianity uses the stick of suffering to discipline his sons. Judaism and Islam also agree in taking evil and suffering as a mark of punishment to the erring man. But here as we have noted earlier, a problem arises before both of these religions as to why even those have to suffer who are innocents. Sometimes, we also find that innocents suffer and the sinful rejoice. Here the justice of God falls in difficulty.

As Judaism and Christianity virtually form two stages of the same tradition, there is naturally much of affinity between the two regarding the explanation of evil. Besides accepting the reformatory character of evil, which we have indicated above, both take evil as good in disguise. According to both of them evil is a signal for better things to come and therefore it is to be tolerated with patience, and not to be scorned. The history of Judaism shows that whenever the Jews suffered, they suffered only to come out with greater faith and prospect. Similarly, the suffering of Christ on the Cross and then his coming out triumphant by resurrection symbolise Christian view of suffering as a boon in disguise. The very birth of Jesus Christ is an example of the fact how evil is to be followed by greater good. Had not people suffered due to the Original Sin of Adam, Christ would not have come down to earth as a redeemer. Thus evil is surely a boon in disguise. Then again, both Judaism and Christianity (along with Zoroastrianism) emphasise the moral value of evil. God has knowingly allowed evil so that an occasion for moral progress of the world may arise and people may have an opportunity to exercise their freedom of will. If there were good alone, no occasion for moral effort on the part of man would have arisen.

Religions of the Indian tradition, as we have noted above, mainly possess a practical attitude towards suffering. Taking evil and suffering as fact, their main job seems to be pointing out ways and means so that people may be saved from suffering. However, all these religions point out the cause of (although not the reason) suffering. Mainly, according to all of them, suffering is due to man's own past karmas generated out of ignorance. In Sikhism, it is due to *haumai*, which also virtually comes to the same. Human ignorance (lack of right knowledge) is then the root cause of suffering. Buddhism and Jainism do not believe in any God and therefore in them there is no question of God being responsible for evils. Hinduism, in so far as it is theistic, believes in God, but then it seems it is not disposed to impose the responsibility for evil upon God. Man suffers due to his own ignorance and past karmas. God does not want to transgress the law of *karma* and he has left it free to work.

Sikhism sometimes tends to hold God directly responsible for evils, but then as we have noted above, it takes them as the gift of God. God's non-interference in the working of law of *karma* may be compared here to the Christian view of God voluntarily imposing a limitation upon his omnipotence so as to grant freedom to human beings. There may also be marked a similarity between the Hindu (also the Buddhistic and the Jaina) view that man suffers due to ignorance and the Christian view that man suffers due to his Original Sin. The comparison consists in the fact that men suffer due to some element present in them from their very birth. It is due to ignorance that man has to take birth and suffer. Similarly, it is due to the Original Sin that man had to take birth on earth to suffer. Moreover, although in both the cases it seems that man himself is directly responsible for his suffering, but really speaking it is God who is responsible. The ignorance in man is said to be beginningless (*Anādi)* in Hinduism and thus it must have been associated with him by the creator himself. Man himself cannot be held responsible for his ignorance, because he comes to earth with ignorance attached with him from beforehand. Similarly, the original man Adam committed the sin due to the freedom of will given to him by God and so God himself becomes responsible for the sin committed by him. God is omniscient and so knowing full well that Adam would misuse his freedom, why did he give freedom to him? Moreover, the descendents of Adam are not or should not be responsible for the sin committed by him. Why should they suffer for the sin committed by their forefather? Taking birth with the burden of Original Sin, therefore, is not the direct responsibility of man, it is God who has attached the burden of sin with him. So in both the cases, virtually it is God who becomes directly or indirectly responsible for man's suffering. But there is an important difference also. In Hinduism man suffers due to ignorance, *i.e.,* due to lack of knowledge, in Christianity it is just the opposite – man suffers due to knowledge. Adam committed the Original Sin by eating the fruit of knowledge in the Eden Garden and it is due to that that he and his descendents suffer. But then this difference must not be emphasised too much. Christianity does not take knowledge as the cause of suffering in the sense that ignorance will bring salvation. In Adam's eating the fruit of knowledge against God's will, what is importantly involved is not so much the acquiring of knowledge by Adam, but his disobedience of the will of God. It is this disobedience which is the real cause of suffering, and not the attainment of knowledge.

We have noted above that Hinduism makes man, rather than God, responsible for his suffering. But in ancient Hinduism (*i.e.*, in the Vedic Hinduism) there are references that show that evils and suffering of the people in the world are due to the working of the various evil spirits (Asuras). There is also the reference of *Devāsura Sangrāma* (Fight between the gods and the demons) which is very much similar to the Zoroastrian conception of the fight between the forces of good and evil. Moreover, in the Vedas there are also references showing that suffering is the result of the displeasure of some god or goddess, who must be pleased through ritualistic acts. Even now, an average Hindu believes that happiness or suffering of a man is directly the result of the pleasure or displeasure of some gods and goddesses. However, the dominant note is that a man suffers due to his own karmas.

5. Life after death

Amidst factors in which a religious outlook differs from a materialistic outlook, perhaps this one is the most important that whereas the latter takes this world to be the final world and the physical life of man to be the only story about him, the former does not believe like that. According to it, this material world is not the final world and the end of man's physical life is not his final end. All the religions of the world believe in a life beyond death, although in the detailed nature of that life they differ. In this again, religions of Indian origin form one set, while those of Semitic origin form another. Zoroastrianism seems to side with the latter, or more properly, the latter set seems to borrow its views regarding post-mortem life from Zoroastrianism. All religions of Indian origin – Hinduism, Buddhism, Jainism and Sikhism – unequivocally believe that after the end of the present physical life, man has to take rebirth by assuming another body in accordance with the deeds of his present life. Every man has got a soul within him, which does not die with the physical death and transmigrates into a fresh body after the death of the present body. The alternative to rebirth is *Moksha,* the nature of which we have discussed earlier. Those who exhaust the fruits of their attached actions and attain knowledge have not to be reborn after death. They attain a spiritual status of immortality and perfection. Hinduism, of course, specially the Vedic Hinduism, speaks of heaven and hell in which the souls of the dead bodies have to go for permanent abode in accordance with their good or bad actions on earth. The Purāṇas also believe in heaven and hell, present graphic descriptions of them as well as of the passages leading thereto, and assert that souls of the pious and virtuous go to heaven while those of the sinful to hell. There is also reference in the Purāṇas of someone (named Chitragupta) taking note of all the good and bad actions of men in a register in accordance with which they are rewarded or punished by being sent to heaven or hell. Yama is regarded as the god of death whose agents bring the souls of the dead before God and in accordance with the account maintained by Chitragupta about their good or bad deeds they are sent to heaven or hell. This aspect of Hinduism has affinity with the eschatology of Zoroastrianism and the Semitic religions. Such references, however, do not seem to be present in Buddhism and Jainism, while a part of them occurs in Sikhism.

The eschatology of the Semitic religions is, more or less, the same. Day of final judgment, resurrection of the dead, taking account of the good and bad actions of each on earth and finally sending him to heaven or hell in accordance with his deeds are the basic ingredients of the eschatology of every Semitic religion. The details differ at some points. Jewish eschatology is somewhat vague, indefinite and multishaded. This is not the case with the Christian or Islamic eschatology. Islamic eschatology is the most straightforward. Judaism, we have seen, sometimes seems to believe that the sinful have no after-life, they perish completely with death. It is only the virtuous who enjoy the privilege of resurrection and then of abode in heaven. Sometimes, it seems that it believes in the final day of judgment on which the whole world is brought to an end by God. On this day, all the dead resurrect and are brought before God. Their good and bad deeds are accounted there and accordingly they are sent to heaven or hell. Judaism does not seem to be clear about the fate of the dead in the intermediary period, *i.e.*, during the period between individual death and the final day of judgement. Islam and Christianety are clear about that period also. These two religions elearly believe in the final day of judgment, resurrection of the dead and the allotment of heaven and hell. According to Islam, the souls live in Albarzahk during the intermediary period and on the final day of judgment they all resurrect and are brought before the Allah by his angels for final assessment. According to Christianity, those whose good actions clearly balance over bad ones are straightway received into heaven, those whose bad actions balance over the good ones are straightway sent to hell and those who come under the latter category but have repented for their sins are sent into the purgatory for purification. On the final day of judgment, all come to life again (resurrect), are brought before God and are finally allotted heaven or hell according to good or bad deeds. Islam, quite in affinity with Zoroastrianism, gives a description of the passage also that leads to either heaven or hell. Before reaching heaven or hell, the soul has to cross a bridge called Al-sirat (called Chinvat in Zoroastrianism). For the sinful, the bridge proves to be as thin as a sword's edge and consequently he falls down below in the abyss of suffering – the hell, but for the virtuous the bridge proves to be quite wide such that he crosses over it easily and goes to paradise. This story is directly taken in Islam from Zoroastrianism. Zoroastrianism differs in its eschatology from that of the Semitic religions in two important respects. Firstly, according to it after physical death, the soul resides with the body for three days and meditates upon its deeds. Then it is brought before God for final assessment of its deeds and allotment of heaven or hell. Secondly, damnation to hell according to it is not eternal. It is only till the bringing of the present world to an end by Ahura Mazdah that the evil souls have to reside in hell. After that all souls equally become the members of the same world, which Ahura Mazdah creates afresh and where there is no evil and suffering but only good and happiness. This is like the final day of judgment of the Semitic religions, but on this day, there is neither any judgment nor allocation of heaven and hell. Rather on this day, all are granted an eternal happy life. There are sometimes indications in Judaism also that the life of hell lasts only for 12 months and after that the souls are purified and all sent to heaven. But, as we have said above, the eschatology of Judaism is not very clear and definite.

6. Human destiny

In respect of the question of human destiny also, as in respect of such other questions, religions of the Indian tradition seem to share, more or less, a common belief, while religions of the Semitic tradition and Zoroastrianism seem to hold another common belief. It does not imply, however, that the two traditions have nothing in common between them, or again that religions belonging to one tradition have everything common amongst them. Similarities and differences are there, but generally speaking, religions of Indian origin form one set, while those of the Semitic origin form another set. Hinduism, Buddhism, Jainism and Sikhism all believe that the final destiny of man is *Moksha* or liberation. This *Moksha* according to all these religions essentially means release from the continuous cycle of birth, death and rebirth on its negative side and attainment of a spiritual status of freedom, perfection, eternity and immortality on its positive side. But again these religions differ amongst themselves regarding the exact nature and contents of the positive side. In religions like Hinduism and Sikhism which believe in God, God is regarded as the paradigm of perfection. And so, in these religions a question arises as to whether the perfection etc. attained by man in *Moksha* is exactly similar to that of God, or it is of a different nature. Then again, whether this perfection means attaining a state of identity with God or merely a state of nearness to or communion with him. On answers to these questions, Hinduism and Sikhism agree in certain respects and differ in certain other ones. In Hinduism itself, there are different answers. Because Buddhism and Jainism do not believe in God, therefore, such questions do not at all arise in them. But again these two religions do not seem to possess exactly similar beliefs regarding the positive contents of *Nirvāṇa* or *Moksha*. Jainism is very much explicit in maintaining unambiguously that *Moksha* is a state of infinity and that by the attainment of it one attains infinite power, infinite knowledge, infinite faith and infinite bliss. But Buddhism is not so very explicit regarding the positive contents of *Nirvāṇa*. It is very much clear in maintaining that *Nirvāṇa* is a state of cooling down of passions, but what positive gains actually accrue by the attainment of *Nirvāṇa* is not very clearly maintained by it, except that *Nirvāṇa* is a state of perfect peace, equanimity and perhaps of bliss as well. Again Hinduism and Buddhism believe that liberation can be attained in this life also (*Jivan-mukti*), but according to Jainism, perhaps, *Moksha* is not possible unless pudgals are completely removed from the soul. Sikhism also believes in some sort of partial liberation in this life, but according to it also final or complete liberation is possible only after the end of the physical life. Moreover, Hinduism sometimes takes heaven to be the ultimate destiny of man, but Buddhism and Jainism (and perhaps Sikhism as well) do not have any such belief.

Religions of the Semitic origin generally believe that attainment of heaven or hell in accordance with one's deeds is the final fate of man. However, what man should aim at attaining as his final destiny is definitely heaven and not hell. Heaven is a place of immortal, eternal, spiritual existence in utter nearness to God. It is a state of permanent communion with God. But again, even in this state man remains finite and never attains equality with God. In heaven although there is neither any physical existence nor any material or sensuous activity, still it is a place of perfect rejoice and happiness. (In Islamic description of the pleasures of heaven, however, there is a smell of sensuousness, although the Judaic description of the same has a clear non-sensuous spiritual touch and appeal). All sorts of comforts are available there. In all these matters, the Semitic religions agree together with greater or less emphasis. The picture presented by Zoroastrianism of the ultimate destiny of man includes within it the above mentioned contents of the Semitic faith, but it goes somewhat farther. According to Zoroastrianism, the allotment of heaven or hell to people in accordance with their earthly deeds are not final. In the final analysis, every one, whether a sinner or otherwise, awaits a good fortune, when the purpose of Ahura Mazdah of creating this world is fulfilled (i.e. when the forces of evil are completely defeated), he brings this world to an end and creates a world, in which there is absolutely no evil and suffering and consequently all people live together in perfect peace and happiness. So the ultimate fate of every man according to Zoroastrianism is very bright.

From the above an impression may amply be created that there is a definite gap between the Indian and the Semitic understanding of the nature of the ultimate destiny of man. But that is not always true. Closely seen, there may be marked points of affinity too. At least there is a lot of affinity between the Christian and the Hindu understanding of the nature of man's destiny. In one sense or other, Christianity also, like Hinduism, takes the life of this world a life of suffering. The very concept of Adam's Fall and his being sent to earth as a mark of suffering suggest that the earth is a place of suffering. And, therefore, the Christian conception of the attainment of heaven may well be taken as the attainment of liberation or salvation. These terms are actually used in Christianity. But it must not suggest that the affinity lies in the use of terms only. On the other hand, the affinity lies in spirit also. According to Christianity, salvation lies in attaining eternal nearness to God. In Hinduism also, this conception is very much present. At least the theistic brand of Hinduism as represented by Ramanuja and the Bhagvadgītā depicts actually this conception of *Moksha. Moksha* according to it consists in attaining a state of eternal communion with God, a permanent nearness to God. Moreover, both Christianity and the brand of Hinduism in reference assert that by attaining communion with God, man only becomes similar in nature with God, and he never becomes as perfect and as infinite as God is. Man is always finite in relation to God. Of course that brand of Hinduism which takes self-realisation of self-perfection to be the nature of *Moksha* is nearer to Buddhism and Jainism in its belief about the destiny of man than to Christianity or any other religion. A similarity between Hindu and Christian conceptions may be marked in this respect also that just as the latter sometimes seems to believe that the Kingdom of God or the reign of heaven will be established on this earth itself, the former believes that *Moksha* can be attained in the present life itself. God's grace is a very important factor in Christianity for salvation. Similarly, in Hinduism also it is regarded as very important, at least in the theistic conception of *Moksha*. Sikhism also takes God's grace as an important factor in this regard.

7. Ethical and other disciplines

Every religion consists of certain beliefs and practices. We have seen that in many respects, the different religions contain similar types of belief, but in many others they differ too. In respect of the practices, the differences seem to be more glaring than the similarities. The ways of prayer, the observance of various rituals and ceremonies and such other religious practices sometimes sharply differ from one religion to another. We can very well mark these differences out by going through the account of various religious practices carried out in different religions that we have given earlier. However, there is an underlying similarity in spirit and that is that all these practices in their own distinctive ways are directed towards the God or gods to secure their grace, so that man may find himself out of the sufferings he faces in the world and may strive for a better destiny. Differences in the actual nature of these practices are bound to be there, because men coming of different geographical and cultural traditions cannot all be expected to observe exactly the same set of practices. What is to be wondered at is not that there are differences, but that there are a few striking similarities. For example, fasting is taken as a very important religious practice in all such religions as Hinduism, Buddhism, Jainism and Islam. Similarly, fire-worship is regarded as very sacred in both Hinduism and Zoroastrianism, pilgrimage is given a great religious value in both Hinduism and Islam. There are striking similarities between Islam and Judaism on the one hand and Judaism and Christianity on the other in respect of many religious practices. Again, reciting of religious texts is regarded as a very important religious duty in almost all the religions. Similarly, every religion gives credence to the erection of religious temples and shrines where people go either individually or in groups to pay their respect and devotion to God. Even religious like Buddhism and Jainism which originally did not believe in any God have found place for such temples. Hence, even if there are not exact similarities in the various details of the various practices of different religions, there are definitely similarities of a general nature in the religious behaviours of the followers of different religions.

There is, however, a very clear and definite similarity in the nature of the ethical practices that the different religions prescribe. No religion is such which teaches enmity with others. Similarly, no religion is such which teaches excessive attachment to worldly objects as desirable. On the contrary, every religion without exception teaches the observance of such ethical virtues as liberality, humility, chastity, purity, love, kindness, truth etc. to be the sacred duty of every religious man. All religions unexceptionally teach universal brotherhood. Similarly, all of them teach abstention from cruelty to creatures. There may be difference of emphasis, but that does not affect the inner similarity of conviction. Sometimes, the similarity is very direct and obvious. The three religions of Indian tradition – Hinduism, Buddhism and Jainism – assert with equal emphasis the desirability of the observance of five ethical virtues – Non-violence, Truth, Celibacy, Non-stealing and Non-attachment. There is a striking similarity between these religions on the one hand and Judaism and Christianity on the other in respect of the importance of these ethical virtues. The latter five items of the famous Ten Commandments are more or less the same as the above mentioned five ethical vows. Although Islam does not explicitly expound the eminence of these virtues, nevertheless it cannot be denied that these are definitely involved in its essential spirit. An obvious similarity may be marked between the religions of Indian tradition on the one hand and Zoroastrianism on the other in as much as all of these equally emphasise the need for observing rightness of thought, speech and action all together. There is, however, a general air of difference between the Indian religions and the Semitic ones in respect of the fact that whereas the former seem to lay repeated and greater emphasis upon virtues concerning individual purity such as those of self-denial, celibacy, chastity, penance, monkhood etc., the latter seem to lay greater emphasis on virtues relating to social morality. The distinction, however, is only of degree and not of kind. Neither this is a fact that Indians religions ignore social virtues, nor this is true that Semitic religions pay no attention to virtues of individual purity.

11

The Possibility of Universal Religion

We have found that religions of the world both agree and differ amongst themselves on several points. It is wrong and one-sided, therefore, to overemphasise either the similarities alone or the differences alone. People of saintly nature have so often overemphasised the similarities with the pious idea of promoting understanding and goodwill amongst the followers of different religions while fanatics have been always active in highlighting the differences. Philosophically or scientifically speaking, none of the attitudes is commendable, but with social considerations in view, the former has of course proved more healthy and desirable than the latter. The latter has been a cause of much strife and struggle amongst people of the world in the name of religion. Differences are there, but, as we have said they are quite natural. Differences are more conspicuous on the level of practices rather than of beliefs and such differences are quite natural in view of the various social and cultural traditions prevalent in the world. But there is no cause for quarrel on account of these differences. Religion in one sense is a means of satisfying the hunger of the soul for attaining a status which is free from the strifes and strains of the mundane existence and there is no reason for quarrel if people of different traditions make efforts for satisfying this hunger in their own different ways. Nevertheless, it is a hard fact that religion has been one of the most striking causes of strain and struggle amongst different peoples of the world. It has bred no less harm than the good it has generated, or is expected to generate. Fight in the name of religion has been our history and even now there are many national and international problems which are purely religious in character. The etymology of the word 'religion' indicates that religion is there to bind men together in one thread of brotherhood, but the actual experience has been something different. It has more divided than bound. The following lines of Vivekanand echo as fresh even today as when they were written – "Nothing has made the brotherhood of man more tangible than religion; nothing has made more bitter enmity between man and man than religion. Nothing has built more charitable institutions, more hospitals for man and even for animals, than religion; nothing has deluged the world with more blood than religion.[1] This is why many have preached the end of all religion to be in the interest of man. But without much of argument, it can be seen that this is a foolish remedy. Saner persons have therefore sometimes foreseen another remedy and that is in the form of the bringing up of a universal religion. What exactly will be the nature of this universal religion is not very clear so far but this much seems to be obvious from the very nomenclature that it will not be one more religion besides the many existing from before hand, rather it will be the only religion prevalent all over the world which will be acceptable to and followed by all religious men alike. It will be the religion of all religious people, and not of one particular group or society. Universal religion will thus be the universally accepted religion. It is felt that once there is a universal religion, all bloodshed and enmity in the name of religion will be completely over and religion

---

1. Vivekanand, *Jñāna Yoga* (Advaitasharam, Calcutta, 1961), p. 373

will then have its real role to play – the role of binding all people together in the thread of universal brotherhood. In one sense, such a situation may be highly beneficial for mankind and may therefore be highly desirable. But the question is, whether such a situation is really possible, *i.e.* whether universal religion is a real possibility. That such a religion is logically possible is undoubted, because there is no contradiction involved in the concept of universal religion. For, if we think of a religion which is universally accepted and observed by all religious people of the world alike, there seems to be no contradiction involved in such a thought.

But here in saying that there is no contradiction in the concept of universal religion, we must be careful about the fact that we are using the term 'religion' in its social sense, *i.e.*, in a sense in which Hinduism, Buddhism, Christianity Islam etc. are all called religions. There may be a religion, as we have seen in our Introduction, which does not cover a whole group or society under it, rather it is confined to an individual alone. 'Religion' is sometimes defined or understood in such a way (as by Whitehead and RadhaKrishnan, for example), that it becomes a purely internal affair of an individual. In this sense we can hardly say that there is no contradiction in the concept of universal religion and that is very clearly logically possible, because in this sense whatever may be universal can hardly be taken as a religion at all. Religion is an individual affair and there is hardly any point in saying that it may be universal. But here we are obviously not dealing with such a religion. We are dealing with that form of religion, which is social in character in the sense that its principles and practices are observed by a whole group of individuals, more often crossing the boundaries of nations and who feel a sense of bond of unity amongst them. And in this sense of 'religion', there is obviously no contradiction in thinking that there may be a religion, the principles and practices of which, are observable by all religious people alike.

The above tells us only about the theoretical possibility of universal religion. But that does not solve our real problem. When we come to the actual or practical plane, matters do not seem to be so easy. Our real problem to be seen here will be whether persons tied to a particular religion in a particular manner will ever be ready to give up their own religion in favour of some other. Religion, we know, is a very touchy and sensitive affair and the bond with which one feels tied to his own religion (which is coming to him through his forefathers for centuries) is more internal than external. For this we will have to go into the details of some of the essential elements contained in any religion to which the followers of that religion are tied up with a sense of internal piety. We will also have to see whether it will be reasonably and emotionally possible for the follower of a particular religion to give up easily these essentials of his own religion and adopt the principles and practices of the newly coined religion called the 'universal religion'. Moreover, it will also have to be seen what exactly will be the form or the nature of this universal religion which an individual may be expected to adopt in place of his own religion. Or in other words, this will have to be decided what the possible universal religion will possibly be like. Let us proceed.

The possible universal religion will possibly be of any one of the following three forms:

(a) One of the prevailing religions themselves may be taken universally by all people of the world to be their religion instead of one which they have so far been following as their own.

(b) Or else, common and essential points of all prevailing religions may be drawn out so as to form common set of beliefs and practices to be observed and followed by all religious people of the world.

(c) Or again, a totally fresh religion in a fresh manner may be evolved and people all over the world accept it as their common religion.

But before seeing whether universal religion in any of these forms is possible, it will, perhaps, be worthwhile to see what actually the acceptance of a religion by a people means. This consideration will, as a matter of fact, bring us very near to the consideration of the problem regarding the very nature of religion.

The question 'What is religion'? may be answered differently and the theoretical discussion on the problem as to what a man has or does or becomes when he accepts a particular religion may centre around various points. But seeing the entire thing on a very general and realistic plane one may very easily find that what a man as a matter of fact has with him in having a particular religion like the Hindu or Christian or any other of this kind as his own religion is that, he entertains certain specific beliefs with regard to the world-and-life as a whole and performs certain specific practices in the light of those beliefs. Religion in this light, as we have also indicated in our Introduction, may conveniently be defined as a specific way of life based on some specific conviction or convictions with regard to the world-and-life as a whole. Hinduism represents one way of life based on some specific kind of conviction or convictions with regard to the world-and-life as a whole, Buddhism another and Christianity yet another. The beliefs include belief in God, belief in a specific nature or status of the world and man, beliefs in a specific kind of life after death etc., and the practices include ways of prayer, various ceremonies and rituals and many ethical virtues and duties. We have seen that all the religions of the world have their own specific kinds of beliefs, and all of them prescribe specific practices for their followers. Of course, there are many similarities as regards these beliefs and practices amongst different religions, but there are differences too. Every religion maintains its separate character due to the specific beliefs and practices that it imbibes and prescribes. Similarly, every religious man is distinctly recognised as a

Hindu or Buddhist or a Christian due to the specific beliefs and practices he entertains and follows. One more thing that we may add as forming the characteristic nature of a particular religion is the presence of certain specific religious stories or myths within it. It is Braithwaite[2], who while analysing the nature of religious language has drawn our attention very significantly towards this aspect of the religions of the world. According to his analysis, every religion consists of two things – (1) a moral way of life and (2) certain stories. The first is primary and the second is only subsidiary, but the two are there in every religion. Every religion, according to him, is an attempt at setting out a moral way of life supported by certain stories. His analysis may or may not be accepted, but in pointing out the role and importance of stories in religions, he has drawn our attention to a very important aspect of prevailing religions. Every religion abounds in certain mythical stories, which are very reverently read, listened and remembered by its followers. On the practical level, these stories play a great role in religions and the specific nature and character of one religion are distinguished to a great extent from those of the others by the presence of different stories in them. Thus every religion, as its people observe and follow it, consists mainly of three things – (1) certain beliefs, (2) certain practices and (3) certain religious stories. Naturally, therefore, accepting one specific religion rather than another by a man means accepting one set of beliefs and practices and entertaining one set of religious stories in mind rather than another by him. Now let us see in this light the question of the acceptability of the so-called universal religion in any of the three possible forms mentioned above by all religious people of the world alike, because practical possibility of universal religion in any of the above forms means its acceptability by all people alike.

2. R.B. Braithwaite, *An Empiricist's View of the Nature of Religious Belief*, Eddington Memorial Lecture, Nov. 1955.

The practical possibility of the universal religion in its first form means the acceptability of the beliefs, practices and religious stories of any one of the prevailing religions by all religious people of the world. For example, if Hinduism becomes universal religion, it will imply that all religious people of the world begin to believe alike in the immortality of the soul, *karma* and rebirth, bondage and liberations etc. and all of them adopt the Hindu way of prayer and worship, perform Hindu rituals and observe Hindu moral principles etc. Not only these, all the people of the world will begin to read, listen and remember with reverence the Hindu sacred stories relating to Rama, Krishna and many other Hindu mythical personalities. But when will it be possible? Perhaps only then when Hindu beliefs, practices and religious stories prove to be the most religiously satisfying, *i.e.*, when they prove to be such which satisfy the religious instinct and hunger of all the people of the world in the most efficient manner. As a matter of fact any religion which claims to be universal or which is taken as being most suitable for this purpose, will have to satisfy this condition, viz. its beliefs, practices and religious stories are most readily acceptable to all the people of the world and are most satisfying in nature. But on what grounds can one prove the supremacy of the set of beliefs and practices of one religion over all others so that it can have the best claim to be the universal religion? Each religion in its own way is most satisfying to its followers, such that its beliefs and practices are most naturally, agreeably and conveniently acceptable to them. What will be the grounds then on which one can claim supremacy for the beliefs and practices of anyone religion?

There have, of course, been attempts by some noted thinkers to prove implicitly or explicitly the supremacy of their own religion in respect of the fact that it contains elements which make it most efficient to serve as a universal religion. For example, George Galloway in his book

Philosophy of Religion expresses the view that Christianity contains within it all such elements in the most efficient manner which may make a religion universal. According to him only that religion may be taken as universal which touches the inner soul of man and which goes beyond all distinctions of class or group such that the ways of deliverance pointed out by it are applicable to all, and not to only a few of a particular class or group[3]. In Galloway's opinion three religions of the world – Buddhism, Christianity and Islam – satisfy these conditions, but it is only Christianity which satisfies them in the most suitable and efficient manner. But we can see it very well that Galloway's opinion is openly one-sided and is based on an unwarranted bias for his own religion. Every religion in its own way tries to satisfy the inner soul of its followers and its principles and practices are never meant for any particular group of people only. No religion in its origin is sectarian in nature. Whatever ways for man's deliverance it deciphers are meant for all, and not for a particular few. It is a different matter that only a few people in the world become the actual followers of a particular religion and such people form a definite religious or social group. If at all there is any religion which at least at its face seems to be a religion meant for a specific class or group of people, it is Judaism, the religion of the "chosen people". But, as the later prophets like Issaiah clarified, God took the people of Israel as the chosen people, not in the sense that salvation was meant for only them, but in the sense that they were the people whom God has chosen to bear the torchlight and spread his message of the Law and the commandments to the people of the world so that all of them might be able to attain their salvation. Thus no religion is really sectarian in its outlook. Its message is universal, although only a few

3. George Galloway, *Philosophy of Religion* (T & T Clark, Edinburgh) 1956, p. 138.

people adopt it and organise themselves under a separate religious group. Galloway's plea cannot make the claim of Christianity stronger than the other religions to become a universal religion. Every religion may claim universality and there is every likelihood of a quarrel on this score as to which religion can justify its claim most for being a universal religion.

With an implicit bias for Hinduism Dr. Radhakrishnan sometimes seems to conceive the possibility of universal religion in the nature and form of Hinduism. In his book *Eastern Religions and Western Thought,* he argues that Hinduism by its very nature has always been very liberal and broad-hearted and its attitude towards other religions has always been one of tolerance. It has always believed that all religions refer to the same reality and they all are just like the different pathways leading to the same goal. History also presents testimony to this universalistic outlook of Hinduism. At times, people of different religions came to India and settled here. The Hindus quite happily allowed those people to settle and observe their own religions. But in course of time, these religions could hardly maintain their identity in the face of the liberal and universalistic outlook of Hinduism and they ultimately merged into it. Buddhism originated in India, spread and survived throughout the universe, but it could hardly maintain its separate identity in India. The liberality of Hinduism absorbed it. Those religions which did not merge into Hinduism were greatly influenced by it and they have hardly been able to maintain their original rigour. All these facts amply show that Hinduism contains within it qualities of being a universal religion. It can very well accommodate other religions within it and form ground for a universalistic faith. But on examination we can see that the grounds on which Dr. Radhakrishnan hopes and believes Hinduism to contain within it the practical possibility of a universal religion are not very strong. The beliefs that the God or gods and goddesses of different religions are basically one and the same and that all the different religions are just the different pathways leading to the same goal do not constitute Hindu religion; they rather constitute Hindu philosophy of religion. Therefore the practical possibility of universal religion in the nature and form of Hinduism does not depend upon the fact that it looks to other religions with a sense of sympathy and tolerance, rather it depends upon the answer to the question, how far the beliefs, practices and religious stories of Hinduism contain elements within them which will be efficaciously able to satisfy the head and heart of all the religious people of the world. And it can definitely be not said with certainty that Hinduism possesses elements which will best satisfy all the people of the world. As we have said above, all the religions of the world contain elements which best satisfy their followers in their own ways. The historical examples also prove nothing. The merger of certain religions at a certain time in some other religion or religions may be a sequel to many local factors of the time. There was a time when other religions merged into Hinduism and today there are several Hindus who are daily undergoing conversion into Christianity. Further, if Hinduism has influenced other religions, the influence of other religions upon Hinduism cannot also be denied. It is quite natural that religions flourishing together influence each other and therefore there is nothing special in Hinduism influencing other religions.

Thus the pervading of one existing religion over all others such that it is acceptable to all religious people of the world alike as their own religion does not seem practicable. The basic question is: which particular religion is competent for the purpose and why? We have seen that all religions may have equal claims and the preference cannot amicably be decided. However, the most basic question in this regard seems to be, whether it is practically possible that the same set of beliefs, practices and religious stories may be able to satisfy with equal efficiency the religious feelings of persons coming of different traditions and living at different places in different times and different situations. The answer seems to be most palpably negative. And therefore the practical possibility of universal religion in the first form seems very much doubtful.

Let us now take up the second possibility which perhaps seems to be the most viable alternative. If the common and essential points of all the religions are drawn out and put together so as to form a common set of beliefs and practices, perhaps that will be acceptable to all the religious people of the world ungrudgingly. But on analysis and examination, the matter does not seem to be so easily practicable. There are, of course, similarities amongst religions on many points and that we have already seen. But how far we can be able to form a religion in the full sense of the term on the basis of these similarities is still a matter of consideration. We have seen that accepting a religion by a man commonly means accepting a certain set of beliefs, practices and religious stories as constituting that religion. Now, the point to be considered is, whether there are any similarities between the mythical stories of different religions, such that their common features may be taken out to form the religious stories of the universal religion. Is there any affinity between stories related to Moses and Jehovah on the one hand and Rama and Krishna on the other? Similarly, is there any similarity between stories about Jesus Christ and others of the Christian tradition and the various religious stories present in Islam, Buddhism etc.? What common mythical stories can be derived out of these? Similarly, on the level of beliefs, we find that some religions strictly believe in only one God, some in two, some in several gods and goddesses and some do not believe in any God or gods at all. Again some take God as personal, some as impersonal and some as super-personal. What are the common points between them? Again, in one religion belief in *karma* and rebirth constitutes the central core, in another religion it finds absolutely no place at all. Further again, some take *Moksha* or *Nirvāṇa* to be the ultimate destiny of man, others take the attainment of Heaven as the ultimate destiny. What are the common points in all these which can be extracted to form the belief of the universal religion. And these points are not trivial so that they may be left out. As a matter of fact, these constitute the essence of the religions they belong to. Similarly again, although there is much common amongst various religions regarding the ethical virtues and duties they recognise, there is very little common amongst them regarding the various rites, ceremonies and rituals they contain. And however little importance one may be ready to give to these rituals and ceremonies from a higher religious standpoint, they possess indisputably great importance for the common religious man. Thus it is difficult to find common religious practices which may be extracted out of various religions so as to form the rites and rituals of the universal religion. And most of all, is religion something so external that certain beliefs, practices and religious stories chalked out, formulated and constructed in an artificial manner by taking points from different religions will give real satisfaction to its followers? Religion is primarily a matter of inner conviction, and nothing can be pressed upon a religious man artificially from without. The way in which the proposed set of common beliefs and practices is to be determined for the universal religion will definitely make it external and artificial which will hardly be able to satisfy the inner heart of the religious man. Such beliefs and practices will be like artificial instructions imposed from outside. They will, therefore, never have that inner anchorage in the heart of religious man which the original beliefs and practices of his own religion find in him. Such a religion, therefore, in short, will not be a religion at all; it may be anything else.

The third alternative of the practical possibility of universal religion is no less dubious. If universal religion comes about as a new religion in any form whatsoever, it is bound to be nothing other than one more religion besides many existing from beforehand. As we have indicated earlier, no propounder or prophet of a fresh religion has ever wished his religion to be the religion of a selected group; he has rather wished it to be a religion of all the people of the world. But it is an irony of fate that everytime when an attempt has been made by a prophet to give man a new religion of universal acceptance, it has resulted merely in giving rise to one more religion besides those existing from beforehand. The same will be the fate of the so-called universal religion, if it comes up in the form of a totally new religion. The mere name 'universal' will hardly be able to make it universal.

Thus the practical possibility of universal religion in any of its possible forms seems very bleak. As a matter of fact, such a religion is not at all needed. What is needed is tolerance and sympathy on the part of the followers of every religion towards religions other than their own. To our mind, if there is ever a religion which is universal in any of the above three forms, that will mark the end of true religion. Religion will then be only a fashion, an external clothing. It will be completely cut off from its root. Religion is a matter of inner conviction and the outer way of life is just a consequence of that. Men, so long as they are men, and not mere automata, have the right to differ from one another in their convictions and are bound to have different ways of life in the light of their convictions. That is the real privilege of man. If a universal religion is thrust upon him from outside in an artificial form, this privilege is withdrawn and there is neither real man nor real religion. Religion, as we have said above, is, from one point of view, a medium of satisfying the hunger of one's soul which arises due to the deficiencies of mundane life. And if there are various ways of satisfying this hunger, where is the ground for quarrel? Every man has the right to differ from others on various points relating to life and existence. Why then debar him from this privilege in the sphere of religion? He has the right to differ and there is no need of evolving any universal religion. We will have only to learn to accommodate and respect differences in matters of religion. Differences are quite natural and they will have to be recognised and tolerated as such. One cannot be both intolerant and religions at the same time. The primary lesson of religion must be to tolerate and accommodate the ideas and sentiments of others. If someone finds himself unable to do it, he has no right to claim himself religious.

Appendix

Religions of China and Japan

A. Buddhism in China and Japan

As has been indicated earlier in the chapter on Buddhism, the branch of Buddhism which found place in China and Japan was the Mahāyāna one. But the history of the entry and development of the religion in the two countries is not one and the same. Therefore, we will deal here with them separately, of course, in brief outlines only.

1. CHINA

Introductory

Buddhism came to China via Central Asia. Although the gust of Buddhist wind was begun to be felt in China in the first century AD itself, the actual conversion began around 150 AD. At that time Indian culture had its headway in Central Asia and China had important political and commercial links with this region at the time. During the first century most of the region came under Chinese sovereignty, but the influence of Indian culture continued to be immense throughout the region. Most of the early Buddhist missionaries came to China from Central Asia during this period and hence during this high time of growing cultural relationship between India and Central Asia, Buddhism had its entry into China through the latter.

Buddhism came to China with a perspective which was incompatible with the mainly naturalised native culture.

Consequently, its progress was marked by a conflict with the indigenous religions – Taoism and Confucianism – and also with the native social values. The Buddhist way of dealing with this opposition, however, was very mild and, in a sense, accommodative, wise and prudent. On the one hand, it respected the native religions and on the other hand it did everything possible to convert people to Buddhism. Yet, even those who were converted did not totally renounce some of the characteristic native beliefs. For example, the Chinese gentries, and specially the youths, did not renounce studying the Classics (the basic texts of Confucianism), which, although moralistic, was basically this-worldly (or world-affirming) in its outlook, which hardly tallied with the essentially other-worldly attitude of Buddhism. The result was that although Buddhism made room for itself in China, it could not obliterate the native faiths.

Chinese Buddhism retained almost all the characteristic properties of Mahāyāna Buddhism – the monastic system, the rites of worship, the sacred writings and the contemplative exercises all evolved mainly through the study of the *Mahāyāna Sutras* in Chinese translation. The Chinese sects of Buddhism differ among themselves principally on the basis of the Sutras they selected for themselves as expressing the essence of *Dharma*. There is a Chinese *Tripitaka* also, which is a unique storehouse of informations about the development of Indian Buddhism. The two largest sections of the Tripitaka are the *Mahāyāna Sutras* and the Chinese commentaries on the *Mahāyāna Sutras*. The believer is free to accept the authority of any text that he selects from the Tripitaka. One speciality of the Chinese Tripitaka is that, although Chinese Buddhism is exclusively Mahāyāna, it includes within itself the complete *Hīnayāna Sutras* (the *Agmas*) also.

Chinese Buddhism also retained all such characteristic beliefs and practices of the Mahāyāna branch of Indian Buddhism as belief in transmigration, belief in the efficacy of good deeds, belief in universal salvation and worship of the Buddha and the Bodhisattvas by observing various ritualistic practices. The idea of transmigration was a totally novel idea for the Chinese land and it made a great contribution in converting the Chinese to Buddhism. The Chinese were much attracted by this novel idea. Belief in the efficacy of good deeds, such as, charity towards the needy, offering donations to the cause of the Three Jewels (The Buddha, The Samgha and the Dhamma), worshipping the Buddha and the Bodhisattvas, also formed important part of Chinese Buddhism, because such deeds were believed to guarantee a good rebirth or the final salvation. (A Bodhisattva is a person who is regarded in Buddhism to have attained his liberation, but so long as he is alive, he works for the salvation of others also. Buddhism believes in the ideal of universal salvation, because everyone is inherently a Buddha. And in this attainment of universal salvation, the role of a Bodhisattva is very important. A Bodhisattva, therefore, is regarded as a very holy person, and is an object of worship). The chief Bodhisattvas who attracted Chinese devotion and worship were the following: Amitabha, Maitreya, Bhaisajyaguru (Yaoshih), Avalokitesvara, (Kuan-yin), and Kshitigarbha (Ti-tsang). Amitabha, once a bodhisattva, later on attained full Buddhahood and created a Buddha land or a Pure Land with a vow that those who would remember his name with sincerity must get a rebirth in the Pure land. Bhaisajyaguru was regarded as the Master of healing, who saved his worshippers from different diseases. Avalokiteshvara was believed to save his believers from fire, poison, wild beasts, sword, dragons, demons etc. Kshitigarbha saved people from hell.

Sects

There have been several sects in Chinese Buddhism of which the following deserve mention: The T'ien-t'ai sect, The Hua-yen sect, The Chen-yen sect, The Pure Land sect and the Ch'an sect. Let us have a few words about each of these.

1. *The Tien-tai Sect:* This school was founded by Chih-I, who in the main pointed out that the teachings of the *Lotus Sutra* are perfect and they must be followed. He also propounded philosophical doctrines which seem to be a combination of *Shunyavāda* and *Vijñānavāda*. He established a system of meditative exercises which consist of correct posture, correct breathing etc. as well as a contemplation upon the sentences from the *Lotus Sutra*. This sect has been very popular in China and perhaps survives in the land even to this day. Again it is this sect which served as the ground for the establishment of the Tendai sect in Japan.

2. *The Hua-yen Sect:* Fa-tsang is its founder, although some regard it to be founded by Tu-Shun and brought to perfection by Fa-tsang. This sect has for its basis the *Avatamsaka Sutra*. The chief Buddha of this sutra is the Vairocana or the Sun-Buddha. This sect came up before people more as a philosophical school than a religious sect and therefore it could not become very popular. The chief tenent of its philosophical teaching is that all sentient beings inherently possess the nature of Buddha. So like Confucianism and Taoism which said that all men could become sages, the Hua-yen school preached that everyone could become a Buddha. It preached the philosophy of all-in-one and one-in-all.

3. *The Chen-yen-Sect*: This sect is chiefly based on the authority of the two sutras – the *Mahāvairocana sutra* and the *Vajraśekhara sutra*. Chen-yen practice consists in contemplating symbolic representations of the five Buddhas, of their attendant Bodhisattvas and of a great number of other holy personalities. These symbolic representations are contemplated in the mind and mantras are chanted. This sect abounds in some or other kind of occultism which conveys sense only to those who are initiated.

4. *The Pure Land Sect:* This sect is based on its exclusive

faith in the *Amitabha Sutra* and exclusive devotion to the Amitabha Buddha. It is only by having sincere faith in and devotion to Amitabha that one could insure his birth in the Pure Land of Amitabha.

5. *The Ch'an Sect:* This sect lays exclusive emphasis on meditation or *dhyāna* to be the only method of attaining Buddhahood. Bodhidharma, who hailed from South India, is regarded as the first patriarch of this sect. It is this sect which is generally regarded as the progenitor of Zen sect of Buddhism in Japan.

Buddhism in China today

It is very difficult to tell in exact terms what is the actual status of Buddhism in China today. With the advent of the Communist regime, religion as a whole has suffered a set back, but the Communist Government has allowed many Buddhist institutions to function on certain conditions. The monasteries have been allowed to possess land and farm them, but on the condition that they will have to pay proportionate taxes. Moreover, the administration has always been taking steps to preserve the old Buddhist buildings, books, works of art etc. as national treasures. Also Buddhist delegations are sent to the international conferences on Buddhism.

As a matter of fact, in spite of its speedy spread over China for many centuries since its inception, Buddhism could hardly ever win the minds of the literates and the elites of China due to its other-worldly attitude and monkish tradition. The Chinese, by and large, have been people of this-worldly attitude. The literates, specially the youths, have always cherished a regard for the Classics of Confucianism and therefore they have been much concerned about their society and social values, and less about *Nirvāna* and enlightenment. Buddhism in China has hardly ever got state patronage, and the Government has drawn its administrators from the literates whose careers have always been influenced by the Classics. So with the exception of a few early centuries, Buddhism has hardly been in a very dominant position in China. It is in the present century that a youth monk of revolutionary calibre, T'ai-hsu made vigorous efforts to renovate Buddhism in China. But about a year before the advent of the Communist regime T'ai-hsu died and his disciples fled to Formosa along with the Nationalist regime, where Buddhism still flourishes as the prominent religion. However, let us hope with Richard H. Robinson that "No other religion is likely to take the place of Buddhism in China, and there is no reason to think that the aspirations which have prompted Chinese to follow the Buddhist course in the past will not continue to rise.[1]"

2. JAPAN

Introductory

Buddhism entered Japan by way of Korea. Between 550 and 600 AD., various Korean princes sent gifts of images, the *Sutras* and missionaries to the emperors and these became instrumental in the introduction of Buddhism in Japan. The most important role was played in this connection by the King of Pekche, Sungwang, who sent emissaries to the court of King Kimmei of Japan in the year 552 AD. A big image of Buddha and certain Buddhist books were sent as presentations to the Japanese King in return to the help that he extended to his Korean counterpart to face attacks from the enemies. For many years, it was a question whether the new faith would be accepted in Japan. All opposition was, however, overcome in the year 588 and Buddhism thence forth began spreading unhindered. In the same year another mission from Pekche brought monks and expert builders of monasteries. It is with their assistance that the first Buddhist monasteries were built in Japan and Buddhism began taking hold in the land.

1. R.C. Zaehner (ed.), *The Concise Encyclopedia of Living Faiths* (Hutchinson, London, 1959), p. 337.

As is clear from the above, unlike China, Buddhism started spreading in Japan from the imperial house and it almost always got the imperial patronage. It is during the seventh century under the devout prince Shōstoku and a series of other devout sovereigns that Buddhism became part of the affairs of the state in Japan. Temples were constructed, ceremonies were performed publicly for promoting national good, monks were given prominance in administration and so on. And in this way by getting imperial patronage, Buddhism went on taking hold in Japan.

Buddhism was introduced in Japan against the background of an unorganised, or at most a loosely organised, religion which was later on called the Shinto. Under it, the Japanese believed in a host of spirits known as *Kami*. These indigenous spirits were supposed to control the fate of the Japanese people and various kinds of crude rites and ceremonies were associated with them. Thus for want of any organised indigenous religion, Buddhism had a very easy and smooth sailing throughout the land. The imperial patronage added immensely to this smooth and speedy passage of the growth of the religion. Later on, of course, a few nationalist scholars wanted to revive and renovate the Shinto as a national pride, but hardly any substantial set back could be effected against the spread, survival, and growth of Buddhism. Buddhism, thus, once introduced, went on growing in Japan and it is the primary religion of the land even today.

For the most part, however, the history of the spread and growth of Buddhism in Japan is a history of the development of several sects, the construction of several temples and monasteries and the growing introduction of the Buddhist art and architecture. No less than a dozen of sects (and several sub-sects) came about, of which the following six gained important ground: Tendai, Shingon, Jodo or Pure Land, Jodoshinshu or True Pure Land, Nichiren and Zen. The former arose in the eighth-ninth century, whereas the rest in twelve-thirteenth. As a matter of fact, during 12th-13th century, Buddhism became a religion of the masses and during this period popular saint-reformers founded new sects. The teachings of these sects were simple which appealed to the hearts of the farmers, soldiers and fishermen. Let us have a cursory look at the chief tenets of the six sects.

Sects

1. *Tendai Sect:* The sect was founded in 805 by a Japanese monk Saicho, better known as Dengyō Daishi. He was a supporter of the T'ien t'ai sect of China, the doctrine of which was based on the *Lotus Scripture*. Being disillusioned by the moral decadence of the clergy in Nara, Saicho founded a temple on the top of the forest hill, Mt. Hiei. There he tried to lead a disciplined spiritual life based on the teachings of the *Lotus Scripture*. He took the following five vows and expected his disciples also to follow them –

(a) Not to engage in the act of charity until a state of purity comparable to that of the Buddha was attained.

(b) Not to be concerned with his talents and accomplishments, until mind was enlightened by truth.

(c) Not to participate in religious services unless purity was attained.

(d) Not to be involved in worldly activities, unless transcendental wisdom (*prajñā*) was attained.

(e) Not to monopolise the merit earned, but rather to distribute it to all men so as to help them in attaining enlightenment.

Thus by meditation and other such practices, Saicho endeavoured under Mahayana discipline to increase the altruistic ideal of the bodhisattva.

2. *Shingon Sect:* It is the counter-part of the Chen-yen sect of China and was founded in Japan in 807-808 by Kūkai. He was ordained to the priesthood at Nara where

he came across the great *Mahavairocana Sutra* (the great Sun Scripture). Kūkai taught that the heart of Mahavairocana (The Great Sun Buddha) is full of compassion. Without his teaching men could not be saved. Enlightenment must be acquired by one's own realisation, and not by the effort of others. Men are capable of it, although they do not ordinarily know it.

3. *Jodo or Pure Land sect*: Founded by Hōnen in the twelfth century. Hōnen was a Tendai monk and was much troubled by a sense of sinfulness. He studied the Buddhist literature thoroughly but not being satisfied by his erudition, he went into seclusion for enlightenment. Ultimately at the age of fortythree, he had the realisation that only complete reliance on Amitābha could save himself as well as other people. He then preached the path of salvation by faith in Amitābha, which could guarantee rebirth in the Pure Land. He, however, advised people not to abuse other paths or sects. He rather told them that Buddha's teaching include many doctrines, and anyone of these could lead to salvation. But faith in and devotion to Amitābha was the surest method.

4. *Jodo Shin Shu or True Pure Land Sect*: Founded by Shinran, who was disciple of Hōnen. Shinran's speciality lies in his exclusive emphasis on the reciting of the name of the Amitābha to be the sure means of salvation. He renounced monastic life and returned to household lfe, but did not relinquish his religious vocation. He said, "As for me, Shinran, I have no other recourse except to believe in the salvation by Amitābha (Amida) by reciting his holy name, which is the teaching I received from my master, Hōnen"[2] One should not be afraid of the power of evil, because there is no evil which could obliterate Amida's original vow.

5. *The Nichiren Sect:* Also known as the Reform Tendai Sect, was founded by Nichiren. He proclaimed that only

2. *The Great Asian Religions* (Macmillan, 1969), compiled by Wingtsit Chan and Others, p. 280.

the *Lotus Sutra* should be worshipped, and all other sects should be suppressed or abolished. He was militant in his attitude and due to this he was ousted from his monastery. Still he did not change his attitude and firmly preached that there should be one and only one national religion based on the Lotus scripture. Only that could save the nation from insecurity and disturbance of mind. "Let me exhort you to be converted straightway to the true teaching of the Lotus, and when people follow the teaching of the Lotus, the Three Worlds and the ten regions will be transformed into the Buddha Land, and be it noted that the Buddha Land will never be destoryed by any calamity or trouble. When the nation thus attains security, we will all attain the safety of the body and peace of mind. You should believe and respect this statement."[3]

6. *The Zen Sect (Zen Buddhism):* As this sect or school of Japanese Buddhism has gained much popularity in certain lands outside Japan, specially of the West, I shall try to deal with it in somewhat greater detail as compared to other sects mentioned above. This is really the counterpart of the Chinese Ch'ain sect. 'Ch'ian' is actually pronounced as 'Zen' in Japanese, and therefore the Japanese Zen Buddhism is really the Ch'an sect of Chinese Buddhism imported into Japan by Eisai and (later) by his pupil Dōgen around 1200 AD or so.

As indicated above, 'Zen' is the Japanese wav of pronouncing the Chinese word 'Ch'an' which is equivalent in its meaning to the Sanskrit word '*Dhyāna*' or 'meditation'. More fully, it may be taken to mean contemplation leading to a higher state of consciousness of union with Reality. Zen Buddhism is generally regarded as a branch of the Mahayana school of Buddhism and its stated aim is said to be nothing other than the aim of the Buddha himself, *i.e.* the attainment of an absolute or ultimate knowledge lying

3. *Ibid.*, p. 283.

beyond all change and transformation. The state of consciousness to be attained is known as *Satori* in Zen and is comparable to state of consciousness that the Buddha attained under the Bodhi tree. Zen exhorts in a similar vein as that of the Buddha: "Look within, thou art the Buddha". Or again, "Be a light unto yourself."

It is very difficult to grasp the fundamental standpoint of Zen. It depends more on intuition rather than description and explanation, on experience rather than doctrine. There are no sacred gospels, well defined dogmas and creeds, and set beliefs and rituals in it. Sometimes, it seems to be a bundle of paradoxes, an unusual type of mysticism like that of Taoism. As a matter of fact it seems to have drawn much from Taiosm, specially from its doctrine of Wu-wei. It also seems to have drawn the human and humanitarian aspects of Confucianism. So, more often than not, it seems to be a blending of Buddhism, Taoism and Confucianism, all the three. Dr. Suzuki takes even the Shinto to have blended in it. As he says in his book *Zen and Japanese Culture,* Zen teaching is concentrated on an "intuitive experience" and a Zenist may be ostensibly a "Taoist, a Confucian, even a Shintoist – which is the original religion of the Japanese people." Similarly, N.W. Ross characterises Zen as a "subtle blend" of all the three Chinese faiths – Buddhism, Taoism and Confucianism. As she says, "Together, in time, these three philosophies might be said to have created a fourth, a subtle blend of them all – Indian metaphysical abstraction, Taoistic paradox and Confucian pragmatism – Zen."[4]

We have said above that Zen depends more on intuitive and meditative experiences rather than on description or doctrine in written or spoken terms. Although it makes use of certain Buddhist scriptures in its training centres, its specific attitude of silent searching after one's own soul by

---

4. N.W. Ross, *Hinduism, Buddhism, Zen* (Faber and Faber, London, 1973 ed.), p.140.

one's own meditative effort is clearly set forth in the following lines:

> A special transmission outside the scriptures;
> No dependence on words;
> Direct pointing to the soul of man;
> Seeing into one's own nature.[5]

Zen is terribly self-reliant in its search after one's true nature. It advises not to depend even on the Buddha in this regard. The Characteristic Zen attitude is very well expressed through the following: "If you meet a Buddha, kill him! If you meet Daruma (the Japanese name for the first Patriarch) or any other great Master, kill him!"

A True Zenist is not supposed to effect withdrawal from the world, he rather encourages participation, although not involvement in the world. The way consists not in anything far and away, but in everyday life. The characteristic Confucian saying 'The way is near, but men seek it after' is wholeheartedly endorsed by the Zenist. The way consists in the depth of silence, in non-action, in naturalness and stillness. These we can see are the characteristic virtues contained in the Taoist Wu-wei. Zen draws inspiration from the Taoist stillness and non-interference as well as from Buddha's silence. The story goes that once Buddha was seated before a large gathering supposedly to teach the *Dharma*. The Buddha by holding a flower in his hand which had been given to him kept completely silent. Everyone in the gathering was puzzled by his silence save one disciple, Kashyapa, who later on became Bodhidharma. Kashyapa looked at the golden blossom in the teacher's hand and smiled, signifying in the eyes of the Buddha that he alone understood the truth. Bodhidharma himself is reported to have his silent sitting for nine years. Zen's way is the way

---

5. *Ibid.*, p. 145

of silence, of meditation. Again, the aim of Zen realisation is not seeking something superhuman, rather it is simply to "recover, uncover and discover" one's true self, to become totally what one potentially is.

One of the most important contributions of Zen Buddhism to Japan is in the form of various works of art, architecture, painting, designing etc., without which the growth of Zen in Japan can hardly be understood and appreciated. All these arts and architectures constitute the various ways of Zen, considered to be the expressions of Zen enlightenment in practical life. Qualities like simplicity, naturalness, stillness, tranquility. emptiness etc. have been given expression in these architectural beauties. Zen temples and monasteries in Japan contain many beautiful statues and paintings of the Buddha and the Bodhisattvas, which are as a matter of fact Japan's most important national treasures. These images are not worshipped, but are regarded as objects which remind that the attainment of enlightenment lies within the power of man. Zen monks and lay men alike practise daily the Buddha pose of meditative serenity as depicted in the traditional sculptures and paintings of the Buddha image. The correct posture of the body as imitated from the image of the Buddha is deemed essential for true meditation and thereby to the attainment of self realisation.

There are two chief Zen schools (or sects) in Japan today – the Rinzai school (also known as the 'Sudden' school) and the Solo school (also known as the 'Gradual' school). The first was founded by Eisai in 1191 and the second by Dogen in 1227. The two schools differ between themselves mainly regarding their methods of concentration or meditation. It has been seen earlier that the aim of Zen is to attain enlightenment, to know or realise one's own nature, and the method adopted for that is, by and large, the method of meditation. The method that is adopted by the Rinzai school may be broadly termed as the Kōan-method and the method adopted by the Solo school is what may be called the Zazen method. Let us now try to understand the two methods.

The word 'Kōan' is related to the Chinese legal term 'Kung-an' in its origin, which literally means 'public document', *i.e.*, a document brought into being in consequence of a decision in some case which becomes a precedent for any subsequent case of similar nature. In Zen tradition, however, it refers to some statement made by a Zen master usually in baffling or paradoxical language which transcends all logical reasoning, but which when meditated upon silently, deeply and persistently leads to the sudden intuitive realisation of ultimate truth. A Koan is used as a means of opening up the disciple's intuitive mind in its depth. Usually, it consists of a question of some baffling or paradoxical nature, which is unsolvable by way of the process of reasoning. As a matter of fact, Koans are presented with an intention to defy all logical analysis and ratiocination so as to create a mental impasse in the student and force him to meditate with perseverance such that an enlightening comes suddenly as a flash of light. Each Koan has generally a 'Classic' answer, and so the student or the disciple has to come to an answer which is approximately the same as that answered by some Zenists in the past (Here it is that the significance of the word 'precedent' in the meaning of the Chinese term 'Kung-an' may be seen.) Answers are neither required nor given in appropriate words or phrases, rather they are to be given in terms of actions, responses etc. which go far beyond correct or clearcut language. Mere silence sometimes is an answer as in the case of Buddha's wordless communication with Kashyapa. Zen believers accept it unreservedly that Koans do not admit of explanation. They are as a matter of fact intentionally designed to go beyond words and explanations, because explanatory words hold us merely to the world of multiplicity and change. Zen, on the other hand, is in search of an experience, an enlightenment which cannot be stated in explanatory or descriptive language. An enlightenment cannot be confined within the boundary of words.

It is said that there are some seventeen hundred koans in the Zen tradition. They reveal very little to the uninitiated. The student is advised not to think about the koan presented to him, but simply to "gaze at it closely." This type of concentration involves not the brain, but specific parts of the body. This is also a type of meditation. Some of the typical koans are as follows:

1. You can make the sound of two hands clapping. Now what is the sound of one hand?

2. What was your original face – the one you had before your parents gave birth to you?

3. Whether a dog also is inherently a Buddha?

This koan is very famous in Zen. This is known as the "Joshu's Mu" koan. Joshu was a Chinese Zen master. He was once asked the above question by a young monk. Joshu said simply 'Mu' in reply, which means 'No'. He uttered the word 'Mu', however, in a manner which indicated that he refused to answer the question. This implies silence which in its turn implies that such questions cannot be answered through words, their answers are to be directly experienced or realised.

Similarly, the "sound of one hand" koan (the first koan above) is said to have the implication that two hands make a sound in relation with each other. In the Absolute, however there are no relations or distinctions. So the koan is the one of many ways in which the Zen pupil can be made to understand the real nature of the final goal, i.e., the goal of absolute oneness. Hence, we can see that the koans are the indirect, paradoxical, or rather, mystical methods to teach the people the deeper aspects of truth. The Rinzai school in recommending this kind of method is obviously influenced by the paradoxical beliefs, statements and practices associated with Chinese Taoism.

The Solo school or sect, in contrast, teaches the direct method of meditation by sitting patiently and continuously in specific bodily postures. This method or practice is known as the zazen, and is described as follows:

"If you wish to attain enlightenment, begin at once to practise zazen. For this meditation a quite chamber is necessary, while food and drink must be taken in moderation. Free yourself from all attachments, and bring to rest the ten thousand things. Think of neither good nor evil and judge not right or wrong. Maintain the flow of mind, of will and of consciousness; bring to an end all desires, all concepts and judgments. Do not think about how to become a Buddha.

In terms of procedure, first put down a thick pillow and on top of it a second (round) one. One may choose either a full or half cross-legged position. In the full position one places the right foot on the left thigh and the left foot on the right thigh. In the half position, only the left foot is placed upon the right thigh. Role and belt should be worn loosely, but in order. The right hand rests on the left foot, while the back of the left hand rests in the palm of the right. The two thumbs are placed in juxtaposition.

The body must be maintained upright, without inclining to the left or to the right, forward or backward. Ears and shoulders, nose and navel must be kept in alignment respectively. The tounge is to be kept against the palate, lips and teeth are kept firmly closed, while the eyes are to be kept always open.

Now that the bodily position is in order regulate your breathing. If a wish arises, take note of it and then discuss it. In practising thus persistently you will forget all attachments and concentration will come of itself. That is the art of zazen."[6]

---

6. Quoted by N.W. Ross in her *Ibid.*, p.147 from H. Dumoulin's book *A History of Zen Buddhism*.

Dōgen, the founder of the Solo sect, taught about the supremacy of zazen over koan as a matter of attaining enlightenment in the following words: "Zazen is the most supremely important matter in Buddhism. Many persons in China attained enlightenment by practising zazen....... Although you might have a feeling that you understand the koan, it causes you to depart from the way of the Buddha. Devote yourself to zazen without any desire to receive either reward or enlightenment that is the path of the Buddha. Although both koan and zazen were taught by the masters of the past, the latter was considered as more important."[7]

The status of Buddhism in Japan today

As we have hinted above, in spite of certain efforts by a few Japanese scholars from time to time to revive the indigenous Shinto and to push the alien religion in the background Buddhism could not be dethroned from its royal place. A brief account of these efforts may be seen in our brief survey of the Shinto, the indigenous Japanese religion. Of course, Shinto exerted some influences on Buddhism and certain elements, such as emphasis on purity, were introduced from the former into the latter, but the Mahāyāna brand of Buddhism by and large, has survived as the primary religion of the Japanese islands even today.

---

7. *The Great Asiān Religions*, p. 288.

B. THE GREAT ANCIENT ASIAN RELIGIONS OF CHINA AND JAPAN: TAOISM, CONFUCIANISM AND THE SHINTO

In the section 'A' above, we have outlined the nature and status of Buddhism as it has flourished in China and Japan. But these two great Asian countries have experienced on their land some other religions also, besides Buddhism. In fact, they have experienced two types of religions, one indigenous and the other imported. Buddhism has been the imported religion of both the countries, but they have their own indigenous religions also. Taoism and Confucianism are the indigenous religions of China and the Shinto has been the indigenous religion of Japan. We shall try to present here a brief outline of these religions.

None of these religions neatly exhibit such features which may be bound within the frame which we have stipulated for our study of the living religions of the world. This is one reason why we have not included these religions in our regular chapters. The second reason for doing so (i.e. including them as regular chapters) is that they can hardly be taken as living religions now. So far as Taoism and Confucianism are concerned, many have raised doubts whether they are religious at all. But again some have regarded them not only as religions, but as great examples of ancient human faith and philosophy which have in some form or other influenced not only the Chinese life and culture throughout centuries, but also the faiths and philosophies of the other societies and nations of the world. This is why we have thought it desirable to present here at least a brief account of the main features of these ancient Chinese faiths. Shinto, the indigenous faith of Japan, has all the characteristics of a primitive religion found in any corner of the world. It can hardly be taken as a living religion of Japan, but some indirect influence of some of its features may be well seen on the manners and customs of the even the present Japanese society. This is why we would like to acquaint our readers with some of the features of this ancient Japanese religion also.

(a) Religions of China

1. TAOISM

Introductory

Taoism is generally regarded as one of the oldest indigenous religions of China, although there are many who question whether it is a religion at all. They regard it rather as a metaphysics depicting the nature of the ultimate reality, Tao, and its 'ways' in relation to the universe and man. But if at all it is to be regarded as a religion, as many regard it to be, it is to be taken as a mystical religion, because its chief constituent, the Tao, is an inscrutable mystery. There are other mystical and occult elements involved in it too. In a different perspective, it can be said to be a non-theistic religion, because it does not recognise any personal God to be at the source of affairs. The Tao, which is the supreme reality is impersonal, whose exact nature can hardly be described in words. Of course, like many other religions of the world, Taoism has in course of time given place to a pantheon of deities to whom appeals may be made by means of different ways of prayer and worship, including several occult and mystical practices. Also many kinds of superstitions and popular beliefs became associated with the religion in course of time.

In its original form, however, Taoism has been a purely absolutistic faith, a metaphysical or mystical religion, as it has been called. Before Taoism proper, which is generally associated with the name of Lao Tzu, many kinds of animistic beliefs and concepts associated with certain personalised deities were prevalent in China, but Lao Tzu absolutely surpassed these early ideas in his thought and developed a full-fledged metaphysics around the absolutistic concept of Tao. This metaphysics, again, has somehow or other, given place to a religion also which has much influenced, directly or indirectly, the Chinese way of life in the past as well as in the present.

Taoism has no definite creed and no set of moral and religious codes to follow. It takes Tao as an impersonal, all-pervasive reality out of which everything comes about. However, the Tao is never regarded as the creator. Creation takes place spontaneously throughout the interaction of the two principles inherent in Tao itself—Yin and Yang. Here, there is in Taoism an Upanisadic ferver in as much as it believes that creation takes place spontaneously from the original impersonal source. It seems that like the Upaniṣads, Taoism also believes in the principle of joy working behind the spontaneity of creation, because it takes the world as a place of joy. There is a legend according to which the originators of the three great religions of China (Taoism, Confucianism and Buddhism) stood around a jar of vinegar, the symbol of life itself. Each in turn dipped a finger into the jar to taste its content. Confucius pronounced it sour, to Buddha it was bitter, but Lao Tzu found it sweet. This certainly shows that according to Taoism the world is a place of joyous living. It is basically good and there is no place for evil in it. This is why original Taoism has no doctrine of evil. Evil is a product of specific viewpoint or interpretation.

One of the most important teachings of Taoism is non-interference with the course of nature and keeping harmony with it. This doctrine of non-interference carried on systematically leads to the doctrine of non-resistance and non-violence. One of the paradoxical, but at the same time outstanding, teachings of Taoism is the strength of weakness. The power of passivity is more enduring than the force of direct action. The former has controlled and sustained power, the latter is quickly spent and dissipated. "That the yielding conquers the resistant and the soft conquers the hard is a fact known by all men, yet utilised by none."[1]

Confucianism has a strict moral code, Taoism has hardly any. In fact, it believes that virtue is not a quality to be taught. It is inherent in man and its realisation depends upon one's consciousness that he is dependent on the Tao. Hard and fast rules destroy the spontaneity of morality. Ignorance about man's identity with the Tao is the root cause of all moral malice. True virtue consists in being in perfect harmony with nature.

As we have said earlier, Taoism is generally associated with the name of Lao Tzu. There is, however, an uncertainty regarding the actual period of LaoTzu. Traditionally, he is placed in the 6th century BC but some scholars put his time around 300 BC. The former, however, seems to be more convincing, because it seems certain that Confucius once met Lao Tzu and this could not have been possible, unless the two were contemporaries. *Tao Te Ching* is the basic text on which original Taoism is based, and it is taken to be the work of Lao Tzu himself. As the story goes, when Lao Tzu left Chou (where he resided most of the time of his life) and came to the frontier with a mind to retire in the mountains, the frontier warden, Yin Hsi, requested him to pause for a while and write a book regarding his teachings. Lao Tze conceded to his request and wrote *Tao Te Ching* in two parts consisting of around five thousand words. The first part is concerning the 'Tao' and the second concerning the 'Te'. After that Lao Tzu travelled towards the High pass and never returned.

Amongst those who played significant roles in rendering

---

1. *Tao Te Ching* (Tr. by Waley), Chap. lxxviii, p. 238.

the principles of Taoism more elaborate, manifest and instructive, the name of Chuang Tzu is leading. His work is known as The Book of Chuang Tzu or simply Chuang Tzu. It is through this work that we are able to understand the basic concepts of Lao Tzu more clearly.

It may be clear from the above that 'Tao' and 'Te' are the two basic concepts which Lao Tzu has dealt with in his book *Tao Te Ching*. Therefore, to have the basic conception of Taoism, we will have to understand these two basic concepts very properly, besides some others such as, the concepts of Yin-Yang, Wu-wei etc. The word 'Tao' is taken to mean the 'Way' in Chinese and the word 'Te' is generally taken to mean 'Virtue' although some take it to mean 'Power' also. The addition of 'Ching' to any work implies that it is a Classic or a Canon. So 'Tao Te Ching' means 'The classic of the way and the virtue (or power)'. Let us now try to understand in somewhat greater details the two basic concepts of Tao-Te-Ching along with some other important ones.

The Tao

Although the word 'Tao' is usually translated in English as the 'way', it is very difficult to decipher in exact terms what 'Tao' means or what Tao is. It seems to have two different sorts of connotations – one metaphysical and the other ethical. In its metaphysical connotation the word may generally be taken to mean the 'way of the universe', *i.e.* the course of nature and the fundamental principle immanent in it. Ethically, it may be taken to signify the 'way of man', *i.e.*, human conduct. However, in *Tao Te Ching*, Lao Tzu seems to have made the primary and direct use of the term in the sense of the fundamental principle of the universe, *i.e.*, in the sense of a metaphysical reality, and the use of the term in the sense of human conduct seems to be only derivative. As a matter of fact, Tao is manifested in everything and so the way of man is also basically the way involved or implied in Tao itself. So, naturally the way becomes the way of man also. But directly Lao Tzu seems to be mainly concerned with developing the metaphysical connotations of the Tao. As we have said earlier, the term 'Tao' perhaps pre-existed Lao Tzu and at that time it might have contained the meaning of the way mainly in the sense of the way of man, which perhaps, has lingered prominently in Confucianism. But in Taoism of Lao Tzu it is mainly its metaphysical sense that has remained prominent and therefore in deciphering below the nature of the Tao in brief, we will be mainly concerned with this sense.

Fundamentally, the Tao is an ineffable mystery whose nature can hardly be deciphered in linguistic terms. Nevertheless, like all other mystical concepts, it is attempted to be described in several words. Perhaps it is best to be described in negative terms like the Upanisadic *Brahman (Neti, Neti)*. It is emptiness, non-being, the indefinable, the nameless, the void, and so on. But yet it is taken by Lao Tzu as the timeless, all-pervading first cause of everything. Sometimes, it is also called "The Mother" of everything. Everything has come out of the Tao, but the Tao by itself is self-caused and self-sustained. It is the source of everything, but by itself, it is nothing. We read in *Tao Te Ching* as follows –

> "There was something formless yet complete,
> That existed before heaven and earth;
> Without sound, without substance,
> Dependent on nothing, unchanging,
> All-pervading, unfailing,
> One may think of it as the mother of all
> things under heaven.
> Its true name we do not know;
> 'Way' is the by-name that we give it....."[2]

2. *Ibid.*, XXV, p. 174.

Before Lao Tzu, there was prevalent in Chinese faith a goddess who was regarded as the progenitor of all beings. It seems that this progenitor of all beings is converted by Lao Tzu into the metaphysical Tao, whose exact nature cannot be described. Chuang Tzu writes about the Tao, "The very name Tao is adopted for convenience sake. . . . Tao is beyond material existence. . . . it may be transmitted, but it cannot be received. It may be attained, but cannot be seen. It exists prior to Heaven and Earth, and indeed for all eternity."[3] Thus, the Tao is an invisible, intangible, mysterious, all-pervading power which inheres in everything and can be realised everywhere, but as an existent, it is nothing. It is the uncaused cause, the primordial basis of everything, but yet by itself, it is nothing; it is absolute non-being.

The Te

As indicated above, it is usually translated as 'virtue', but sometimes it is understood in the sense of 'Power' also. It is Tao made manifest. It is through Te that the Tao manifests itself in the world. The Tao is non-being, non-action etc., but it is not without its efficacy or power. Te is that mysterious power or efficacy of the Tao through which it manifests itself in the world and also sustains it. So it is written in the *Tao Te Ching* "Tao produces and Te rears all beings." It is the efficacy or power inherent in everything. As virtue, Te is not conventional virtue; it is natural goodness which is the outcome of enlightenment. What is enlightenment? The *Tao Te Ching* says, "To know the eternal is called enlightenment."[4] Thus enlightenment is nothing

3. Quoted by J.C. Cooper in her book *Taoism* on p. 11.
4. This quotation has been taken from the extracts of *Tao Te Ching* included in *The Great Asian Religions* on pages 151-156.

other than knowing the true nature of the Tao. It is being in accord with the Tao. But what is again this 'being in accord with the Tao? *Tao Te Ching* again says, "To know harmony means to be enlightened."[5] So attaining harmony with nature and with all other beings is the greatest virtue. Chuang Tzu defines Te as the "perfect attainment of harmony". About the greatness of attaining harmony with nature, the *Tao Te Ching* again says, "Being one with nature, he is in accord with the Tao. Being in accord with the Tao, he is everlasting, and is free from danger throughout his life."[6]

The sage is the living example of the presence of Te in him. He is not a moral man in the conventional sense of the term. He is so perfectly adjusted and harmonised with his surroundings that he acts with spontaneous perfection. Thus true virtue is spontaneous and natural, it is not learnt. It is the inner quality of every being, the inner enlightenment. "He who knows the Tao is sure to understand how to regulate his conduct in all varying circumstances. . . . ." Thus no moral code is required for the guidance of man so that he may act morally. As a matter of fact, laying down of hard and fast rules of morality, as is the case with Confucianism, is deprecated in Taoism, because it destroys spontaneity and naturalness.

The truly virtuous man has no assumptions about him. He is very simple and unassuming. The *Tao Te Ching* says, "He who possesses virtue in abundance may be compared to an infant."[7] Again, if such a man does any great virtuous act, he does not boast about it, does not take any credit for that. As is said in the *Tao Te Ching*:

> To produce things and to rear them,

5. *Ibid.*
6. *Ibid.*
7. *Ibid.*

> To produce but not to take possession of them,
> To act but not to rely on one's ability,
> To lead them, but not to master them –
> This is called profound and secret virtue."[8]
> Or again, "He who knows glory but keeps to humility,
> Becomes the valley of the world,
> He will be proficient in eternal virtue,
> And returns to the state of simplicity."[9]

Thus, humility, simplicity, unassumingness are the chief qualities of a truly virtuous man.

Aquinas calls the virtue related to Te an intellectual quality. This implies that virtue in man depends upon his knowledge or understanding about his true nature as well as the nature of the Tao. Sin is, therefore, a result of ignorance. In his true nature man is "in accord with the Tao", and being in accord with the Tao means being in harmony with Nature. Sin consists in the violation of the cosmic harmony and it results due to our ignorance about Taós essential unity with nature. Sin is, thus, not an infringement of the divine command, it is rather a breach of the harmony of the universe. J.C. Cooper very ably remarks in this connection, "what, in theistic religions is an obligation to conform to the will of God is, in Taoism, a natural co-operation with the harmony of the universe."[10]

Yin-Yang

The two – Yin and Yang – taken together represent the principle of duality involved in the manifest or phenomenal world. The two emerge out of the Tao, and it is through them that the universe comes out spontaneously out of Tao.

---

8. *Ibid.*
9. *Ibid.*
10. Cooper, *op. cit.*, p. 22.

Yin is the principle of negation, of darkness. It is also regarded as the female principle. On the other hand, Yang is taken as the positive principle, the principle of light and also the male principle. Sometimes, the duo is taken to represent Earth and Heaven – Yin representing the Earth and Yang the Heaven. Yang is symbolised as round, Yin as square. Roundness symbolises dynamism, movement and creativity, square symbolises the static and the passive.

Characterised as above, the two seem to be opposed to each other, but really speaking they are mutually interdependent. The two are completely balanced powers held in an all-pervasive unity. Everything harmonious, regular or balanced in nature or in individual is a result of Yin-Yang equilibrium. The regular occurrence of seasons and other regularities in nature is the result of yin-yang balance and co-operation. In the case of an individual, the perfect man or the sage is an example of perfect Yin-Yang harmony. Wherever the two forces work in perfect balance, there is order and harmony. Whenever the harmony between the two is disturbed for some reason or other, there is maladjustment or disharmony. So, by promoting natural or cosmic harmony, man should help maintain the Yin-Yang balance.

The Yin-Yang duo is also known as the "Two Essences". The essences emerge from the First Principle, the Tao, and are responsible for all sorts of change and transformation in the world. The Tao is immutable, but the phenomenal world is changing and the change is due to the two essences working all through the world. There is nothing absolute in the world. Consequently, there is no absolute good or absolute evil also. Evil is a product of perspective. The something which is good with one standpoint may change into evil from another and *vice versa*.

One thing worth noting about the Yin-Yang is that it is neither exclusively Taoist nor exclusively Confucianist in origin. In fact, it was prevalent in Chinese thought from before the two and both have used them throughout as the dual principle working in the phenomenal world right from its creation through its sustenance and maintenance.

Wu Wei

Like Tao and Te, this term also defies exact translation, but generally speaking, it is taken to mean 'non-interference' or 'letting go'. This obviously implies non-action or inaction. But really it is not so. Quite in consonance with the Te, it is the principle of naturalness or spontaneity. It implies non-interference with the natural go of things. "It is the secret of mastering circumstances without asserting oneself against them; it is the principle of yielding to an oncoming force in such a way as it is unable to harm you. Thus the skilled master of life never opposes the things. . . . he changes them by acceptance, by taking them into his confidence, never by flat denial.......he accepts everything until, by including all things, he becomes their master."[11] This acceptance and non-interference along with naturalness and spontaneity is basic to Taoism.

After attaining the spontaneity of the Tao, actions become motiveless. Thus on a higher plane Wu-Wei implies disinterestedness, dispassionateness, desirelessness, etc. The letting go attitude, which Wu-Wei teaches requires utmost courage, perseverance and patience, because it is "a state of interior silence and quietitude from which, at the right time, right action emerges without any volition"[12] Volition is the main source of tension, so letting things go in their natural course and acting only on the right time with a sense of naturalness and spontaneity is the greatest wisdom.

The doctrine of "no action" thus has its great advantages and achievements. Things which seem quiet, tranquil and apparently non-acting really do the marvel.

---

11. Cooper, *op. cit.*, pp. 76-77.
12. *Ibid.*, p. 77.

The softest things in the world overcome
the hardest things.
Non being penetrates that which has no space.
Through this I know the advantage of taking no action.
Few in the world can understand teachings
without words and the advantage of taking no
action."[13]

An obvious consequence of non-interference or non-activity is non-resistance and non-violence. Lao Tzu declares, "What others have taught, I teach also:

> Violent and fierce people do not
> die a natural death.'
> I shall make this the father (basis
> or starting point) of my
> teaching."[14]

This shows the utmost faith that Lao Tzu reposed in non-violence. However, this non-violence is not based on any cowardice, rather it is based on a true sense of restraint, which requires inner courage and perseverance. It is perhaps in this sense that Taoism speaks of the great strength of weakness. Lao Tzu had such a faith in the greatness of non-violence, that even for the rulers or the kings, he prescribed rule without any force. According to him, as according to Confucius also, he was the best ruler who used the least or no force.

"Weapons are the instruments of evil, not
the instruments of a good ruler.
When he uses them unavoidably, he regards
calm restraint as the best principle.
Even when he is victorious, he does not regard

---

13. This quotation has been taken from the extracts of *Tao Te Ching* included in *The Great Asian Religions* on pp. 151-156.

14. *Ibid*.

it as praiseworthy,
For to praise victory is to delight in the slaughter of men.
He who delights in the slaughter of men will
not succeed in empire."[15]

Thus we can well see that non-violence can hardly be taken as the sole property of the ancient Indian religions like Buddhism and Jainism from which perhaps Gandhi took them. It can be taken as much a strong faith of ancient China as of any other place in the world. And there is no wonder that Gandhi might have been influenced in his ideas of non-violence and satyagraha by the lofty ideas of Lao Tzu regarding non-interference, non-action, non-resistance etc. Lao Tzu advocated not only non-violence but also advised responding to evil with good. Although this ideal did not find favour with Confucius who maintained that enmity should be rewarded with justice and not with unqualified goodness, but it can definitely be taken as a precursor of the great Christian ideal of paying good for evil and the Gandhian ideal of taking non-violence as positive love.

Other ideas and decadence

Besides the above lofty ideas that the ancient Chinese religion has to its credit, it also seems to have, more or less, a definite idea regarding the ultimate destiny of man. It believes that finally everything returns to his root, the tranquil Tao. Everything arises from the Tao, and finally everything returns to it.

All things come into being,
And I see thereby their return.
All things flourish
But each one returns to its root.
The return to its root means tranquility

15. *Ibid.*

It is called returning to its destiny.
To return to destiny is called the eternal (Tao)."[16]

But in spite of these high beliefs and ideas that early Taoism contained, later on the religion degenerated into various superstitions and a variety of occult magical practices. An idea about physical immortality seems to have developed very early in Taoism and various unseemly practices including the magical ones were adopted to achieve it. In general, two sorts of practices were adopted for the purpose, which may be designated as religious and physical. The religious practices included observation of commandments, prayer, incatenations etc. The physical practices included excessive diets, medicines, chemicals, breathing methods etc. Later on, these elaborate and cumbersome practices were substituted simply by taking a miracle drug, by which transformation of body could be affected in a moment. Later on, such alchemic practices were given further support by a person known as Pao-Pu-Tzu. He spent all his life experimenting with cinnabar to produce the drug which could prolong life. Gradually, Taoism remained hardly anything more than a complex of superstitions beliefs, mystical cults etc. Small cult societies sprang here and there and many persons began claiming as possessed by spirits and special revelations. Different tiny sects came about and secret societies were formed where peculiar sort of occult practices such as the planchettes, the practice of the secrets of finger signs and various other magical and charming practices were carried on. It is for a long time that such secret societies captured the minds of the Chinese people by terrorising them and also by holding real sway over them. When however, Mao-Tse-Tung came to power, he began exterminating such societies by arresting their leaders and demolishing their secret places. Such degenerate practices perhaps no longer exist in China.

---

16. *Ibid.*

Taoism today

However, Taoism as a faith cannot be said to be totally defunct and dead in present day China. Its basic principles have become somehow integrated with the Chinese way of life. For example, extreme respect for Nature and the natural ways which was initiated by early Taoism in China persists in some form or other even today. The peaceful life of the early Taoist temples, their architectures, the quiet struggle of Taoism for purification and union with Nature by meditation and some of its lofty ideals will perhaps never lose their charms for the average Chinese mind. Because Taoism became linked up with degenerate secret societies, it was exposed to persecution, but the Taoist temples have not only been preserved, rather they are being repaired and the images are placed under protection. They are treated as treasures of ancient Chinese culture. In Taiwan, however, as it is reported, Taoism even today has the place of a leading religion and that way it may be regarded as a living religion too.

2. CONFUCIANISM

Introductory

It is very often a matter of controversy whether Confucianism is a religion at all. There are many who regard it not as a religion, but simply as a code of individual and social conduct. So far as Confucius is concerned, he was not a religious teacher, but it does not imply that he was not a religious man too. It is of course a fact that the chief concern of Confucius was man and his duties towards the society in which he lived. His major attention was devoted to the organisation of society in accordance with moral principles. Nevertheless, he was a religious man and what he advocated and preached may be taken as a religion, of course, in some special and restricted sense. There is no contradiction in this kind of position taken regarding

Confucius. He, of course, primarily discussed questions of human conduct and character and the social affairs, but he never forgot that these were all rooted in Heaven. He had a sense of personal relationship with Heaven and he believed that whatever he said and did was in accordance with the Mandate of the Heaven. He used to say very often, "No man knew him, but Heaven knew him." He further believed that the course of Nature was dependent upon Heaven and that Heaven could not be cheated. He believed in spiritual beings, but preferred not to talk about them, because he did not want people to have reliance on these spirits. According to him the spirits including those of the ancestors should be respected, but simply as a matter of filial piety and not as a bargain for blessings. His famous but at the same time puzzling statement is often quoted in this connection: "Respect spiritual beings and keep them at a distance." The full Confucian statement in this regard is translated (by Ku Hung-ming) as follows: "To know the essential duties of man living in a society of men, and to hold in fear and awe the Spiritual Powers of the universe, while keeping aloof from irrelevant familiarity with them, that may be considered as understanding."[1] Again, when asked for a definition of wisdom, Confucius replied: "Devotion to one's duties as a subject, and respect for the spirits while keeping them at a distance, may be called wisdom."[2]

On the basis of the grounds enumerated above and some other grounds, Confucianism may, then, be regarded as a religion. We have noted above that belief in Heaven and its 'decree' (Everything that happens on earth is in accordance with the 'decree' of the Heaven and all things have to follow the regular courses of nature, "The way of Heaven".), belief

---

1. Quoted by Jack Finegan in his *Archaeology of World Religions* (Princeton Paperback 1965), p. 349.
2. *Analects*, VI. 20.

in spiritual beings and paying respect to them in terms of traditional rites and ceremonies including scarifies, etc. are some of the grounds on which Confucianism may be regarded as a religion. In The *Great Asian Religions*, Wing-tsit Chan enumerates the following four grounds to claim that Confucianism may well be taken as a religion. To quote him in full, "It is often asked whether Confucianism is a religion. It is certainly not if one thinks of religion as an organised church with holy scriptures, a clergy and so on, for there is none of these things in the Confucian tradition. But it is unmistakably religious because, first of all, Confucius and his followers have always affirmed the reality of a purposive and powerful Heaven; secondly, Confucianism has promoted traditional rites such as sacrifice to Heaven and Earth, sacrifice to ancestors, and so on; thirdly, it has exercised an influence and control on Chinese society as religion has done in other countries, and finally, its classics have served as the fountain of truth as religious scriptures have done elsewhere."[3]

Confucianism is so named, perhaps, on the general impression that whatever goes by this name, whether a religion or anything else, was founded by Confucius. But that is perhaps not true. Confucius is not the originator of the principles and practices he laid down for the people to follow, they rather came down from tradition. Confucius himself also did not claim any originality for them. Confucius is perhaps the last of a chain of sages who contributed much to the formation of what was later on known as Confucianism. Very little is known about these sages, so the credit for what is known as Confucianism almost exclusively goes to Confucius.

Confucius was born in the year 551 BC (according to some in 552 BC) in the city Chou of the state of Lu. Even in

3. The *Great Asian Religions*, p. 105.

his early years he manifested special religious interest. He set up sacrificial vessels in his childish play. By the age of 30, he established himself as a scholar of repute. He was also known amongst people as a perfect gentleman. As he was poor he accepted employment very early as a petty official, but his worth and ability raised him to the high positions of Minister and Acting Chancellor. But certain zealous people could not tolerate all these things and at the age of 56 years he gave up all sorts of job and took to fourteen years of wandering. Finally, towards the end of his days, he devoted himself solely to his literary work and teaching. However, throughout his life, barring a few who were zealous of him, people took him in high esteem. Of his habitual ways and manners, the following description is given. "In every day life, Confucius was altogether modest, as though he were not able to speak. In the ancestral temple and at the court, he was eloquent, yet his speeches were always cautious. At court, he conversed with the upper dignitaries in exact and definite terms; with the lower dignitaries he was free and open. Whenever he entered in at the Duke's door, he walked as though bowed over, with quick steps; he approached as if on wings. Whenever the Prince commanded his presence at a reception of guests, his appearance was serious. Whenever a command of the Prince summoned him, he left his house without waiting for the horses to be put to chariot."

Confucius spent his last days in a relative obscurity. He felt it deeply and once said with a deep sigh, "Alas, no one knows me! I do not murmur against Heaven. I do not grumble against man. I pursue my studies here on earth, and am in touch with Heaven above. It is Heaven that knows me!" Once he wept and said to one of his disciples, "For a long time, the world has been unregulated; No one understood how to follow me. . . ." Such statements clearly show how deeply Confucius was concerned for teaching people the right way, but perhaps during his life time people did not pay adequate attention to his teachings. He died in 478 BC at the age of 73.

The 'Classics' are regarded as the basic texts of Confucianism. These Classics were six in number at the time of Confucius – the Songs, the History, the Rites, the Music, the Changes and the Spring and Autumn Annals. According to tradition Confucius edited some of the Classics and himself wrote the last one and the appendices to the Changes. Classics thus contain the teachings of the whole succession of sages including Confucius and those existing prior to him. The 'Anelects' are exclusively attributed to Confucius and thus they may be taken to possess the specific teachings of Confucius. Besides these the Mencius is regarded as one of the very important texts of Confucianism. This contains the sayings of the most prominent of Confucius, successors, Mencius.

We have said above that although Confucius believed in Heaven and Spirits and he also advised to pay respect to the spirits, his main concern was man and the society in which he lived. He wanted that even while offering sacrifices to the heavenly spirits or to the spirits of the ancestors, men should possess a detached attitude. The sacrifices were to be offered simply as a mark of respect to them and never as a means to please them so as to utilise their powers. This is why he advised to "keep aloof" from them. In matters of life and existence, Confucius wanted people to possess a perfectly this-worldly attitude. According to the *Anelects*, "Chi-lu asked about the service of the spirits. The Master said, 'until you can serve men, how can you serve spirits? When he said, 'I should like to ask about death', the Master replied, 'until you understand life, how can you understand death?" Regarding the problem of survival after death, the typical view of Confucianism is taken to be that men have no business except with the living and should not concern themselves with what happens after death. From the repeated advice of Confucius to offer sacrifices to the ancestors, it might be supposed that he definitely believed their survival, but that would be a mistake. Confucius sacrificed to the spirits as though they were present.

According to him what mattered in such sacrifices was the sense of reverence and obligation towards the ancestors, and not their existence. So the Confucian attitude in these matters was purely pragmatic and not philosophical or mystical.

Social and Moral Code

As indicated above, Confucianism has been chiefly concerned with moral and social teachings which could give the individual and the society a code of conduct and behaviour leading to a regulated way of life. The code is very extensive and concerns various aspects of life, but we will be concerned here only with some of the virtues recognised by Confucianism which are moral and social in implication. There are five such virtues recognised. They are – (1) *Jen* (Benevolence), (2) *Yi* (Duty), (3) *Li* (Manners), (4) *Chih* (Wisdom), and (5) *Hsin* (Good faith). Following these virtues means following the "Way of Heaven". A Confucian who offends any of these virtues is supposed to feel ashamed not only before others, but also in his own eyes. Let us now see these virtues one by one in brief.

(1) *Jen*: Of the five virtues enumerated above, this one is taken as the most important. But its exact meaning seems to be uncertain. Although it is generally translated as benevolence, sometimes it seems to be a collective name for many moral qualities, so much so that it seems to embrace the whole moral ideal. Sometimes again, it seems to be used for persons who possess these qualities. Once when asked for a definition of *Jen*, Confucius said that the possessor of the following five qualities will be regarded as *Jen* – politeness, liberality, good faith, diligence and generosity. Elaborating them further, he said, "Being polite, you will not be slighted; being liberal, you will win the people; having good faith, you will be trusted by others; having diligence, you will be successful; being generous, you will be worthy to employ others." The word has also been employed sometimes to connote certain moral precepts, such as,

"Behave in office, as though you were receiving an important guest." Or again, "what you do not like yourself, do not do to others." Confucius said, "The Jen wishing to stand themselves, help others to stand; wishing to arrive themselves, help others to arrive. An ability to appreciate the needs of others by comparing them with one's own may be said to be in the direction of Jen". Here it seems the word has been employed to connote an altruistic principle.

From the time of Mencius, however, *Jen* has generally been taken in the sense of benevolence or love. It has also been taken in the sense of universal love, specially by the neo-Confucianists. Han Yu, the great Confucian revivalist in the 9th century AD declared that universal love is what is meant by benevolence (Jen). But in actual practice Confucians generally does not seem to believe that one should love all equally. He has for his first concern family and filial piety.

(ii) *Yi*: This means 'duty', which is an ordinary moral term implying doing actions which are morally right and avoiding those which are morally wrong. Such right and wrong actions are generally laid down as a social code either in written or conventional form. What is duty has also a sense of moral obligation associated with it. It also implies a sense of shame on the part of some one who either fails to do some right action or performs some wrong action.

(iii) *Li*: This may be taken to mean 'manners' but the term 'manners' itself should be taken here in the context of Confucianism in a very comprehensive sense, including rituals, customs, conventions etc. It is therefore more appropriate to translate it in the sense of 'rites'. The Book of Rites (forming part of the Classics) contains three hundred major and three thousand minor rules of li, *i.e.* manners of behaviour, customs, conventions etc. One of the major instructions contained in the rules of li is that ruling by moral influence, by politeness and sympathy is always better than ruling by force or punishment. This is primarily applicable to the rulers or kings, but this may be taken as a general moral or social principle of Confucianism too. Confucius said, "If you govern them by regulations and keep them in order by punishments, the people will avoid trouble but have no sense of shame. If you govern them by moral influence, and keep them in order by a code of manners, they will have a sense of shame and will come to you of their own accord.[4]

Along with the manners or the rites, Confucius attached great importance to music as a social force, as a power of arousing and controlling emotions, as a factor contributing to the harmony of the universe. Therefore, he said. "Education begins with the Odes, is confirmed by the practice of rites, and is completed by music."[5] Music harmonises the passions, while the rites keep the desires within limits.

(iv) *Chih*: means wisdom, which implies moral and practical knowledge. Although this virtue is expected to be possessed by all, it is particularly expected to be possessed by a ruler or minister.

(v) *Hsin*: means good faith. According to this virtue, one should have the quality of trustworthiness, *i.e.*, as one whom people could trust. This implies keeping promises, speaking the truth etc. But on the whole the Confucians do not take it as an obligation to speak the truth in all circumstances.

As a matter of fact, morality in Confucianism is hardly a matter of consistent obedience to absolute or universal standards. It depends on a sense of timeliness and an instinct for the mean between the extremes. It is said in the *Book of Rites* that the gentleman strikes the mean according to the times. Confucius himself said about this mean, "to exceed is as bad as not to reach." Confucianism also does not advise repaying evil by unqualified goodness. In this it sharply differs from Christianity and many other, rather almost all, religions. It is really such instances which render it doubtful that Confucianism is a religion. In these instances it clearly

4. *Anaelects*, II.3.
5. *Ibid.*, VIII.8.

backs in the sense of religious piety and seems to work on a sense of worldly prudence.

Neo-Confucianism: In face of Buddhism, many Confucians tried to give Confucianism a face-lift by systematising it and making it more rational so as to enable it to complete with the former. This kind of effort involves hundreds of thinkers over hundreds of years, of whom Chu Hsi is perhaps the most important. The kind of religion or philosophy which came about as a result of the effort of these thinkers is known as Neo-Confucianism. Neo Confucianism kept all the basic Confucian faiths and ideas in tact, but tried to develop a philosophy out of them which could well compete with the philosophy of imported Buddhism. The two main concepts of Neo-Confucianism are – Nature and the Principle involved in it. In fact, the system is called *Hsing-li-hsiieh, i.e.,* the learning of Nature and Principle. Thus, the two main subjects of neo-Confucianism have been the nature of things and man and the principle underlying them. Its chief aim, however, has been to investigate the nature of things, to realise one's nature completely and to fulfil one's destiny. This has really been the sum and substance of the religion of the enlightened Chinese, although the masses have remained engaged in worshipping all kinds of gods and spirits.

Neo-Confucianism believed in the unity of man and Heaven. According to it the principle involved in man is the moral principle. It is sometimes obscured but may be aroused by moral education. *Jen* (Benevolence or Love) is the highest morality. Neo-Confucianists generally took *Jen* in the sense of universal love. Treating others as one treats oneself has been the basic moral principle. They also did not generally question the spirits and took them operative through mountains, rivers and such other natural objects. The importance given to the spirits of the ancestors and paying respect towards them were also not in the least questioned. So, the unity between Heaven and man, universal love, filial piety, self-realisation etc. were some of the themes which were given importance by the neo-Confucianists.

(b) Religion of Japan: The Shinto

Introductory

Before the introduction of Buddhism in Japan in the sixth century AD the life of the Japanese people was controlled by a host of indigenous spirits known as *Kami*. These *Kami* were both good and bad, benevolent and malevolent. The term 'Shinto', which literally means 'the way of the *Kami* or gods', was introduced simply with a view to distinguish this early Japanese faith in the indigenous *Kami* from the newly inducted Buddhism. There are varied opinions regarding the etymology of the word '*Kami*', but according to majority opinion, it is taken to mean something which is strange and mysterious, awesome and powerful. It may also be taken as the '*mana*' of the primitive religions, which is generally regarded as a supernatural, mysterious power manifesting itself through various natural objects and events. In the words of the great 18th century Shinto revivalist, Motoori, "Anything whatsoever which was outside of the ordinary, which possessed superior power or which was awe-inspiring, was called *Kami*."[1] However, for the most part these *Kami* were very vaguely conceived. It is only in the case of Amaterasu, the Sun goddess, and Susanoo, the withering wind of the summer, that some definite arthropomorphic form was given. The purpose of various religious observances was to praise and thank the

---

1. Quoted by G. Bownas on p. 343 of *The Concise Encyclopedia of Living Faiths*; ed. by R.C. Zaehner.

Kami to ensure their blessings and avoid their worth. Important religious rites, however, consisted mainly of the fertility cults with emphasis on purification.

Early Shinto was a loosely organised religious cult which hardly possessed any definite sacred canon. As such, there are hardly any religious texts which can be regarded as the basis of Shinto faith and practice. Nevertheless, the two literary texts, *Kojiki* (Record of Ancient Matters) and *Nihon Shoki* (The written Chronicles of Japan) of early eighth century may be regarded as the broad basis of this religion. The former is written in Japanese, and the latter in Chinese.

Creation Myths and the Purification Rite

There is a creation myth prevalent in Shinto which reveals much about the early Japanese belief and attitude. According to the myth, in the beginning, heaven and earth were not separated. They together formed a chaotic egg-shaped mass, which contained the life principle. The purer and clearer part of this mass gradually went up wards and formed heaven, while the grosser and heavier element settled down and became earth. Something like a red-shoot was produced between heaven and earth which became transformed into a god called Kunitokotachi no Nikoto, the one who established the Land Eternal. Six generations later, one-divine-couple came to be by spontaneous creation, the male known as *Izanagi* and the female *Izanami*. The subsequent creation can be understood as a product of this married couple. The islands, rivers, seas, mountains etc. of Japan as well as the spirits of the various aspects of Japan's climate and natural features – all came into being gradually.

However, at some point *Izanami* was burnt and died in the process of giving birth to the spirit of fire. Izanagi followed her in the Land of Darkness and looked at her. Izanagi was greatly shocked at the sight of the putrefied and swarmed body and exclaimed, "Nay! I have come unawares to a hideous and polluted land!" So, he immediately ran back and purified his body from pollutions. Deities were produced by his plunging down and washing at the bottom of the sea in course of this pollution cleansing. By his washing of the left eye, a deïty was produced who was named Amaterasu Omikami, the Sun goddess. By the washing of his right-eye, another deity named Tsukiyomi no Mikoto, the Moon God was produced. Then he washed his nose and by that the deity named Susanoo no Mikoto, the God of the withering wind of summer was produced. At some point Tsukiyomi was forgotten and only Susanoo and Amaterasu remained who also parted company.

Some of the points that may be gathered from the above creation myth are the following –

(1) The Heaven is a 'High Plain' situated above the earth.

(2) The Land of Darkness is the home of horrible pollution, the home of the decaying dead.

(3) Purification is good, impurity is evil.

(4) Consequently, stress is laid down in Shinto on rituals which remove the stain of pollution. As a matter of fact, purification from pollution is the chief feature of Shinto belief and ritual. It has perhaps remained the chief practice of the Japanese throughout the ages. It is believed that it is by purification and ritual perfection that man comes near the divine. We have seen above that it is by such practices of purification that the *Kami* have come about.

Examples of purification may be seen in various rituals that the Japanese of Shinto faith observe on various occasions. At the time of death of some body mourning is observed for more than ten days. When the funeral ceremonies are over, all members of the family go together in the water to cleanse themselves of the death pollution. Another example of purification can be seen in the early Japan's history of the regular change of capital on the death of the king. The ritual of the great purification was celebrated twice a year at the end of the sixth and twelfth moon to secure purification from pollutions and calamities affecting the whole population.

There were three primary methods of securing ritual purity: *Imi, Misogi & Harai*. The first was purity by abstention. It consisted, by and large, in avoidance of anything that caused pollution, viz., strong drink, food not purified by a holy flame, relations with women, etc. The second was performed by a person actually involved in some accidental defilement such as spilling of blood, child delivery by women, menstruation etc. Purification by use of salt, by taking bath in rivers or sea, etc. were taken to come under this method. The third can be taken as a method of purification by 'paying.' This paying took the form of presentation of offerings by way of fine on the offender or polluter. This was done by a priest on offender's behalf.

All the above ways of purification by rituals are clear examples of the fact that the Japanese used only the external methods, such as reciting of words, bathing, sprinkling of salt, paying fine for offences etc. and they hardly seem to have any idea of internal or moral purification. Impurities and pollutions recognised as well as their remedies – both were only external in nature. G. Bownas perhaps rightly remarks in this connection, ". . . . the pollution about which concern was felt was external; the priest prayed for the cleansing of your impure state through external contamination; neither he nor the *Kami* whom he approached took note of your internal or moral state. Nobody was trying to save your soul."[2]

Ryobu or Dual Shinto

Although Shinto came about in consequence of the earnestness and anxiety of the believers in local *Kami* to distinguish their faith from the incoming Buddhism, it could

---

2. *Ibid.*, p. 349.

not for long save itself from the immense influence that Buddhism exerted on Japan within a short period. Dual Shinto is a resuit of that influence. In less than two hundred years of the arrival of Buddhism in Japan, Buddhist elements were begun to be incorporated into Shinto. Shinto itself was begun to be understood as a local manifestation of the eternal truths of Buddhism and its *Kami* were interpreted as the local versions of the Buddhist deities. Amidst the growing influence of Buddhism on Shinto, the influence of the Shingon sect of the former proved crucial. Shingon's influence on Shinto was mainly felt through Vairocaṇa, the Great Sun, who was actually identified with the Buddha. This identification of the Sun with the Buddha was sure to find attractive place amongst the Shinto believers. If both Amaterasu (the great Sun-Goddess of Shinto) and Vairocana were the Sun, then the way was clear for the identification of both Buddhism and Shinto. The two were begun to be treated as the two aspects of the same belief and hence Dual Shinto came about.

The amalgamation of Buddhism with Shinto had many external influences on the latter, as, for example, in most Shinto shrines, a special inner sanctuary was built in which the Buddhist cult was observed. But the thing to be noted is the internal or moral influence that both Buddhism and Confucianism exerted on Shinto. We have seen that in the early Shinto what mattered was pure externalism and there was no place for internal moral purity. But now virtues like truthfulness, sincerity etc were incorporated in Shinto and such feelings as envisaged in the following had their abodes in Shinto: To do good is to be pure; to commit evil is to be impure. The *kami* dislike evil deeds because they are impure." Or again, "If we wash ourselves in sea water and are cleansed of bodily filth, this is outer purity. But if we are pure in mind and body our soul is united with the divine, and divinity in humanity is thus realised." Even the *kami* are now made to utter as follows." Even though a man provides me with a nice clean room, offering me rare and precious treasures of the land. . . . I am unwilling to favour a house with my presence whose owner is dishonest, harsh or greedy. But even though one, by reason of deep mourning for a deceased parent, is polluted and therefore cannot invite me, yet if he be always kind hearted towards others, he may expect me to appear in his dwelling, because I, the *kami*, am truly the very incarnation of Mercy."

Revival of Shinto

We have seen above that from the eighth century Shinto came to be subordinated to Buddhism under the syncretistic system called Ryōbu or Dual Shinto. But from the fourteenth century onward, there developed a gradual sense of indigenous pride and various movements came about for restoring the glory of Shinto. As Buddhism was too deeply rooted to be ousted in toto, therefore efforts were made to restore the glory of Shinto within the structure of the Shinto-Buddhist syncretism itself. By altering the strategy or by altering the outlook to see things in a changed perspective. For example, instead of taking the Shinto *kami* as the manifestations of the Buddha and the bodhisattvas, it was now declared that the latter were the manifestations of the former. Similarly, it was said that Buddhism and Confucianism were to be valued, because they contained the partial truths of Shinto.

Of the various movements trying to restore the glory of indigenous Shinto, one was Unitarian Shinto. This movement adopted a very wise step by declaring that Kunitokotachi (In the creation Myth, we have seen, it was the first *kami* to come about), and not Amaterasu, the Sun Goddess, is the primary *kami* of Shinto. The idea was that because the latter was identified with the Vairocana of Buddhism, so Buddhist influence had stolen the identity of Shinto. If Kunitokotachi would be taken as the primary deity of Shinto, its distinct identity could be maintained.

It was further declared by the Unitarians that Shinto was the primary source of Confucianism, Buddhism and of all other religions.

During eighteenth century, with the vigorous efforts of some of the Japanese schools of National Learning, like Kamo Mabuchi, Motoori Norivaga, Hirata Atsutane, the revival of Shinto assumed a new vigour. They argued that as Japan was a land of gods, her people were naturally endowed with the knowledge of what ought to be done and what ought not to be done. Japanese hearts have always been pure and they needed no moral teaching from any external quarter.

During the nineteenth century, however, when there was a fresh consciousness and confidence amongst the Japanese people and a strong anti-Buddhist wind was blowing, some thirteen popular messianic cults grew during the Meiji period (1867-1912) with the "Sect-Shinto" denomination, although hardly any of these sects had anything to do with the main traditions or tenets of Shinto. This was really a misleading denomination. Thus in spite of attempts from time to time to revive the indigenous Shinto, Japan has remained by and large, a Buddhist country.

INDEX